Dancing at the Crossroads

For Derick
with very best wishes,
Helena

Dancing at the Crossroads

Memory and Mobility in Ireland

Helena Wulff

Berghahn Books
New York • Oxford

First published in 2007 by
Berghahn Books
www.berghahnbooks.com

© 2007, 2009 Helena Wulff
First paperback edition published in 2009

Library of Congress Cataloging-in-Publication Data
Wulff, Helena.
Dancing at the crossroads: memory and mobility in Ireland / Helena Wulff.
    p. cm. -- (Dance and performance studies)
Includes bibliographical references and index.
ISBN 978-1-84545-328-2 (hardback: alk. paper) -- ISBN 978-1-84545-590-3 (paperback:
alk. paper)
1. Dance--Ireland. 2. Folk dancing, Irish--History. I. Title.

GV1646.I8W85 2008
793.3'19415--dc22

                            2007043684

British Library Cataloguing in Publication Data
A catalogue record for this book is available from the British Library

Printed on acid-free paper

ISBN 978-1-84545-328-2 hardback
ISBN 978-1-84545-590-3 paperback

Contents

But beneath the words is another sound:
the echo of tapping, stamping, drumming feet.
They reverberate down the centuries and resound
from the floors and walls of deserted cabins,
the timbers of emigrant ships,
the stages of the cities of America and Britain,
the platforms of roadside 'dancing decks';
from tables, barrel tops, half-doors;
indeed, from any surface which could amplify
that most insistent beat of Irish life
– the rhythm of the dance.

Helen Brennan
The Story of Irish Dance

Acknowledgements

When I first arrived in Ireland, I was struck by a sudden sense that I had been there before.

It may have been my childhood summers on Gotland, the Swedish island in the Baltic Sea similar to Ireland in flat landscape resting on cliffs and beaches, which made me feel at home. I had long known about Ireland as a place of poetry, literature and drama. I was also aware of some of its plights in the past. As my field research unfolded, I was to learn about a new confidence that had come with the economic boom.

Applying my longstanding interest in the anthropology of dance and culture to Ireland turned out to be most rewarding analytically: dance in Ireland reflects larger theoretical issues such as memory, mobility and place as well as tradition and modernity not only in Ireland but further afield. The study was also most rewarding to do. This is a study I have thoroughly enjoyed. However, it would not, and could not, have happened without a number of colleagues and friends in dance and academia, to whom I am immeasurably grateful.

Hastings Donnan's profound knowledge of Ireland, North and South, coupled with a creative cutting-edge approach, provided major inspiration and analytical clarity. His authoritative advice has been crucial. Helen Brennan bridged the dance world and the academic world. It was her MA thesis 'Dancing on a Plate' which sparked this study. I can still recall the moment of joy of discovery when her rendering of dance competitions opened up a new avenue of research for me. Later, she would share her vast experience of Irish dance on a number of enjoyable occasions. It was because of Sean Corcoran, traditional musician and music collector, that I found my way to a competition in *sean-nós* (old style) dance in Connemara, one of the high points of my field research. I thank him very much for this and also for seeing to it that I went to a *céilí*, a dance gathering, in Monkstown outside Dublin.

A versatile scholar, folklorist Diarmuid Ó Giolláin, has followed my study from beginning to end. I am most grateful for his continued support and well-informed interest. With his considerable insight into (Northern) Irish society and politics, Andrew Finlay supplied astute comments on my study. He was an excellent guide on many great nights in Dublin, some of them began at dance theatre performances. Hilary Tovey put me up in her house, which was very nice, every time. Her sociological ideas on dance in Ireland were most useful. A highly competent anthropologist of Irish competitive dancing and a musician, Frank Hall has been a main source of information and camaraderie. I have certainly appreciated our conversations. Fintan Vallely, a fountain of knowledge about traditional Irish music but also dance, who combines the perspectives of musician, writer and academic, was always very helpful and considerate. I am most grateful to him and also to Evelyn Conlon whose great literary writings often comment on contemporary Irish life. Barbara O'Connor contributed in many ways to my study, not least through her well-crafted sociological work on dance and gender in Ireland. I also wish to thank Catherine Foley, Chair of Ethnochoreology and Dance Research Forum Ireland at University of Limerick, and Victoria O'Brien and Orfhlarth Ní Bhriain.

John Cullinane, member of the Gaelic League, adjudicator of Irish dancing and noted historian of this dance form, was delightful company at dance championships and conferences. I was impressed with his Cork house archive of Irish dancing. In Tralee, Co. Clare, I had a momentous meeting with Father Pat Ahern, gifted musician and theatre man, who used to direct *Siamsa Tíre* (The National Folk Theatre of Ireland), a community dance theatre group. I also got to interview and see Jonathan Kelliher, one of the dancers, perform, which was an important experience.

One of the key points of this book is to acknowledge connections between different dance forms. Many of the people who appear in my study were thus around in more than one dance form and capacity. Here I will put them into the context where I met them most often during the time of my field research. (There are only a few pseudonyms in the book).

I got to know Seona MacReamoinn in her capacity of an eloquent dance critic for *The Sunday Tribune*. I owe very special thanks to Seona for her warm hospitality, for putting me up time after another in her Dublin flat, for arranging dinner parties, taking me to wonderful (sometimes hilarious) events, introducing me to central people in the Dublin dance world, to her friends and family. It was a great privilege to get to know Seona's father, the late Seán Mac Réamoinn, a legendary broadcaster who took a kind interest in my study. Among other things, he taught me that 'the Irish have a long memory'. And once when Seona was away, her sister Laoise MacReamoinn and I stayed in her flat. We too had a lot of fun!

Early in my field research I met Anthea McWilliams in Belfast, the founder of the Dance Collective (later renamed Dance Northern Ireland), an organisation which promotes dance classes, performances and community projects. Anthea is a brilliant performer and choreographer, which together with her academic qualifications in arts administration and an intellectual inclination, have made her a real resource for my study. I wish to thank her very much indeed for hospitality and fabulous times, for connecting me to dance people in Northern Ireland, even driving me around places in her white van. I was pleased to be introduced to her mother Norah and her late father Leslie Boyle. They told me stories about ballroom dancing. Anthea also took me to see Jeanie Peak, one of the few people I met who remembered having danced at the crossroads in the past. This was obviously a meeting I cherish. Anthea also put me in touch with Patrick O'Donnell who does set-dancing very well.

In Dublin I had the opportunity to spend quite a lot of time with the late Carolyn Swift, then senior dance critic for *The Irish Times*. She generously gave me complete access to her files which turned out to be a veritable gold mine of information. Meeting and getting to know Carolyn was a turning point in my study, from then on it was much clearer defined. Sadly Carolyn died in November 2002. I remember her, fondly admiring her fine writing style, passion for dance in Ireland and caring, strong personality.

Another Dublin dance critic I wish to single out is Michael Seaver. His engaging and knowledgeable reviews were always to the point. I found his approach to dance and Irish society most stimulating for my study. I thank him for keeping me up to date with the dance scene in Ireland when I was not around, and for many useful conversations and enjoyable meals when I was. Don Smith also took a great interest in my study, both through our meetings and his reviews that were enlightening. Liz Kennedy who did dance reviews on the radio in Belfast was good to talk to. So was Sam Smyth, an insightful journalist who has written on *Riverdance* among many other current affairs. I also wish to thank Diana Theodores and Deirdre Mulrooney. Father Dermod McCarthy, editor of Religious Programmes at RTÉ (Irish television) combined dance and religion on television in the most elegant way. I am very grateful for his engagement in my study.

It was when I spotted the novel *The Dancers Dancing*, by Éilís Ní Dhuibhne, in a bookshop that I began making active use of Irish fiction in my work. Trained in Irish folklore, Éilís has an acute awareness of ethnographic detail that makes her portraits of people and their relations revealing of human life both in Ireland and applicable more generally. She has continued to contribute to my study by way of quick succinct email replies to my queries, by providing contacts and elaborate views on Ireland's cultural and historical life. Our meetings have been significant. One such occasion was when I gave The Phyllis Kaberry Commemorative Lecture at the University of Oxford in May 2006 on Éilís' writings.

Bo Almqvist, Professor Emeritus of Irish folklore, has also been very supportive of my study for which I thank him deeply. At the Department of Irish Folklore, University College Dublin, I had a pleasant and rewarding conversation with Ríonach Uí Ógáin. Bairbre Ní Fhloinn and Emer Ní Cheallaigh were very helpful with photographs, as was Sara Smyth at the National Photographic Archive, the National Library of Ireland. I made a number of visits to the Folklore Collections. I also visited The Irish Traditional Music Archive where Nicholas Carolan was a great help.

The choreographers and dancers in my study range from being funded full-time by the Arts Council to supporting their choreographing in other ways, which is the usual situation in Euro-American contemporary dance worlds. Some of the choreographers in Ireland have worked for decades, others are new to the job. There was also a noticeable difference between those who did one or two new dance productions occasionally, on one hand, and on the other, those who seemed to be unstoppable, constantly choreographing. All of them were very willing to contribute to my study and allow me to hang around. The Dublin choreographers I wish to thank most especially are Michael Keegan Dolan, David Bolger, John Scott, Robert O'Connor, Loretta Yurick, Liz Roche, Finola Cronin, Cathy O'Kennedy, Ann Maher, Patricia Ryan-Collins and Fiona Quilligan. I am indebted to David Bolger's well-organized producer Bridget Webster for her assistance. Mary Brady, Director of the Insititute for Choreography and Dance in Cork, generously provided thoughtful views, as did choreographers Mary Nunan and Ríonach Ní Néill in Limerick and Jools Gilson-Ellis in Cork. I very much enjoyed talking to dancers Lucy Dundon and Lucy Hickey. An excellent anthropology student at National University of Ireland, Maynooth, as well as a ballet teacher and dancer, Yvonne McGrath has both anthropology and ballet in common with me.

As Irish dancing was a new dance form for me, I wanted to try it in order to get a feel for what it is like to dance. Aware that I would never be able to dance like the people in my study who had grown up with it, I nevertheless went to a set-dancing class taught by Mary Fox, renowned set-dancing teacher, in Belfast. She also took me to my first session in traditional music in the Belfast pub, The Kitchen Bar, where the *craic* was good, really good! In Stockholm, Mick Mulkerrin gave a great class in Irish dancing and talked to me very usefully about dance in Ireland.

At the Association of Professional Dancers in Ireland (APDI) in Dublin, Emma Richardson supplied statistical information and archival material. Gaye Tanham at the Arts Council in the Republic of Ireland told me about funding policy and visions for dance. Kathy McArdle talked about curating art, dance and theatre. In Belfast, at the Arts Council of Northern Ireland, Ivan Amstrong, Martin Dowling and Imelda Foley provided details about funding for traditional dance, theatre and the arts. Vicky Maguire, efficient Director of Dance Northern Ireland gave me important access to dance festivals and other events. I thank her very much and also her associates Sophie Bryson and Chris Ball as well as Chris Scullion, salsa instructor and dancer. In connection with EarthQuake, a dance festival in Belfast, I was invited to take part in *The Artery Show* at Northern Visions radio station, hosted by Royce Harper. Majella Flanagan at the Crescent Arts Centre, Anna Cutler, a dance consultant, and Hilary Headly who teaches set-dancing, were all informative about dance in Northern Ireland. David Grant, theatre director, described the Northern Irish theatre and drama scene. I had a number of great meetings with Fiona Campbell, Marie Mannion and Rana O'Brien who teach ballet in Belfast. Other ballet teachers who were very helpful were Graham Drake in Bangor and Clare Novaes in Moira. In Belfast, I also had many inspiring talks with Nic Bryson and Sandy Cuthbert. I will never forget the September day when I first visited Helen Lewis, choreographer and dance teacher. A holocaust survivor, Helen told me how she miraculously had survived Auschwitz. Later she had married an Englishman and made a good life in Belfast. In her memoir, *A Time to Speak*, Helen recalls her ordeals in the concentration camp. A sweet personality with a fine sense of humour, she seemed remarkably unbroken.

I am greatly indebted to Gearoid Denvir for first alerting me to the *sean-nós* dancing competition in Connemara, to Colm Ó Méalóid who chaired it and certainly to Paraic Hopkins, the fantastic winner! Terry Moylan, renowned set-dancer at the Brookes Academy in Dublin, supplied eloquent views about this dance form.

In the Irish dancing world I wish to thank in particular Tomás O'Faircheallaigh, President of the Irish Dancing Commission, and ninety-five years old when I interviewed him in 1999. I also interviewed the chairperson, Séamus O Shea, his son Cormac O Shea, a dancer also with the original cast of *Riverdance*, dance teacher Antony Nolan and assistant Moira Nachorberd, and thank them all. I enjoyed following champions Alice Reddin, Michelle Lawrence and Nicole Rankin and talking to them around championships.

At *Riverdance*, the offices in Dublin and backstage in Stockholm, my warm and deep thanks go primarily to Gerry Lundberg, in charge of press relations, and also to producer Julian Erskine, to Robert Ballagh who designed the sets and to award-winning composer Bill Whelan, dance coordinator Carol Leavy Joyce, and Patricia Carroll. In long interviews, dancers Joanne Doyle and Orla Griffin introduced me to Irish dancing, *Riverdance* as a show and the culture around it.

My study has benefited from feedback to papers I have given at Queen's University Belfast, National University of Ireland, Maynooth, Trinity College Dublin, University College Cork and the Merriam Summer School in Ennistymon, Co. Clare. Apart from friends and colleagues in Ireland, North and South, already acknowledged, I would like to thank Suzel Reily very much. In her capacity as music scholar Suzel first pointed out the impact of the percussion beat in *Riverdance*. I am also most grateful for Graham McFarlane's kind interest. Not only did he give me useful contacts but also a couple of videotapes of dancing. They have added wonderful visual imagery to my talks on many occasions. I also wish to thank Ulrich Kockel, Máiréad Nic Craith, Tracey Heatherington, Maruška Svašek and Fiona Magowan. Thomas Wilson deserves special mention for warm support and good company. Tom's expertise on the anthropology of Ireland was indeed helpful. I have certainly enjoyed Larry Taylor's advice and views. I thank him and Maeve Hickey for offering major insights and good times. I am indebted to Séamas Ó Síocháin, Abdullahi El-Tom, Pauline Garvey, Steve Coleman and Jamie Saris for comments, hospitality and fun. Other scholars of Ireland who contributed to the study were Judith Okely, Martin Stokes, Thomas Taafe, Kelli Ann Costa, Robin Whitaker, Stuart McLean and Susan Cahill.

I always felt welcomed in Bernadette Flynn's comfortable B&B, Willow House in Dublin, where I stayed many times. Bernie took a real interest in my study, and even gave me a lift when the buses were on strike.

My special thanks go to Jonathan Skinner for his boundless energy and enthusiasm for the anthropology of dance. I have highly valued Jonathan's contributions to this study.

At a popular summer school for anthropology PhD students, the Socrates–Erasmus Intensive Programme, University of Vienna, I have had the opportunity to present two papers on this study. I am especially grateful to Thomas Fillitz, Andre Gingrich, Anna Streissler and Sabine Strasser for arranging such a stimulating event both for students and teachers over the course of a number of years. Outside Ireland and Irish Studies, my deep thanks go to Moshe Shokeid, Don Handelman, Michael Herzfeld, Nigel Rapport, Danny Miller, Mukulika Banerjee, Brian Moeran, Roger Sanjek, David Lowenthal and Hélène Neveu-Kringelbach. Kirin Narayan's perceptive creative writing comments on one of the chapters have been very useful. Our sister spirits mean a lot to me.

I have also had many useful comments to papers on my study at conferences such as the annual meetings of the American Anthropological Association in San Francisco, 2000, in Washington, D.C., 2001 and 2005, in New Orleans, 2002 and in Chicago, 2003; at the European Association of Social Anthropologists in Krakow, 2000; at the Conference on Understanding Tradition in Cork, 2001; at the Anthropological Association of Ireland in Maynooth, 2001; at the Association of Social Anthropologists of the UK and the Commonwealth in Durham, 2004; at the ESRC Research Seminar in European Ethnology in Belfast, 2002; at the annual conference of the Society for Dance History Scholars in Limerick, 2003; at the Nordic Forum for Dance Research, in Copenhagen, 2000 and in Stockholm, 2004; at the Conference on Making a Difference in Dance, in the Theatre Academy, Helsinki, 2004; at a Seminar on Memory and the Social Sciences, Swedish Institute of International Affairs, Stockholm, 2004; and at Dance Research Forum Ireland panel, International Dance Festival Ireland in Dublin, 2004. I am also grateful for suggestions in response to papers I have presented at University College London, the Institute of Ethnology, Stockholm University, University College of Dance, Stockholm, and University College of Arts, Crafts and Design in Stockholm.

In Sweden, Irene Gilsenan Nordin has, with enthusiasm and excellence, built a thriving Dalarna University Centre for Irish Studies in Falun. I have appreciated ideas on papers I have given at the Conferences of Nordic Irish Studies Network in 2004 and 2006 there. Mícheál Ó Flaithearta, Celtic Section, Uppsala University, has also been helpful. Other important input has been provided by Barbro Klein, Orvar Löfgren, the late Karl Eric Knutsson, Lena Gerholm, Åke Daun, Eva Persson, Karin Becker, Jill Kennedy and Staffan Kylberg. My friend Cecilia Olsson, dance scholar and critic, has had a continued keen interest in my study for which I thank her very much. At my home Department of Social Anthropology, Stockholm University, I have had useful responses to papers on my study by Christina Garsten, Johan Lindquist, Mattias Victorin, Susann Ullberg, Katja Sarajeva and Hasse Huss. Virva Basegmez has a special place in this study as she was my doctoral student and had started her PhD study *Irish Scene and Sound: Identity, Authenticity and Transnationality among Young Musicians* before I set out on this study. It is probably unusual that supervisor and doctoral student share as much as we do.

It has been a great pleasure to work with Marion Berghahn. I am very grateful indeed for her encouragement and enthusiasm over this book. It has also been a real joy to work with Mark Stanton, editor at Berghahn.

The study was first funded by a small Stockholm University Social Science Faculty Grant in 1998, and by the Bank of Sweden Tercentenary Foundation 2001–2003.

The photographs are as credited, and copyright for all photographs remains with the photographer or organization named. I thank them very much for granting permissions to publish their photographs: Kip Carroll, Abhann Productions, John Egan of FeisPix, Delargy Centre for Irish Folklore and the National Folklore Collections at University College Dublin and the National Library of Ireland. Some sections are reprinted by permission of Sage Publications Ltd from Helena Wulff (2005), 'Memories in Motion: The Irish Dancing Body', *Body & Society*, 11(4): 45–62. I also acknowledge permissions to include revised sections from Helena Wulff (2003), 'Steps on Screen: Technoscapes, Visualization and Globalization in Dance', in Christina Garsten and Helena Wulff (eds), *New Technologies at Work*,

Berg. Helena Wulff (2003), 'Steps and Stories about Ireland', *Choreographic Encounters*, 1: 70–74, (2003). A few revised sections are included from Helena Wulff (2002), 'Yo-yo Fieldwork: Mobility and Time in a Multi-Local Study of Dance in Ireland', *Anthropological Journal on European Cultures*, 11: 117–136, (2002).

My niece Victoria and nephew Ludvig have been with me in this endeavour contributing thoughtful comments. They have grown up during the course of the study, into diligent students who, among their many interests ranging from literature to LARP (live action role-playing), also know a lot about Ireland.

A fellow Ireland fan, my husband and colleague, Ulf Hannerz, has enjoyed listening to my stories from the field, even accompanying me on one of the trips. When I made use of cheap but uncomfortably scheduled flights between Stockholm and Dublin, Ulf loyally got up at four o'clock in the morning in order to drive me to the airport and picked me up when I came back a week later arriving after midnight. And once in the depths of the Stockholm winter, he drove me to the airport in a snow storm, and between different terminals as my flight was being rescheduled. It took me two days to get to Dublin where the spring sun was out and the daffodils in blossom. As all authors know, the completion of a book requires a special concentrated push. When I got down to the momentous completion of this book, Ulf understood how much time I needed for writing at my desk. I thank him very much for his patience, and also for inspiring and interesting conversations all along. My thanks to Ulf are truly heartfelt.

Helena Wulff

Pic. 1: The Riverdance troupe. Used by kind permission of Abhann Productions.

Pic. 2: Champions in Irish dancing. Used by kind permission of John Egan and FeisPix.

Pic. 3: Dancing at the crossroads c. 1930 in Glendalough, Co. Wicklow. Courtesy of the National Library of Ireland. VAL 96436.

Pic. 4: Sean-nós dancer in Co. Galway. Used by kind permission of UCD Delargy Centre for Irish Folklore and the National Folklore Collection.

Chapter 1

Into the Rhythm of the Dance

On St Patrick's Day in 1943, Eamon de Valera, the founding father of the Republic of Ireland and Prime Minister, delivered his 'dream speech' on the radio. This speech famously depicted an ideal Ireland, and the vision of 'comely maidens dancing at the crossroads'. Half a century later, in 1994, *Riverdance*, the commercial Irish dance show, became an overnight sensation as a seven-minute interval entertainment in the annual Eurovision Song Contest broadcast fr om Dublin.[1] The show, which appeared at a turning point in Ireland's historical and economic development, went on to unprecedented global success. These two manifestations of Irish life, crossroads dancing and *Riverdance*, represent two poles in what follows here. As Helen Brennan (1999: 14) says, 'the rhythm of the dance' is 'that most insistent beat of Irish life': dance is integral to Irish life. Since de Valera's speech, the notion 'dancing at the crossroads', has been a key metaphor in Irish cultural and political life, referring to historical junctures although with shifting meanings. As a key metaphor, dancing at the crossroads very usefully crystallizes the analytical perspective of this book: Ireland is now to be found in a crossroads situation which connects a distinctly Irish tradition with European modernity and the world in a new way.

The aim of this book is to analyse in ethnographic detail what dance conveys about Ireland, North and South. The book combines an anthropology of dance approach with cultural analysis contextualized in Irish Studies. By focussing on how Irishness is creatively negotiated through social memory and mobility in different, but interrelated dance forms, I will discuss expressions of Irish national identity that on a larger scale have played some role in the building of an Irish nation, first as a part of the Gaelic cultural nationalist revival, now as a part of a European nation-state formation. There are in particular three such dance forms: Irish dancing, which is a competitive solo step, 'folk' dancing, out of which *Riverdance* grew, and Irish dance theatre. The latter is a type of contemporary or modern stage dance with Russian roots which came about in the United States and Germany as a part of the modernist movement in the arts in the early twentieth century (Wulff 1998). Yet Irish dance theatre is notable for including Irish traditional steps, song and music, as well as modern steps. There is also a fourth dance form, *sean-nós*, old-style step dance. These different dance forms are linked together through networks of people (dancers, musicians, choreographers, teachers) who move between them, and also in the dance practice through Irish themes, steps and music.[2] Irish themes that run through the dance forms refer to Irish mythology and legend, the history such as the Great Famine and emigration waves, as well as political circumstances especially the Troubles in Northern Ireland. This is in many ways one dancing community, which extends abroad.

Most studies of dance focus on one dance form[3] while in this study it makes sense to conceptualize different dance forms within a single framework. This reveals how popular culture, 'folk' culture and an experimental 'high' culture weave into each other. It is important, and one point where the book has wider theoretical implications. Where my analysis is distinctive is in the way it pulls together the existing debates on memory and mobility, tradition and modernity, and relates them to dance and culture in Ireland. While the captivating case of Irish dance brings out tensions and ties among these debates, this book also aims to extend broader understandings of nationalism, postcoloniality and cosmopolitanism. In line with the objective of an anthropology of dance which identifies the emotional and expressive nature of dance as a special means for uncovering social and cultural circumstances, the analysis shows how dance provides an alternative arena for Irishness. As dance moves back and forth across the Irish border with tours, championships and festivals (and through the use of Northern and Southern steps and stories in the dance), an all-Ireland perspective is necessary.

In this social and cultural analysis of dance and dance culture, I intend to explore the social organization of meaning produced by different dances, and connect these to historical and political circumstances. As a part of this, I report on cultural debates and audience responses to performances, also commentaries by dance critics and writers and other intellectuals including anthropologists. This aspect of my method entails examining 'cultures of expertise' in a global context as recently suggested by Holmes and Marcus (2005). Instead of 'others', these people we now study are our counterparts and colleagues. And this is an increasing trend in anthropology, which is reshaping fieldwork and the writing process.

Designing a Dance Study

One evening in the winter of 1997 I happened to watch the signature section of *Riverdance*, the long line of Irish dancers beating out their steps on Swedish television. I remember being impressed as a dance scholar with the 'togetherness' of the troupe, meaning both perfect coordination in steps and expressive energy between the dancers. But it was the explosive cross-cultural commercial success of the show, on different continents, which later provoked my anthropological curiosity. Here was a dance show which worked as a performance in many different cultures, despite the fact that dance usually requires some cultural introduction. It was evident that *Riverdance* spoke on a general level to people from a number of cultural backgrounds. I early reflected that it was this particular combination of Irishness and crossover, which reached a vast audience. And by presenting the themes of displacement, nostalgia and longing, that every one of us can relate to, in a suggestive rhythm of music and step dance, the success was a fact.

To be able to understand *Riverdance* in greater detail, I soon realized that I had to learn about the tradition, such as sean-nós, the old step-style dance from Connemara in the west of Ireland, but above all about competitive Irish step dancing since that was the dance form from which *Riverdance* had developed. With my background in the European dance theatre world from my previous study of career and culture in the transnational world of ballet and dance (Wulff 1998), it was obvious to include Irish dance theatre, not least because this dance form often uses traditional steps, song and music. It was, however, reading Helen Brennan's (1994a) MA thesis 'Dancing on a Plate: The Sean-Nós Tradition of Connemara' which made me decide to embark on this study: I found her account, especially of the widespread custom of dance competitions in Ireland, completely fascinating. For in my view, one cannot really compete in dance (nor in music). What happens is that the best dancers or people who dance a lot reach a certain level of technical proficiency. In the selection of the winners, other aspects, social aspects such as taste and tradition, style and fashion, tend to be the determining factors. I could not wait to find out the determining factors in Irish dance competitions.

I had done fieldwork for two previous studies in Britain, one on female youth culture and ethnicity in an inner city area of South London in the early 1980s (Wulff 1988, 1995a, b) and more recently for the one on ballet and dance with the Royal Ballet at Covent Garden (mainly Wulff 1998, but also 2000, 2001, 2002, 2004, 2005a, 2006, forthcoming). These two studies took place in different ends of the class and race structure in Britain, and were useful experiences when I learnt about Britain from yet another angle: that of a past colonizer of what is now the Republic of Ireland. I started my study of dance in Ireland in 1998 on a small Faculty of Social Sciences grant from Stockholm University, which enabled me to go to the field for a week every other month, third or even fourth month, when something important was happening in the dance world. Inspired by the Swedish travel agency Vingresor's sensationally cheap air fares with uncomfortable departure times between Stockholm and Dublin, advertised as 'Yo-yo tickets', I thought of this as a yo-yo fieldwork (see Afterword).[4] Going back and forth turned out to be the right strategy for doing research on dance performances, festivals and competitions, as they take place all over the island at irregular intervals. A full-time research grant from the Bank of Sweden Tercentenary Foundation from 2001 to 2003 made it possible to expand my early investigations into a major study.

The Field is Coming

After the television breakthrough of *Riverdance*, the seven-minute act was extended into a full-length show, which premiered in Dublin about a year later, in 1995. Since then the show has only performed live a few times in Ireland, but I was able to watch it in Stockholm both from the auditorium and back stage, as well as during rehearsals. *Riverdance* came to Stockholm five times during the course of my study. I also conducted interviews with people in the *Riverdance* management at the office in Dublin, where I experienced a strange emptiness, however, a sense of acute deterritorialization. For there I was, at the *Riverdance* office in Dublin, at the heart of a global structure, talking to people who orchestrate the show in capacities such as executive producer, press officer, video producer and dance coach, but there were no dancers around! They were all abroad, touring in the United States and Germany. Later I would spend time in a participant observation manner with dancers at dance championships and in the dance theatre world in Ireland.

Although most of my fieldwork took place in Ireland, it was not all of it. One small, yet significant, part of this fieldwork was done in Stockholm. In fact, my first entrance to this field was the opening night of *Riverdance* in Stockholm in August 1998. It had been almost a year since I had seen the signature section of *Riverdance* on television, but already I was becoming aware of the critical debate in Ireland over commerce versus artistry, tradition versus modernity, the local versus the global. For an anthropologist it is, again, especially interesting to try to understand why something like this, an Irish commercial dance show, works cross-culturally on different continents. The explosive success of *Riverdance* cannot be sufficiently explained by social or cultural circumstances. Marketing strategies, such as television trailers in the form of programs of and about the show that are broadcast before *Riverdance* comes on tour, have clearly been important, however. For just like the live show, the television programmes convey the catching percussion beat during step sections that makes the pulse go faster. This bodily reaction happens to audiences across a variety of cultures, men and women, old and young.

It was impossible to get a ticket to the opening night in Stockholm, so I put on my dance-journalist hat and called the editor of the Swedish dance magazine. She gave me a press ticket in exchange for an article about the show (Wulff 1999). The opening night was going to take place in Globen, a sports and concert arena in Stockholm. I met with some of the dancers and watched the general rehearsal in the afternoon before the show. The general rehearsal was a relaxed and joyous event, contrary to many other rehearsals I have watched. In the evening, members of the Swedish Irish diaspora and their friends stood out among the many thousands of people in the audience, wearing green. I enjoyed the show, especially the speed and skill of the dancers. References to displacement and longing in the story, produced by the Irish emigration to the United States, struck a chord. The show finished with a happy ending, a homecoming to Ireland. The audience rose in a standing ovation for Ireland.

Mapping the Irish Dance Scene

In Ireland, my field was scattered all over the island, although Dublin was the centre, most of the time, and sometimes Belfast. Between the two poles of de Valera's vision of crossroads dancing and *Riverdance,* the Irish dance scene is spread out on a continuum, where dance forms sometimes overlap: crossroads dancing is portrayed in dance theatre for example, and sean-nós steps are often used in this dance form. There is thus a certain mobility back and forth along this continuum. The Irish dance scene also moves around geographically, with centres being constituted temporarily, such as for the championships that change location every year. My fieldwork consisted of multi-local stints of participant observation, interviews and archival work in connection with dance events, mainly numerous performances, festivals and competitions in Dublin, but also in Belfast and elsewhere on the island. I travelled to the World Championships in Irish Dancing, the 'World's' for short, when it was held in Ennis, Co. Clare and to the All Ireland Championships in Killarney, Co. Kerry. I was also present at an annual informal dance competition in traditional sean-nós step dancing held in a pub in the small village of Carraroe in Connemara in the west of Ireland. Participant observation around performances often started out with me watching rehearsals and hanging around in studios and theatres as premieres were being prepared. Then I would watch the premiere and spend time with dance people and critics at receptions and dinners afterwards. These social occasions not only provided observational and interactional data, but they were also good opportunities for making new contacts that would lead me further along the dance networks. As Ullrich Kockel (1993) has suggested, listening, not only watching, is also a prominent part of participant observation, listening to the voices of the people we study. In the case of Irish dance, there is the additional point about listening not only to the music, but also to the dancing, to the sound of the steps, a matter I will come back to.

In addition to a multitude of informal interview-like conversations that I carefully steered towards certain topics I wanted to know more about, or double check, I conducted eighty-one formal interviews (using the same questionnaire in order to facilitate comparison and other analysis) during my fieldwork period with different categories of people who were involved in dance in various ways, from professional choreographers of international repute and seasoned critics in Dublin to sean-nós dancers in the countryside in the west of Ireland and first-time winners of major championships in Irish dancing. There was also the Catholic priest, Father Dermod McCarthy, who produced television programmes about liturgical (religious) dance. He told me about liturgical dance, television and morality in Ireland where Catholicism has defined so much of private and public life (Wulff 2003). And Father Pat Ahern, director of *Siamsa Tíre*,[5] a folk dance company, offered long stories about crossroads dancing. A handful of people were interviewed twice, among them my key informant in the North, choreographer Anthea McWilliams, and my key informant in the South, Seona MacReamoinn, a dance critic.

A number of dance and art administrators and officers at the Arts Councils both in the Republic of Ireland and Northern Ireland informed me during interviews about the infrastructure of dance and funding policy. I also interviewed the directors of the Association of Professional Dancers in Ireland (APDI) and Dance Northern Ireland, both rapidly growing associations. In Dublin, I interviewed the then director of The Project, an experimental theatre and gallery, which often feature dance performances. In Belfast, I interviewed the director of the annual City Dance Festival, in Cork the director of Institute for Choreography and Dance (Firkin Crane). All directors were incidentally women. I interviewed ballet teachers and dance instructors, some of whom were teaching Irish dancing, all over the island. The dance teachers were young and middle-aged, a few were retired, but most of the dance teachers were women, except in the Irish dancing world where there were about as many men as women dance teachers. Some of the ballet and dance teachers also worked as choreographers.

I interviewed members of the Irish Dancing Commission, which the Gaelic League established in the 1890s in order to cultivate Irish dance, rather than foreign, mostly English dance. The Irish Dancing Commission still regulates dancing styles and steps worldwide for the ubiquitous championships in Irish dancing.

As a part of my field studies I took part in one of the most famous Irish annual national rituals, St Patrick's Parade on 17 March 2002 in Dublin. The parade displayed dancing and a so called 'monster céilí', a huge dance gathering in a park which was held afterwards. I also attended dance festivals: the Belfast City Council Week of Dance in May 2001, the International Dance Festival Ireland in Dublin in May 2002 and Earthquake: Northern Ireland's Festival of International Dance in March 2003. I participated in the conference 'Dance in the Community' in October 2002 in Derry, which was an opportunity to interact with community dance specialists who organize dance classes on a community level for disabled people and children from disadvantaged areas, as well as salsa and hip hop classes for teenagers, and tea dance for senior citizens. A part of community dance in Northern Ireland is the policy to teach Catholic and Protestant children to dance together in dance classes at school, as a way to promote future understanding between the two 'sides of the community', as the expression goes. And I was invited in May 2004 to give a paper in a panel organized by Dance Research Forum Ireland at the biannual International Dance Festival Ireland held in Dublin. I went to conferences both as a colleague and a fieldworker.

For this study I also did archival work, more than I have done in any of my previous studies, at the Linen Library in Belfast, the Irish Traditional Music Archive in Dublin and the Folklore Collection at the Department of Irish Folklore at University College Dublin. But the most remarkable archival work took place in the home of a dance critic: early in my fieldwork I met Carolyn Swift, at a reception for a new choreographer-in-residence at University College Dublin. Two months later when I came back the next time to Dublin, I made my way to her house in Upper Lesson Street, according to her instructions to look for a 'yellow door and a forsythia in blossom', where I did an extremely productive interview with Carolyn. Born in London, but having worked for many years in the Dublin theatre world, she had written dance reviews since the 1970s. Not only was her experience and knowledge of the Irish dance world colossal, but she had also kept every single document that had come her way during all these years: programmes, press releases, personal and business letters, reviews and feature articles written by herself and other critics and dance writers. The documents were meticulously collected in bulging beige files in her little study at the back of her garden. I was to spend many hours over the following years in Carolyn's little study going through her files, amazed and endlessly grateful. For there I found data about debates in the dance world that weaved into larger Irish society, biographical information about dance people, information about repertories and companies among many other things. I was able to add to, even correct in some instances, data from participant observation and interviews.

Dance, Anthropology and Ireland

Despite the rich scholarly literature on music, poetry, drama and literature in Ireland, the scholarly literature on dance in Ireland is surprisingly small and quite focussed on historical descriptions of traditional Irish dancing or competitive step dancing. An important source for this book is the comprehensive *The Story of Irish Dance* by Helen Brennan (1999). It is an accessible account of traditional and competitive Irish dancing. There is also the well-crafted *Dancing as a Social Pastime in the South-East of Ireland, 1800–1897* by Mary Friel (2004), which shows the significance of dancing in the social life of people during the nineteenth century, especially in Wexford. There (as in other parts of Ireland) dance took place in connection with seasonal farm work such as harvesting, religious ceremonies, fairs, races and weddings, and was an area where 'rich and poor, young and old, and even clergy and laity' came together. A literary study titled *The Plays of W.B. Yeats: Yeats and the Dancer*, by Sylvia C. Ellis (1999), takes early Irish dance theatre into some consideration. Ellis focusses on the significance of dance in the narrative of plays by W.B.Yeats, so called dance plays, and especially those that were performed in collaboration with Ninette de Valois at the Abbey Theatre in Dublin in the late 1920s and early 1930s. Ellis also mentions dance in Yeats' poems such as the famous line 'How can we know the dancer from the dance?' (1990[1928]: 245). Contemporary dance theatre is the topic of the interview book *Dancing on the Edge of Europe: Irish Choreographers in Conversation* edited by Diana Theodores (2003), a critic and choreographer. Dance writer Deirdre Mulrooney's (2006) detailed *Irish Moves* is, as the subtitle says, an illustrated history of dance and physical theatre in Ireland. *Riverdance – The Phenomenon* by Barra Ó Cinnéide (2002) considers the show as a business enterprise while Sam Smyth's (1996) *Riverdance: The Story* is a popular description of the show's first years.[6]

The book *Dancing in Ireland* by Breandán Breathnach (1983, see also 1996[1971]), an authority on Irish traditional music, is a major historical review on dance customs such as dancing at christenings and wakes, patterns (celebration of a local saint's day) and pilgrimages, and practices such as taking down a half door, clearing a table or dancing on a flagstone in order to get a good surface. Breathnach discusses the lack of descriptions of dancing and an Irish term for this activity in ancient sources, and disputes the claim that this would prove that the Irish did not dance in pre-Norman Ireland. It depends on how dancing is defined, Breathnach argues, referring to documents about music playing and says that this 'must have created reflex movement among those listening' (1983: 10). Dancing in Ireland seems first to have been documented around the year 1300 in the Middle English dancing song 'Ich Am of Irlaunde', although Breathnach (1983: 11) is not convinced that the line 'Come and dance with me in Irlaunde' is an indication of dancing as an aspect of social activity among Anglo-Irish at the time. Breathnach (1983) states that the Irish (Gaelic) terms for dancing, *rince* and *damhsa*, go back to the sixteenth century. It is likely that the so called 'carol', a group dance with a love song, which has been found in poems from the twelfth century, was brought with Norman invaders to Ireland. Brennan (1999), Breathnach (1983) and Friel (2004) all write about the importance of travelling dancing masters who went around the island teaching dancing (and decorum) to country people and gentry. As an indication of the disciplined movements of a good dancer, Breathnach (1983: 53) refers to the imaginative idea of being able to 'dance on eggs without breaking them and hold a pan of water on his head without spilling a drop'.

With a reference to the Middle English dancing song, William Butler Yeats (1990[1933]: 303) expressed his Irish nationalism through a poem in the 1930s titled 'I am of Ireland' where the first verse reads:

I AM of Ireland,
And the Holy Land of Ireland,
And time runs on,' cried she.
'Come out of charity,
Come dance with me in Ireland.

This is probably what has made the line 'Come dance with me in Ireland' famous. Ninette de Valois (1959), who built the Royal Ballet in London, made use of its poetic tone in the title of her memoir and at the same time as a way to emphasize her Irish background. Yet another level is added to the many meanings of the classic line in Barbara O'Connor's (2003b) article '"Come and Daunce with Me in Irlande": Tourism, Dance and Globalisation' where she discusses dance, tourism, globalization and authenticity in Ireland through an empirical case of a *Riverdance*-like dance show in Fitzsimon's pub in the summer of 2000 in the Temple Bar area in Dublin. Elsewhere O'Connor (2003a: 50) distinguishes between two periods of heterosexual discourses in her study of Irish popular dance and gender: the first in the 1920s and 1930s, which was characterized by 'ruin and sin' and linked to the formation of an Irish nation, the second beginning in the 1940s and 1950s of 'romance' which she connects to the growth of consumption and urbanization in Ireland. Although gender and sexuality are taken into some account in this study, as well as in Wulff (2003), these topics are more in focus in articles by O'Connor (1997b, 2003a, 2005).

Frank Hall (1995) has analysed Irish dancing quite substantially as a competitive sport steeped in nationalism; the characteristic stiff torso in terms of the posture puzzle (1995, 1996); and the stress for competitors and dance teachers at the competitions (1999). There is a series of booklets which provides a wealth of detailed documentation of the history of Irish dancing, written by John Cullinane (1990, 1996, 1998, 2003 among others). Catherine Foley's (1988a,b) work deals with traditional step dance in Co. Kerry and Co. Cork. Ruth Fleischman (1998) has edited a volume, introduced as 'Material for a History of Dance in Ireland'. It is a collection of memoirs primarily by Aloys Fleischmann, musician and composer, but also by dance people, family and friends of Joan Denise Moriarty, founder of the Irish National Ballet.

A report by Peter Brinson (1985), a dance educator in London, on theatre dance and ballet in Ireland, which was commissioned by the Arts Council in Dublin, resulted in major withdrawal of funding, forcing a closure of dance and ballet schools and companies in Ireland in the late 1980s. This traumatic watershed was often referred to during my fieldwork. Carolyn Swift's succinct formulation of the event as 'when the Arts Council pulled the plug' says it all. With dance classes at the Dublin Contemporary Dance Studio in the 1970s, and its Dublin Contemporary Dance Theatre directed by Joan Davies, Irish dance theatre had emerged as an art form in its own right. But one day in 1989 when Irish–American dancers Robert O'Connor and Loretta Yurik came in to work, the company had closed down because of lack of funding. It happened overnight. They then decided to start a company of their own, and this was how Dance Theatre of Ireland was formed. It is now one of the major dance theatre companies in Ireland, which tours abroad and performs at international dance festivals. One of these festivals, the biannual International Dance Festival Ireland, takes place in Dublin. To this festival, and on other occasions, Irish choreographers living abroad come back and show their work, sometimes collaborating with choreographers who are still living in Ireland. After many years in London, Michael Keegan Dolan and his Fabulous Beast Dance Theatre have moved back to Ireland. This is an award-winning company, as is Liz Roche's Rex Levitates Dance Company from Dublin.

This study moreover relates to the extensive literature on the *anthropology of Ireland* which has been reviewed in an authoritative reference work by Thomas M. Wilson and Hastings Donnan (2006) spanning topics such as social and economic transformations and traditions, policy issues, as well as new racisms, politics of identity, sport and parades in a global context. As Wilson and Donnan point out, the anthropology of Ireland has focussed on rural harmony, family farms and community, history and nationalism, as well as political and religious conflict.[7] This study is also a contribution to the gradually developing and increasingly theoretically advanced research field of the *anthropology of dance*. Dance has been included in anthropology as long as the discipline has existed, usually as a feature of ritual, without much analytical consideration. It was in the 1960s and 1970s that an anthropology of dance began to be formulated around the ability of dance to express certain circumstances about its society. Direct reflection is one type of dance expression, other types are social commentary and critique, even parody, as well as political and social statements. Dance is often an element of socialization. There is moreover the power of dance to release erotic feelings that usually are kept at bay. It is common that dance is used in the service of nationalism in rituals of nation-states, sometimes exhibiting one national or ethnic dance form at the expense of another in a situation of political domination. Political and religious control of dance, up to the point of legislation, has triggered resistance, particularly in colonial contexts: people have found ways to dance forbidden dances, and to make and revive ethnic dance forms (Wulff 2001).[8]

Shifting Meanings of a Key Metaphor

I can remember as a child growing up, in the evenings and listening from a distance, hearing the music coming across the fields – from this crossroads dance. I didn't ever go there, because we were too young, and it had ceased when I had grown up.

This soundscape memory was formed on a small farm in North Kerry in the west of Ireland in the 1940s, and the little boy who was listening to the music coming across the fields would become a Catholic priest, as well as the director of the acclaimed dance theatre company, Siamsa Tire. Father Pat Ahern learnt to dance from a travelling dancing master and to play the fiddle from his grandfather. Imagining, more than fifty years later, what this scene of dancing at the nearby crossroads would have looked like, Father Pat told me:

> The picture of a lone musician, an accordionist usually, because the accordions were loud enough to carry over the noise, sitting on a fence, under a bush maybe. On a summer evening after all the work was done and people just relaxed for an evening. It was a unique, unusual kind of experience. And the boys would meet the girls, and they would accompany each other home. It was very, very popular. It was probably the only cases when men and women, boys and girls, would meet socially in the week. The other time they would come together would be Sunday when they went to mass.

But everything was not idyllic at the crossroads. Father Pat continued:

> The Church frowned upon them, the crossroads dancing. They used to preach about them, against them. It was usually individual clergymen who would think like that. There were occasions when young people would misbehave. That's only in passing. They were quite innocent evenings of enjoyment.

Still, Catholic bishops were powerful enough to initiate the Public Dance Hall Act in 1935, a law which restricted dancing to dance halls – thus preventing crossroads dancing, dancing in barns and even in people's homes, so called house dances – on the grounds that these informal dances were associated with immorality. In order to avoid this, and significantly, to collect tax money, dance had to take place in licensed dance halls (Brennan 1999; Wulff 2003; O'Connor 2003a). The fact that there were conflicting views on what was actually happening at the crossroads, relates to the anthropological concern with place as a site for contestation and power struggles, as observed by Steven Feld and Keith Basso (1996). Feld and Basso also include issues of displacement and diasporas, as well as annexation and resistance in their perspective on place. Writing about the musical construction of place, Martin Stokes (1994: 3) brings in collective dances in his analysis of how the musical event 'evokes and organises collective memories and present experiences of place with an intensity, power and simplicity unmatched by any other social activity'.

After dancing at the crossroads, in barns and at house dances had been condemned by the Catholic Church, it happened that priests, in their persecution of dance, set fire to dancing platforms at crossroads, or drove their cars backwards and forwards over them (Mac Mahon 1954), or even beat those who were dancing with a big stick, such as in this story which goes back to the 1890s collected by Seán de Buizléir (1936: 35–38) in Duncormick, Co. Wicklow, for the Irish Folklore Collections in 1936:

There was a priest in Rathangan about forty years ago by the name of Father Williams. He was a very holy man and was awfully strict on boys and girls. He would go around the road with a big stick in the night time. He wouldn't allow dances at all. One time there was a set of mummers started in eRathangan, and they were partly afraid to start far they thought he would be putting a stop to them.[9] The priest heard of the mummers alright but said nothing only he wouldn't allow them to have any ball and they would have to finish it every night at ten o'clock. They were satisfied enough with that. They mummed for about three months and then it was into the New Year and it was time for them to leave it so ...They all came to the conclusion that it would be worth anything to have a whole night's fun. They decided to carry out the ball unknown to the priest.

But 'the priest had a boy working with him and he was also going to the ball'. The boy found out that the priest knew about the ball and was planning to 'put a stop to their little game'. So he hurried down to the ballroom where people were arriving for the ball. The boy warned them that the priest was on his way, so when the priest entered there was no sign of a ball, just the family kneeling down saying the Rosary. After that the priest 'never said anything about dances until the day he died'. And when he had left the barn, the guests all came down, 'and they lit the lights in the barn' and had their 'good night's fun'!

There was also an old man I met in the small village of Carraroe on the Connemara coast in the west of Ireland who told me about dancing in the past, and how 'All people, at that time, were afraid of priests. Father Connolly, he went around and he kicked all the accordions out of the house and chased those who were dancing!' In her extensive documentation of Irish dance, dance collector Helen Brennan (1999: 121) writes about police raids in homes, even court cases, but also a cheeky resistance: 'despite such opposition, dancing continued unabated'. The ban did not stop the Irish from dancing at crossroads and in their houses. Dancing was a widespread custom. In the words of the old Irish dancing master, Joe Donovan, '*everybody* danced!'[10] Impromptu dancing and dancing endurance tests were common enjoyments, as was dancing on flagstones and halfdoors. People danced away at parties, called 'sprees', even at wakes. And when someone was emigrating, a special wake, an American or an Australian wake, took place on the emigrant's last night in Ireland. Irish writer Fintan O'Toole (1999: 10) explains the use of the term 'wakes' with the belief that the emigrant was 'passing away to another side, probably for ever'. It is interesting to note that *Riverdance* includes a scene titled 'American Wake'. Brennan says that although dancing at the crossroads has become a cliché, it is still the most prominent memory of dancing from the past and thought of with much affection by those who took part in them. Jeanie Peak in Killinchy, Co. Down, who was in her early 80s when I met her in the winter of 2000, recalled how people walked from far away 'to dance at the corners' as it was called:

Those were good times. There was a corner there just where we lived and that's where we danced, ten of us, siblings and other girls, six girls and four boys, all gone out to the corner to dance. My mother and father were dancers themselves. The people all knew each other. When we were young we took our bicycles and didn't come back until 4 o'clock in the morning. We played rounders with a ball. It was no badness, it was clear pure fun, you know!

But with time young people in the country would find other ways to meet than at the crossroads dances. This dance form thus gradually subsided and turned into more of a rare tourist activity, which it is on the whole today. And so the fond memory of dancing at the crossroads in the past turned into a romantic memory of a lost Ireland.

As to Eamon de Valera's line 'comely maidens dancing at the crossroads', it has become something of a classic saying with shifting meaning in Ireland. It has been fondly and regretfully remembered, but also critiqued even in the form of irony or ridicule. Choreographer David Bolger does think that this speech was 'quite poetic and romantic, it has a lot of movement' yet he points out that that the role of women has changed since then: 'now they have taken over businesses'. In fact, the whole society has changed, David continues, with the grip of the Catholic Church starting to loosen, but he also sees greed around him. All this, as well as the multivocality of de Valera's speech, spurred David to open a dance production, *Reel Luck* (note the play with the name of an Irish dance step, reel, and the idea of real, true luck) with a tape of the speech: de Valera's voice is coming out, a thin but determined greeting from the past about a dream of a frugal and spritual Ireland. The voice is soon drenched in accelerating electronic music, and gone when the dancing starts.

In *Jiving at the Crossroads*, journalist John Waters (1991: 82–3) describes how Modern Ireland emerged as detached from the Past in the 1980s. Ardent advocates of Modern Ireland 'spoke disparagingly about de Valera's dancing-at-the-crossroads vision of a people content with hard work and simple pleasures'. I was well into my research before I discovered that de Valera did not talk about 'comely maidens dancing at the crossroads'. The mistake has occurred partly because the version of the speech which was printed in the *Irish Press* (1943) diverges from what de Valera actually said. This I have been able to confirm by listening to a tape of the speech recorded at RTÉ. de Valera actually said 'happy maidens' on air, but it was printed as 'comely maidens'. Nowhere does 'dancing at the crossroads' appear.

Ironically, it was a Catholic priest, Father Dermod McCarthy, who first told me that crossroads dancing still exists. It was in the mid-1990s in Co. Kerry that he saw people dancing on a plywood platform outside a pub. Later my choreographer friend from Belfast, Anthea McWilliams, called me in Sweden to tell me that her new boyfriend had promised to show her where they still dance at the crossroads. Anthea had prepared me in advance on email and when I replied that it looked like I would have to do some rewriting since I had assumed that crossroads dancing had more or less disappeared, she reassured me:

I wouldn't re-write anything yet if I were you, for, like the fairies, these cross-roads dances may be hard to find even for us Irish folk. But we will do a modern day version and see what happens.

It became a fun holiday for the new couple, which was reported to me on email with Irish eloquence and wit, including the typical (self-)parody, in this case of the style of traditional Irish storytelling:

Gary knew just the spot and Anthea followed, eyes, ears and feet a kimbo eager to snatch and catch a ready reel or a tricky 2–step. The destination? Well, Finuge in Co. Kerry not far from Listowel and Tralee, of course. That sunny afternoon in June found them calling at the Anglers Rest, the public bar at the Finuge crossroads where only cars and lorries scuttled by en route to somewhere else, but the entrepid 'danceplorers' were not fooled by this typical Irish scene with thatched cottage and roadsigns. Could it be that if they listened hard enough they could hear the footfall of dancers of years gone-by, the rhythm of the 'sets of yesteryear' or the murmer of music tinkling through? It was tough choice, but someone had to go into the bar just to ask. They both entered, it was empty, (and no drink was taken) but the barman was soon eager to provide the information they were looking for, and yes, there was to be dancing at the crossroads, in the summer months only and the night would be a Friday. Terrific.

Later they had indeed been dancing:

in the middle of the road (ensuring juggernauts and tractors clearance) to polka to breathlessness (a small Irish village 1km along the road!!!) laughing all the way.

But it would take two more years and another holiday before they actually found a group of people dancing at the crossroads. It was in August 2004, and as far from the original 'innocent evenings of enjoyment' where shy young men and women would meet, as one can get. Anthea wrote to me about a dismal event:

Sadly, although the night was dry and all looked promising for the cross roads dancing at Finuge, quite simply . . . I didn't dance at all. The music was dirge-like (man on keyboard, lady on accordion & cigarette) and not even the locals step foot on the dance floor within the first hour. A cry went up from the musician for 'The siege of Ennis' and the response was nil. The cry went up again and after several minutes of this trying, a trickle of people approached the floor, but still not enough for a full set. Even though the drink was flowing, eagerness was clearly not. The musician resorted to free drink offers to anyone, yes anyone who would get up and dance. I nearly did, but I seemed to be asphixiated (?) to my seat. Slowly, 2 local women ventured up to join the flagging set and Ennis was eventually sieged![11]

It is, again, not really as a practice that dancing at the crossroads lives on in Ireland, but as a key metaphor for major aspects of a changing society where tradition and modernity meet, and are being negotiated in many ways in different contexts. Theoretical discussions on tradition and modernity often postulate that they are not only oppositional categories, but also that they occur during different stages in a linear development, and that this applies to all sectors of society. From my ethnographic exploration in the Irish dancing community, tradition and modernity seem to coincide there albeit not always in perfect harmony. It even looks like I have found an instance of a circular development, of modernity reinforcing tradition: the success of *Riverdance* triggered a new wave of traditional and competitive dancing. *Riverdance* has made Irish dancing more accessible and known, and led to a professionalization of this dance form. The show also created a new genre: the Irish dance show. There have been about ten Irish dance shows modelled on *Riverdance*, but none of them has come close to the success of the original one. As the following chapters will suggest, modernity and tradition also overlap: tradition appears in new versions and then becomes a part of modernity. And this development is driven by travel and other forms of mobility.

Notes

1. The Eurovision Song Contest, which has been arranged for over fifty years, is an annual popular song contest where European countries can send an act to represent their country. The song contest is broadcast from the country that won the previous year. In the past, a jury in each participating country voted for best act, now voting is done via telephone by the viewers of each country. With the transformation of the political map of Europe, the number of acts has increased.

2. Set-dancing (originating from *quadrilles* with four couples) is yet another dance form, which is connected to these dance forms and also included in sections of dance theatre, *Riverdance*, and competitive dancing. Although a common dance practice in Ireland not least with a revival since the 1980s, set-dancing does not appear as a separate dance form here as much as the other three or four forms.

3. See Hélène Neveu Kringelbach's (2005) study for a prominent exception. This anthropological study analyses three interconnected dance forms in Dakar, Senegal: saba, women's dances, folkloric performances, and choreographic performances, so called contemporary dance. Neveu Kringelbach brings out sophisticated and original theoretical points pertaining to how dance, both on stage and in everyday performances, is a means for social mobility, a pawn in the politics of ethnicity in Senegal, and a scene where gender relations are being negotiated.

4. Maxine L. Margolis (1994: 263) has used the term 'yo-yo migration' to describe the back and forth movements of Brazilians in New York.

5. Siamsa Tíre means 'coming together for an entertainment' in Irish (Gaelic). This dance company is, again, also called the National Folk Theatre of Ireland.

6. There are early and more recent handbooks in Irish dancing, from O'Keefe and O'Brien (1902) to Murphy (1995, 2000), and small decorative 'coffee table' books such as Flynn (1998).

7. It all began with the by now classic community studies in the 1930s by Arensberg (1959[1937]) and Arensberg and Kimball (1968[1940]), followed by works such as

Messenger (1983[1969]) seeking to depict the 'true' nature of people in the west of Ireland, and Brody (1986[1973]) on its decline. The latter has recently been challenged by Okely (2005: 16) who, as the partner in the field, not yet trained as an anthropologist, quietly observed a different scene of 'resistance and continuity'. Examples of anthropological studies of Northern Ireland are Harris (1972) on prejudice in a rural border community, Glassie (1982) on storytelling and music, Jarman (1997) on parades and visual displays, Nic Craith (2002) on plural identities, and recently Lanclos (2003) on children's folklore and Kelleher (2003) on the Troubles, memory and identity. Taylor (1995) investigates religion, the influence of the Catholic Church in the Republic of Ireland. There is also a critique from Irish anthropologists of 'stereotypical images' of Ireland, calling for more research attention to the urban everyday life of the majority of the people on the island (Curtin, Donnan and Wilson 1993). In an examination of borders, the Irish border has been discussed by Donnan and Wilson (1999), and especially Northern Ireland's border Protestants by Donnan (2005). Peace (1997, 2001) has studied environment politics and local identity and modernity in an Irish village. McLean (2004) is a postmodern reading of the Great Famine. The peace process and multiculturalism are dicussed in Finlay (2004b). There is also the study by Scheper-Hughes (1979) on mental illness in the west of Ireland. Other studies conducted in Northern Ireland are Jenkins (1983) on youth, Sluka (1989) on popular support for the IRA and INLA, Feldman (1991) on violence and narrative, Aretxaga (1997) on violence and women. Symbols in Northern Ireland are analysed in a volume edited by Buckley (1998). Gmelch (1985[1977]) deals with Travellers in Dublin and Salazar (1996) with rural economy in the Republic of Ireland. The tendencies to portray Ireland in extreme terms either as an 'arcadian' or a 'pathogenic' society, are critiqued by Peace (1989). Wilson (1984) early suggested that it is time to move away from the influence of Arensberg and Kimball's model of kinship in an isolated rural community, urging attention to the impact of the European Common Market on Irish political economy.

8. See Royce (2000[1977]; Hanna (1987[1979], 1988); Spencer (1985a); Grau (1993); Reed (1998); Wulff (2001) among others. Based on her research in Tonga, Kaeppler (1985) was among the first to discuss 'dance' as a Western category. The impact of gender and sexuality in dance is examined in Hanna (1988). Van Nieuwkerk (1995) writes about the problem of dance and 'honour and shame' for professional female entertainers, singers and belly dancers, in Cairo. Cowan's (1990) study of Greek dance and Novack's (1990) study of contact improvisation in the United States regard dance as an embodied discourse, and the body as culturally constructed. This also concerns Ness's (1992) interpretation of the *sinulog*, a Philippino dance form. The theory of semasiology, the meaning of human movements as action signs, was introduced by Williams (1976; see also 2003[1991]) and applied by Farnell (1995) on Plains Indian sign language. There is the study by Daniel (1995) on how ballet replaced rumba as national dance in postrevolutionary Cuba. Recently, dance anthropologists have added Western stage dance and culture, and the unity and diversity of the transnational world of ballet (Wulff 1998), as well as European folk dance, to their previous focus on non-Western dance and movement. A way to illustrate the movement of dance through a text is seen in Taylor's (1998) *Paper Tangos*, where small black-and-white photographs have been included in the margin. Turning over the leaves produces a moving image of couples dancing the tango. Willis and Chisanga (1999) analyse dance in terms of a curative spiritual possession while Mendoza (2000) develops ideas on national identity and ethnicity through a ritual dance in the Peruvian Andes. Sklar (2001) details ritual events, especially dance, in connection

with Virgin of Guadalupe fiestas in New Mexico in the United States. The volume *Dance in the Field*, edited by Buckland (1999), reports on methodological issues in dance ethnography, at home and abroad in Polynesia, Asia, Europe, North America, Australia and Africa, relating to questions of representation and reflexivity, and including a consideration of how dance is documented.

9. Mummers wore masks, performed pantomimes, even danced in connection with festivals or celebrations such as Christmas (cf. Friel 2004).

10. This is a quote from the television programme Emerald Shoes: The Story of Irish Dance (1999).

11. The Siege of Ennis is a couple dance (done in a group) to a particular piece of music (or tempo group dance, referring to the town of Ennis, Co. Clare, in the west of Ireland.

Chapter 2

Tradition Reinvented

Searching for authenticity and tradition in Irish dance, I flew in early September 2001 to Dublin and then on to Galway, in the west of Ireland, where I boarded a local bus which drove along the Connemara coast to the small village of Carraroe. The sun had just come out after a spell of rain, making the pastoral landscape shine in the late afternoon light. I watched low walls running through the fields, and white houses, sheep and horses against a backdrop of the Aran islands. Arriving at the B&B in Carraroe, I met two American sisters on holiday, one of them a linguist who was doing research on the Irish language. They were also going to the competition in sean-nós dancing, it turned out, but for entertainment. We went early, around 7p.m. to the pub An Chistin, paid our entrance fees and received our tickets, each with a number. I told the people at the door that I was there for my study and in order to establish credentials I asked for one of the locals (who teaches at National University of Ireland, Galway), who I knew was coming with his wife. As the pub began to get crowded with local people who spoke Irish around us, I was beginning to wonder how this would go since I 'don't have any Irish', as the expression is. I was also getting tired, having travelled all day. I wanted the dancing to start so I could go back to the B&B and get some sleep. 'They are doing a raffle', the Irish-speaking linguist explained. I noticed that a man was drawing the raffles from a bucket held out to him by a big blond woman in a red blouse. I did not pay much attention to this, however, as I was busy trying to remember the layout of the pub and the people, and figuring out how to approach potential interviewees. Suddenly the linguist pushed my side excitedly: 'They're calling your number!' I had caught the word 'T-shirt' so I thought that as I rose in this packed pub, which now was getting warm and expectant, that I was going up-front to collect a T-shirt with a picture of a sean-nós dancer. But it turned out that I had been selected by chance to be one of six adjudicators of the competition! The man in charge of the competition, Colm Ó Méalóid, was a bit embarrassed, and so was I, but we soon got over it. Being an adjudicator would give me a unique insight into the dynamics of the competition.

This was a field opportunity I could not miss, but I would not have been able to make use of it unless I had had my extensive experience of dancing and watching dance (Wulff 1998, 2000, 2002, 2003). And even though my own participation in

Irish dance was extremely limited – I had taken one class in Belfast and one in Stockholm – I had watched a substantial amount of Irish dance by then. My point is that dance is a bodily activity which like all bodily activities contains knowledge in the actual practice (Wulff forthcoming). This is why virtually all dance, music, and sports scholars at some point take part in the activity they study, although they do not always make an explicit methodological point about it.

In Ireland, the idea of tradition is both cherished and contested, loaded with claims of authenticity and authority. The idea of Irish tradition is cherished because of the memory of the long colonial history when expressions of Irishness often were suppressed, and it is contested because of recent European integration and globalization. In these processes Irishness sometimes is reformulated, which may be experienced as a threat to authenticity and independence. However, tradition relies on transmission between generations or cohorts when it is bound to change somewhat, otherwise it will not survive in the long run. This circumstance is, and is not always, accepted in the dancing community. In this chapter I will discuss the many meanings of tradition and conflicts of authority in relation to ideas of modernity, especially in and around two dance forms: sean-nós dancing and *Children of Lir*, a dance theatre production based on an Irish legend. Both these dance forms have high claims to authenticity and tradition.

While respecting that certain cultural forms may be regarded as emblems for traditions, as well as making account of conflicting interests of such traditions, I had taken the analytical stance that everything is authentic in its own way. No life form, cultural expression or artefact is more authentic than any other, just produced at different points in time in different contexts than the very first form and expression. In my view, *Riverdance* is as authentic as traditional formal competitive Irish dancing, that is for what it is, namely a commercial dance show. *Riverdance* is culturally meaningful and real to those who participate in it and to its audience.

Still, I was intrigued by the pervasive idea that in the west of Ireland, in the so-called *Gaeltachts*, where Irish remains the first language, 'true' Irishness is said to have been preserved. Since the late nineteenth century, Diarmuid Ó Giolláin (2000: 3) points out, the Gaeltachts have been regarded as 'the repository of traditional rural and Catholic values, as a reservoir of Irishness'. This is where sean-nós dancing originates from and can still be found, this dance form that was a part of the Irish language movement in Ireland, which had an impact on national cultural politics. Sean-nós dancing had been on the verge of extinction, but now experienced a revival (cf. Livingston 1999 on music revivals). Brennan (1999) describes sean-nós dancing as informal and unknown outside Connemara until the 1970s. In fact, many people from students to academics and business people I met during my fieldwork outside the dancing community in Ireland had heard of sean-nós singing, this piercing acappela song, but not sean-nós dancing. It used to be self-taught, but for some time classes have been available. And there is the annual informal competition arranged in a pub in the small village of Carraroe. Dancers wear everyday dress and shoes, sometimes with metal tips in order to produce the characteristic step sound. Sean-nós is mostly a reel and the typical step is the so called *timeáil*, a 'percussive effect, which is produced by the heel' (Brennan 1999: 71). Contrary to formal competitive Irish dancing, the arms in sean-nós are relaxed, and swaying movements of the body are not uncommon. But the tapping dancer stays put on the floor. This is what expressions such as 'to dance on a plate' or even 'on a sixpence' refer to.

Touched by the passionate concern for sean-nós dancing I had read and heard about, my curiosity as a dance scholar was evoked: I had to see this dance form live! And despite having an analytical stance about everything being authentic, I had formed a continuum of the Irish dance scene in my mind where sean-nós dancing occupied the most 'authentic' pole on one side and the English group that performed a short *Riverdance* version late one night at a rural festival in Southern Sweden the other pole, with formal competitive Irish dancing and dance theatre stretching between.

The Sean-Nós Competition

So there I was on a chair in the front row with the other adjudicators, close to the little low stage where the 2001 competition in sean-nós dancing was about to unfold. We were handed pens and note books and I was told to give points on a scale between 0 and 10 points. Eight dancers were waiting in another room. They were going to do two rounds. Three musicians at the side of the stage began tuning their instruments: an accordion, a harmonica and a fiddle that soon came together in catching rhythms. First out was last year's winner, a young girl dressed in blue jeans and step shoes, so called hard shoes with big heels. She danced very well, raising the atmosphere in the pub. After her came a man and then a woman, neither of them leaving any particular impression. A little boy about ten years of age took the floor. He danced with a precision and joy that brought down the pub. Two young men appeared, one after the other, filling the stage with their electrifying steps making the audience scream. And I knew: one of them will win. You know good dance when you see it.

That was when a tall, good-looking man in his fifties dressed in worn casual trousers and a modest shirt went out on stage. He did not wear step shoes, just ordinary shoes with iron plates on the front and back of his soles. The music started and he tilted his head as if he was letting the music stream through his body as he listened to the sound, the clicks, of his steps. Everyone in the pub was completely spellbound by this highly skilled, effortless and exquisite dancing. I have no clear memory of the last dancer, although I now read in my fieldnotes that it was a man dressed in dark clothing who got a loud applause. But it was the man in his fifties with the elegant execution who won the competition. His name was Paraic Hopkins. He was in a class by himself.

The next day I went back to the pub, which opened around noon. I had made interview appointments with Colm Ó Méalóid, the man who had been in charge of the competition and with Paraic Hopkins, the winner. The daylight that streamed in through the small windows made the pub look quite different from the night before: harsh and desolate. Two rugged old men were already drinking at the bar. They offered long, rich stories about local dancing in the past, and when I started interviewing Ó Méalóid, they were happy to join in, commenting and elaborating on what he was saying. 'Low and fierce' is how good sean-nós dancing should be, I learnt. Later Paraic strode, in having driven from the small farm where he lived and worked. He sat down and ordered a cup of coffee, which he clutched with his big hands while his eyes were moving quickly around. Something was about to happen that has never happened to me before in the field: he demanded a fee for the interview. 'You will write a book and get money from it', he began and he went on to tell me that when had taught the President of Ireland to dance or when he had been on television, he had received IR£100. I told him that academics do not earn a lot of money on their books, and that I had no money to give him. 'When I teach classes', he persisted, 'I get IR£60'. The price has dropped, I noted to myself. After some more negotiations, when I tried to lure him into talking about Ireland generally, which he refused, realizing that this topic was also a part of my study, he finally urged me to take out my notebook. And so he talked generously and eloquently at great length about his love of music as a child and how he learnt sean-nós dancing by watching the old people dance at parties, or 'do a party piece' at weddings, christenings and Christmas parties, and how he would imitate them:

> That's how you get into it, same with sean-nós singing. The kids would pick up the words – and that's how the tradition has been kept, handed down from generation to generation. But I guess when television came and the parties moved into hotels, the kids didn't follow.

He also described the joy of dancing: 'When you see somebody who enjoys it, he gets carried away! He's like floating in the air and it is the music that is holding him up!' And about teaching this dance form:

> Sean-nós dancing is a natural dance. The old people used to say 'you can't teach it, you can learn it'. You don't let the body do the music. You get the person to listen to the music, the music will do the dancing. You don't worry about what the feet are doing. You don't worry about music and time and the feet does their own bit! When I started teaching I couldn't slow down to see the steps. I kept saying no for many years, then I learnt to slow down, now I'm teaching young kids. They packed it up very, very quickly. So they taught me back my own steps!!

We talked for over an hour and then he gave me a lift to the bus stop down the road. I promised to send him my book. It was with mixed feelings of having accomplished a lot during the short span of twenty-four hours, but also with regret, that I headed back to Galway and on to Dublin. Having been touched by extraordinary dancing and stories about dancing, I brought many fond memories. One thing I had learnt in this 'Celtic knotwork'[1] network fieldwork, however, was to never think that I would not meet people again. Sooner or later, often in the most unlikely contexts, they turned up.[2]

The initial negotiations I had had with the winner before he started talking to me had given me data about multi-local links between the village and wider Irish society, even globally, such as that sean-nós dancing had been included at Irish festivals in Boston, Milwaukee, Scotland and Isle of Man. The Cararroe competition, which is a part of a larger festival, *Pléaráca Chonamara*, containing music, song, storytelling, drama and sport, is an interesting instance of a cultivation of a local tradition through an association, the Gaeltacht Civil Rights Movement. In fact, the term sean-nós dancing was introduced as late as 1975 as a way to distinguish local old-style solo step dancing from the formal national dance competitions organised by the Gaelic League (see Chapter 6) and the *Pléaráca Chonamara* festival was only set up in 1993. Going back to the issue of authenticity, there are thus elements of invention of tradition here. Paraic Hopkins, the winner, recalled this process for me:

> Twelve–fifteen years ago the old tradition was dying out, and a couple of committees went together and decided to put together singing and dancing. That started to revive sean-nós. The competition here is in remembrance of Martin O'Griffin. He used to dance on a small table. He died fifty years of age. Maybe three of four dancers came from within this area. One day they were in the pub here amongst themselves and they were arguing who was the best dancer. A woman said they should stop the arguing. She got a cup and Ir£ 50, and an adjudicator down from Dublin. Since then the cup was danced every year. *Pléaráca* came in and they sponsored and organized.

While I was in Carraroe I kept asking people if the dancing had changed, but they did not seem to think so, except that in the old times mostly men danced, now both men and women dance, young and old. People in the pub, visitors, other adjudicators and the dancers talked about the individuality of the dancing, however, and that 'every sean-nós dancer has his own style'. Brennan (1999: 143) brings up this focus on 'individuality, freedom of expression and personal creativity' and the notion that personality influences sean-nós dancing. Such individual styles are likely to affect, change as it were, the general dance practice in the long run.

In the past, sean-nós was mostly danced by men, but with the introduction of organized competitions, more women joined in. When it comes to the issue of adjudication of sean-nós dancing, Brennan (1999: 148) paints a complex picture saying that 'the adjudicator should know the style intimately; thus will most likely be local'. Yet there is an unwillingness to judge one's peers, and this is why outsiders may be asked instead. But then there is a risk that these people are not familiar enough with sean-nós and apply unsuitable criteria when deciding about the winner. There is for example the story about the woman outsider who found herself adjudicating a sean-nós competition in the 1960s: unable to distinguish between the dancers, she recalls 'I gave the prize to the fella that had the most children!'

At the same time as the advertising of the sean-nós competition in the form of posters and leaflets have attracted more people to it, thereby contributing to the revival of sean-nós dancing, this advertising is all in Irish, which means that this tradition continues to be a local event after all, few tourists make it there.

Tradition: Dead or Alive

In his influential introduction to the volume *The Invention of Tradition*, Eric Hobsbawm (1983: 1, 14) notes that traditions that 'appear or claim to be old are often quite recent in origin and sometimes invented'.[3] These 'invented traditions' include both traditions that are established gradually over a long time and those that suddenly are formalized. Invented traditions can be more or less permanent repetitious rituals, they can be new versions of old traditions, but they all tend to emerge as reactions to new situations and with reference to 'a suitable past'. Hobsbawm talks especially about creations of nationalism and how the modern 'nation' has to be understood in terms of invented traditions. He also makes a point of separating how the past is featured through the official ideology of nationalism on one hand and popular memory on the other.

Because of the elusive nature of dance, and the problems with documenting movements, dance anthropologists tend to be careful with definitive statements about origins of dance. But there are written sources and images, as well as certain oral narratives that provide some information about historical and cultural developments in dance. At the same time, if we follow Hobsbawm's argument, there is reason to be aware that historical pasts may be redefined according to present national political contexts, and that this process is often repeated at different points in time, changing the interpretation accordingly. In my study, the Great Famine in the 1840s, the cultural nationalist movement which began at the end of the nineteenth century, the Public Dance Hall Act from 1935 and the recent economic boom from the late 1980s and early 1990s were the four main historical junctures that kept coming up as points of reference from the past both in the dance and in verbal and written descriptions by my informants. This was the case among dance people such as dancers, teachers, choreographers as well as scholars such as historians, anthropologists, folklorists or sociologists, many of whom also were or had been active as dancers or teachers.

Although some senior dance people maintained that 'the true origins of Irish dance are shrouded in the mists of time', others had made a career out of documenting the history of dance in Ireland. In light of the fact that John Cullinane is a member of the Gaelic League, his historical work on Irish competitive step dancing must be seen as part of the official ideology of nationalism. So are the Folklore Collections at the Department of Irish Folklore, University College Dublin. With national independence, the Irish Folklore Commission was set up in 1935. The remit of the Commission was to 'collect the tradition' which is now held in the Folklore Collections in the form of written accounts of oral narratives, stories in English and Irish on music, dance and local customs, as well as photographs and black-and-white films (see also Ó Giolláin 2000).

The popular memory of Irish dance in all the different dance forms and communities, from sean-nós and formal competitive dancing to dance theatre and dance shows, was structured by the four historical junctures already mentioned, especially the Famine. That is how far back most popular dance memories seemed to go. The senior female Irish dancer who told me that 'we used to do cake dances', which was a session of dancing where the best couple was awarded a cake, was referring to this as a local custom in her area that she had learnt about from the old people there who remembered it from the nineteenth century, rather than a dance event dating as far back as the seventeenth century as discussed by Breathnach (1983, 1996). Another popular memory was conveyed to me by David Bolger, the Dublin choreographer, who talked with great engagement about dancing in the past in Ireland and how:

> They used to wake the dead. They would revive the corpse, put them in their favourite chairs and lift them up when people came in. They danced at wakes, slip jig and reel, and played games, silly, silly games. You have to be drunk to understand. Singing would be huge. Years ago they used to take the door down if the floor wasn't flat enough. They danced on flagstones making sparks with their heels!

The Great Famine raged in Ireland from 1845 until 1848. The fungus *phytopthora infestans* caused recurring failures of the potato crop. As a result, more than one million people starved to death and two million people emigrated. Identifying the Great Famine as the most central event in Ireland in modern times, Kevin Whelan (2005: 137) holds up the historical facts: major famines were not really a part of the European experience any longer, and that Ireland would be shattered by this kind of plight was 'made all the more unusual in that it then formed part of the richest, most powerful and centralised state in the world – the United Kingdom'. In popular memory in the dance world and in the dances, there were many references to the massive losses of people and the cruel circumstance that food and grain kept being exported to England during the Famine. Friel (2004) shows how the depopulation of the countryside in the aftermath of the Famine changed dancing customs. There was also a movement from rural to urban areas, leaving old customs behind in the places where dancing used to take place, and hence those dances more or less obsolete. Another aspect of the social and cultural transformations of Ireland that the Famine entailed was that towards the end of the nineteenth century dance had lost its ability to unite people, even momentarily, across social boundaries (Whelan 2005; Friel 2004).

The *rince fada*, the long dance, or field dance, on May Day goes back to the sixteenth century, according to Irish dance historians.[4] This dance form also came up in conversations I had with dance people, for instance with a senior teacher of Irish dancing. Attributing a popular memory version to this dance, he told me that 'rince fada, it has to do with Ireland and the fact that lots of Irish people went out to the States because of the Famine'.

One type of competition at the week-long World and All Ireland Championships in Irish Dancing is the so called 'figure dancing' or 'dance drama'. It is one of the highlights of these championships and marks the conclusion of them. These dance dramas feature interpretations of stories from Irish legends and history. Inevitably, the Famine is commemorated on these occasions. At the All Ireland's in 2002, for example,

I saw the dance drama titled 'The Leaving', which was about people having to leave Ireland because of the Famine. And when I asked a dancer with Siamsa Tíre, the National Folk Theatre in Tralee, Co. Kerry, about the origin of the erect posture in Irish dancing, he started out with dark wit: 'it's a tribute to those who died in the famine!' before he went into more conventional explanations about the development of Irish dancing.

Choreographer Michael Keegan Dolan had quite elaborate views on Irishness and the Famine:

> I'm also very interested in nationality and about being Irish and the problems. Every nationality has a kind of karmic weight. Being English has its problems, being Irish has its problems. Being Irish can be pretty problematic. You have inherited all the crisis and all the neurosis from the Famine, from the occupation by an invading power and its corresponding de-masculinisation, from dictatorial Catholicism (Theodores 2003: 119).

There was thus a recurring awareness of the Famine in and around dance during the time of my fieldwork, yet its most manifest presence was the 1999 revival of the dance theatre piece titled *Ballads* choreographed by David Bolger. It was the 150th anniversary of the Famine in 1995 which had first spurred Bolger to make this serious and moving piece. For him, the choreographic process had been a way to learn more about this devastating period in Irish history. I will discuss *Ballads* as an instance of social memory in Chapter 3.

Trustees of Tradition

The significance of tradition both as idea and practice in the different forms of Irish dance did not exclude the opportunity, even necessity of, innovation. In fact, the awareness that a dance tradition has to change and develop in order to survive was more common than not, both among dance scholars and practitioners. What mattered was how this change took place and what it consisted of. There were authenticity debates within one dance form, but critique and condemnation of dance developments were also levelled in relation to other dance forms. In my study the most obvious example was the debate that *Riverdance* provoked in the competitive Irish dancing community, let alone in Ireland as a whole. For years, everyone seemed to have an opinon on this sudden success. Writing about *Riverdance*, Fintan O'Toole (1997a) remarks that traditional forms do change when they are removed from their original setting, but this does not mean that they will perish. Irish dancing has survived displacement before. Neither is Bill Whelan, the composer of the *Riverdance* music, worried about tradition. He believes tradition will always be there, 'tradition is safe', he told me, but added that traditional music will only live if each generation takes it up and uses it creatively. This view of each generation as the trustee of tradition is also common in the dance community.

But not even sean-nós dancing was always regarded as traditional 'enough'. In an interview I did in Dublin with Ríonach Uí Ógáin, song researcher and archivist at the Folklore Collections, Department of Irish Folklore, University College Dublin, she reminisced about a local dancing company in Co. Kerry, which used the back of a lorry for sean-nós dancing. (This was incidentally quite common in the past, also for competitions.) This company was a source of pride and joy, everybody was there from the locality to see it. While characterising this dance form as 'less traditional', Uí Ógáin added that:

> It depends on how you define traditional and everybody defines it in different ways. Set-dancing is traditional. The history of dance is very complex, every place has their own sets. Clare, they don't lift their feet that much while in Kerry they lift their feet. Connemara, Donegal they have their own style. The music, the repertoire and style affects the dancing.

In the many debates over what tradition in general and in dance in particular actually consists of, and what changes are 'allowed', a number of commentators have pointed out that Irish dance from sean-nós and set-dancing to competitive solo step dancing and *Riverdance*, like any dance form, is put together from steps of different origins and then executed in local changing ways as these dance forms move between places and over time.[5] This parallels the development of traditional music in Ireland, another charged area which ties into the dance community since much of the dancing is done to traditional music. The recent upsurge in Irish dancing should be seen in relation to the remarkable expansion nationally and globally of Irish traditional music which has been going on since the 1970s (Vallely 1999; see also Basegmez 2005). Sean Corcoran (1991: 2), a traditional singer, mandolin player as well as song and music collector, starts out by arguing for 'the real thing', to listen to the music, when he is asked to define what traditional music is, and that 'theory can never match practice'. Yet he moves on to a theoretical level, which also is useful here, saying that 'my own experience is that while the form may be conservative, the structures fairly permanent, the actual content may be quite innovative, and often surreal'. In her recent study, *Irish Scene and Sound: Identity, Authenticity and Transnationality among Young Musicians*, Virva Basegmez (2005) shows how young traditional musicians in Ireland include many different sounds in their music making, in a quite innovative manner, and that the Irishness of this contemporary traditional music is a combination of traditional Irish music and other musics of the world such as pop, rock, soul, reggae and folk music from various countries.

Already in 1901, Ó Giolláin (2000: 122) tells us there was a debate 'about the vexed question of the authenticity of particular dances' in the Oireachtas, an annual cultural festival connected to the Gaelic League. At stake was whether a four- and eight-hand reel, which had been introduced by members of the London Gaelic League at the Oireachtas in Dublin, was 'native' or 'alien' (Brennan 1999: 33; see also Cullinane 2003). This distinction kept defining Irish dance up to the Public Dance Hall Act in 1935, but as O'Toole (2003: 12) astutely observes: 'A key part of this institutional conservatism was the very notion that there was a fundamental distinction between native and foreign or, in formal terms, between tradition and innovation'. It is a good point pertaining to dance in a larger perspective where so much dance is crossover of different origins. It is also a good point here since it reveals the relative randomness of what is and has been accepted as 'Irish' dance. At the same time there was an insight into Irish dance as 'a fusion of many influences, both from within Ireland and beyond'.[6] Cullinane's comment in the television programme *Emerald Shoes* about the origin and development of Irish dance applies to many national dances:

> The earliest form of our dances would have been jigs, and hornpipes. The hornpipe almost certainly originated in England. We have made those dance forms our own. We have evolved them. We have put our stamp on them, you know. And they have been in Ireland now, danced for several hundred years.

As to set-dancing and tradition, Terry Moylan, who teaches set-dancing at the Brookes Academy in Dublin says that:

> I'd like to see it become fully modern, popular. The word traditional is an awful albatross around the neck all the time, it raises all kinds of spectres. It's a heritage we have to adhere to, when set-dancing became popular again, when it involved a revival, there was a conflict between tradition and innovation, a structure of revival. It was in Monkstown, I was pushed off the floor once when we were dancing a different set than they were playing. Even in our own little club there's a conflict between 'innovation and tradition'. It was a Jenny Lind set where traditionally the men's arms are around the woman's waist and the other arm on the shoulder of the man in front. This old man said: 'it's not traditional'. Since then we don't dance it, it has disappeared.

So there is a risk of losing the tradition. Some traditions are lost such as crossroads dancing is on the whole by now, at least when it comes to scale and significance for young people in rural areas. In his erudite and versatile *Locating Irish Folklore*, Diarmuid Ó Giolláin (2000: 17, 173) discusses the end of tradition. He points out that 'the death – and protection – of tradition has been a prominent cultural theme in Irish life up to the present day'. When a tradition dies this means 'the loss of the shared past which is a foundation of identity' and this has had 'profoundly political implications'. Still, there are other sides to this process. Ó Giolláin questions the view of an unchanging past controlled by tradition while the present is supposed to be devoid of tradition. For as we move towards de-traditionalization, there is at the same time 'the continuity and constructions of traditions', he says.

Regional Tradition, Myth and Modern Steps

Like all folk traditions, especially in music and dance, Irish dance traditions can be deconstructed into a number of regional styles. At least they could some time ago, before radio and tape recorder made regional music styles less distinct, and television and video began diluting regional dance styles.[7] This I was told on a number of occasions by music and dance people. They also talked about how competitions arranged by formal organizations have tended to turn regional styles into one uniform style both in music and dance. Music people also brought up the momentous advent of the radio, and later the tape recorder, and how both media had contributed to making regional music styles less distinct. The same thing had happened to dance styles through television and video. It seems likely that the disappearance of regional dance styles also is a consequence of a modernity process where regional identities are one part of a generic national Irish identity.

Brennan (1999: 58, 64–71, 152) goes back to the impact of individual dancing masters in the past who often taught their own styles in different regions. She distinguishes three remaining styles in traditional Irish step dancing: the Southern style originating from Munster, the Western from Connaught and the Northern style from Ulster. This leaves Leinster, the region around Dublin, in the east of Ireland, without a specific style, at least nowadays as Brennan says. In the Munster style, which is the style that is taught at the Irish dancing schools: 'the dancer is posed on the ball of the foot with the heel being raised about two inches from the floor'. The Northern tradition is characterized by two dancers placed opposite each other. In solo step dancing there is a 'constant heel–toe balancing movement by the foot not engaged in performing the distinctive features of a particular step. It is what could be described as persistent drumming'. In the North, there is also the Belfast Hop, which is performed with 'very high knee movement' combined with 'very rapid movement forward, back or diagonally, as well as a tendency to spring up and down during the execution of a step'. Sean-nós is the style Brennan identifies with Connemara in the west of Ireland. She describes it as 'kicking the floor twice with the tip of either toe', 'stamping with either foot' and 'a shuffling movement in which the ball of the foot brushes the floor'.

The dance production titled *Children of Lir (Clann Lir)* included sections of sean-nós dancing. *Children of Lir* was performed by Siamsa Tíre.[8] Founding Siamsa Tíre in 1974, Father Pat Ahern went on to build it into an acclaimed national dance company with a firm base in the local community that also toured abroad. The travelling dancing master who taught Father Pat to dance (who is mentioned briefly in Chapter 1) was the legendary Jerry Molneaux. His last name was pronounced 'Monnix', Brennan (1999: 54) points out, and this was how dancers I talked to would spell it to me. It is thus the so called Monnix style which Siamsa Tíre still dances.[9] According to Father Pat 'Monnix rhythmically follows the tradition', and when Siamsa Tíre was a new company:

> We videotaped all the pupils of Monnix, mosty men, only one woman (now it's mostly women who dance). They were old and some of them crippled, arthritic. Some of them danced sitting in chairs. Because I was a pupil of this man, Monnix, I was able to interpret.

This was the basis for the style of this company, which was developed further by visiting choreographers such as Mary Nunan who choreographed *Children of Lir*. This old Irish legend, or myth, begins on the back cover of Scott (1997[1986]):

Lir, Lord of the Sea, has taken a second wife, Aife; Aife is consumed with jealousy of Lir's four children and she is determined to be rid of them. The children cannot be killed, but using extraordinary supernatural powers Aife lays a terrible enchantment upon them – one that will last 900 years...

She turns the children, two male and two female, into swans.[10] And as Ríonach Ní Néill, assistant choreographer to *Children of Lir* continued:

The stepmother takes the children to a lake pretending they are going on an outing. They will be saved by a man with a bell when they have lived through the age of the Celtic and Christianity has been introduced, the transition from the pre–Celtic Ireland to the post–Celtic Ireland, linking our history with the myth.

In Siamsa Tíre's version, Lir was very old, wearing a gold crown and a long red robe. The stepmother was dressed in green and black. The company formed the sea by moving together like waves. The four children threw themselves in, where they 'became' swans. They came back covered in identical white long sleeve polo tops, narrow long trousers with lace-like cloth around the hem.

Mary Nunan told me that Siamsa Tíre is 'very protective about their style' and recalled how she and her assistant during the work with *Children of Lir* sometimes went into discussions over whether what they were doing was authentic, and could they do it? *Clann Lir* was choreographed by improvising the traditional steps. 'The main thing I feel', Mary was saying, 'is that this production was a good way to develop the tradition, contrary to *Riverdance*. She added sections of sean-nós dancing not least since she had a special relationship to this dance form:

I remember going to learn some Irish dancing when I was young and not taking to it for some reason and not being attracted to watching it. But when I saw Sean Nos dancing, which is the dancing of Irish traditional dance before the homogenisation, the regional styles, its earthiness and delicacy, its articulation and its looseness, I thought it was like blues singing (Theodores 2003: 204-05).

At the side of the stage was a little traditional orchestra. Irish song was also integrated into the performance, even though the Monnix dance style was the most prominent element. It was, however, especially interesting in light of my discussion on tradition that the traditional footwork was mixed with arm movements from modern stage dance. The 'swans' now and then had their arms making a circle above their heads and flapping them like wings as if they were flying. This crossover texture between traditional 'folk' dance and modern stage dance lead to a major critical success for *Children of Lir*.

No Tradition

The notion of tradition was central in and around sean-nós dancing, set-dancing, competitive dancing, even *Riverdance*. The only dance form in my study where tradition was not an issue was dance theatre. As Ríonach Ní Néill told me: 'One thing I miss in Ireland is tradition'. She talked at great length about the lack of tradition in dance theatre, this emerging dance form in Ireland, meaning a lack of *Irish* tradition. Drawing on her own upbringing and the fact that Irish was her first language, she made a dance theatre piece titled *Seandálaíocht* (Irish for archaeology) about the last speaker of a language, about losing your language and culture. This is clearly something many people in Ireland can identify with. In that sense it is an Irish theme, one that recurs in Irish dance theatre. Ríonach exclaimed: 'We're obsessed with Irishness! I suppose we're postcolonial'. For like most other Euro-American dance theatre, Irish dance theatre, again, goes back to American and German traditions. Yet there are the Irish themes, steps and music that keep occurring in Irish dance theatre, often in order to accentuate distinct emotional moods.

It is interesting that the idea of tradition in the dance world in Ireland is understood to imply Irish tradition, it is interesting because it is not always the case that national tradition is the most prominent tradition in dance in other countries, especially not where modern stage dance and ballet have been stronger than folk dance. In the transnational ballet world, there is a notion of five national ballet styles: the French, the Russian, the Danish, the English, and the American styles. Importantly, they have moved and increasingly move across national borders. It is in fact more common than not, in the ballet world, to cultivate the national tradition of another country in line with political domination and alliances (see Wulff 1998). The cultivation of the national tradition of *another* country is what is happening when Irish dancing, competitive Irish dancing, is practised in the diaspora: from North America, England and Scotland to Australia and New Zealand where the Irish tradition of competitive dancing is thriving in foreign national contexts.

Dance as a Modern Tradition

The belief that Irish tradition emanates from people living close to the land and thus has a holy quality which must not be changed is certainly appealing, but it does not get us very far in the Irish dance scene where tradition does change and sometimes take the form of modernity. As Friel (2004: 9, 53-4) says 'what is now considered traditional Irish dance was simply contemporary social dancing that took selected elements to itself and carried them on, allowing them to change for better or worse'. Friel singles out the prohibitions as the most important junctures for dance and notes how the Gaelic League 'declared what would or would not be termed "traditional"', which supports the argument that traditional Irish dancing was invented.

According to Richard Bauman (2001: 15821), there is a social organization of tradition where cultural specialists are custodians of 'cultural performances or display events, such as rituals, festivals, contests, or dramatic performances' that express 'knowledge, symbols, and values of the group'. The social organization of tradition also involves socialization, processes of conveying and acquiring practices between generations. This is the case with competitive Irish dancing which continues to be a widespread practice and a part of growing up in Ireland. An education in Irish dancing also includes informal lessons in Irish history and culture, in Irishness in other words. To identify dance as traditional is also a way to cultivate nationalism. As Bauman (2001: 15823) says 'the process of traditionalization – under the rubric of tradition, heritage, patrimony, custom, or the like – is a prominent resource in the service of nationalism, whether cultural nationalism or nation-state formation'.

In the debate on tradition and modernity, we need to consider that one person's tradition is another person's modernity: from the perspective of *Riverdance*, the competitive dancing community represents tradition, while those who do sean-nós and set-dancing as a part of the recent set-dancing revival at céilís all over the island regard the competitions and the schools that provide them with Irish dancers as modern. It is significant that dance that has once been identified as traditional Irish dancing will keep that label, but other forms which were once considered modern will be added to the traditional category. Contrary to the designation modern, 'things traditional' will always be traditional. It is a label that sticks and expands. Friel (2004: 54) concludes that 'tradition, if alive, must keep changing, evolving and adapting. Each generation must find some element within a tradition that it can relate to and make its own. This process is alive today in Irish music and dance'.

In the competitive dancing community, tradition seems to be elusive, however: while there is a notion that people in the Irish diaspora are better at keeping up the tradition than the Irish in Ireland, the diaspora go to Ireland to learn about it (see Chapter 6). When it comes to sean-nós and wider Irish society, we have seen how sean-nós dancing was a part of the Irish language movement orchestrated by the Gaelic League, which had an impact on national cultural politics (Brennan 1999). Now sean-nós dancing has spread to other parts of the island, also to cities, which together with classes and television programmes on this dance form are creating a crossroads situation: the Connemara tradition is becoming a part of national and even transnational contexts reaching across the globe to the United States where sean-nós is performed at Irish festivals.

For an anthropologist, the concept of tradition finally problematizes the relationship between indigenous and analytical concepts, or ethnographic and theoretical concepts, that used to be separate. For here is a concept which is referred to in both senses in my field, sometimes on a sliding scale, sometimes overlapping, since some of my informants, in fact quite a few of them, are not only dance people but also intellectuals, writers and scholars, and thus my colleagues, with theoretical, synthesizing perspectives on dance and its traditions. Together with those who see themselves as 'coming out of the tradition', i.e., as dancers, they all contributed both official nationalist comments on dance traditions to my study, and popular memories, sometimes reflected in cherished or haunting personal memories.

Notes

1. See Afterword for how I owe this expression to Frank Hall.

2. I have not yet met Paraic Hopkins since then, but I have met one of his nephews who also danced very well in this competition. He did a sean-nós section as a part of a performance at the (American) Society of Dance History Scholars Conference held at The Irish World Music Centre at the University of Limerick in 2003. This is the base of Daghadha Dance Company, one of the major Irish dance theatre companies, which Mary Nunan founded in 1988 (see Chapter 4).

3. A discussion on the invention of traditions includes an acknowledgement of the notion of authenticity as constructed, see Handler (1986) and Spooner (1986), and even 'fabricated' as Peterson (1997) puts it in relation to country music. Peterson's point is that what is regarded as authentic changes over time. Stokes (1994) agrees that authenticity is not an inherent quality of music or musicians, but suggests that it has great efficacy as a boundary marker. Kockel's (forthcoming) notion of reflexive tradition is another useful take on contemporary tradition and heritage production.

4. See Breathnach (1983, 1996), Brennan (1999), Cullinane (1999) and Friel (2004).

5. See Breathnach (1983), Brennan (1994b, 1999), Hall (1995), O'Connor (1997a), Cullinane (1998).

6. This is a quote from woman speaker in the television programme *Emerald Shoes: The Story of Irish Dance* (1999).

7. In the same vein, choreographer Fiona Quilligan talked about the introduction of electricity on a small island outside the coast of the west of Ireland, and that 'storytelling was gone with electricity, with television'.

8. The story about the poet and warrior *Oisín*, performed by Siamsa Tíre since 2001, is another example of a dance production which features sean-nós steps, traditional music and Irish song.

9. See Foley's (1988a,b) extensive work on this style.

10. In some versions of this myth, there are three swans/children, two male and one female. Scott (1997[1986]) writes about three males and one female child/swan.

Chapter 3

Memories in Motion

'My sisters were dancing all night', the old man told me as he was drinking his Guinness in the pub in the small village of Carraroe on the Connemara coast in the west of Ireland. He went on:

> When someone was going to America, my sisters were dancing all night. I remember once, when our aunt was going, my sisters were 15–16 years old. Our aunt left on the bus to Galway at seven. When the bus came back the next day – my sisters were still dancing!

The sisters in this story made the most of the goodbye: by parting with their aunt while in motion, they can be said to be holding on to her as long as they possibly could while she was in motion, that is travelling on the bus and later on the boat all the way to America. The sisters thus connected the small village of Carraroe with America, the family which was left behind with the departing aunt through their bodily marathon movements.

Emigration and exile, travel and mobility have been a vital part of Irish culture for a long time. In the previous chapter, I considered emigration waves during the mid nineteenth-century Famine when, again, two million people left the country. Later emigration waves have been triggered by unemployment. The Irish diaspora is now many times larger than the population of Ireland.[1] Members of the diaspora have kept going back to Ireland for visits, and recently return migration has gathered force. Dance can be said to travel around Ireland, North and South, as well as back and forth to Ireland. This has been happening for quite some time through emigration, when Irish people have brought Irish dance to their new countries, and it is now an expanding practice. Irish dancers living outside Ireland go back to Ireland for championships in Irish dancing and Irish dance theatre companies and *Riverdance* (as well as other Irish dance shows) go on European and global tours.

Against a backdrop of historical and geographical mobility of Irish dance, this chapter combines theoretical perspectives on mobility on the one hand and social or popular memory on the other with the idea of the body as a site of culture. This analytical triad brings out the idea of embodiment of Irishness through dance, and how dance itself is also a case in point for mobility. This is where *Ballads*, the dance theatre production which features the Famine as a topic, is an instance of how history from the more distant past is managed in popular memory. The dance theatre production *Macalla* (Irish for echo) featuring the Troubles in Northern Ireland is an illustration of such memory of recent, lived history which Irish people who were included in my study, had experienced themselves.

An understanding of dance in Ireland needs to be anchored in the unique history of Ireland, North and South. The postcoloniality in the South is particularly significant for this study, and its links to the long period of English colonialism which ended as recently as 1921. This uneasy circumstance has been addressed primarily by scholars of history and literature[2] rather than anthropologists, although there is a recent discussion by McLean (2004). Some of these scholars have compared Ireland to colonized non-European countries, while others have argued that Ireland is more like any other country in Europe. There is also the standpoint that Ireland is too special a case to be analysed with imported theoretical models. In the many interpretations of Irish history, national narratives versus more diversified perspectives, such as so-called historical revisionism, have been a part of the academic debate.

The memory of history leads to the idea of social memory, and Paul Connerton's (1989) crucial argument that images of the past are remembered by way of ritual performances that are 'stored' in a bodily memory. Connerton points to Paul de Man's (1970) suggestion that forgetting is crucial for the experience of modernity, to make a new departure possible. Yet de Man argues that a pronounced rejection of the past in fact creates a strong dependency on previous times. Irish history is haunting Irish people, and is negotiated through Irish themes and steps in dance theatre and dance shows in order to come to terms with the memory of the past.

In his seminal book *The Collective Memory*, Maurice Halbwachs (1980) contrasts the documenting logic of history with the fragments of collective memory, especially as the latter is always changing and shaped by the present. Collective or social memory may be distributed unequally in the minds of the members of a group, but it can be united at rituals and performances. The colonial past of Ireland is often referred to as unresolved because of its long duration and recent ending. Yet it seems plausible to add another explanation to the lingering memory of colonialism: I am thinking of the complex differences, including internal suppression, between groups of Irish people (some Anglo-Irish versus some Irish, some rural versus some urban etc.) during colonialism. This circumstance diversifies the memory of the past quite substantially. Dance is an area, however, where different kinds of Irish people can meet and manage the past together – even if their experiences and memories are diverse and fragmented. Because of the multivocality, of the many possible interpretations of a dance performance, it provides a versatile forum for investigation of the past. Yet the way this is done, through reflexivity in connection with cutting-edge dance theatre performances, grand dance championships and the showbiz of *Riverdance*, this memory is a type of modernity, an issue I will come back to. It can be seen as an instance of the reflexivity of modernity as suggested by Anthony Giddens (1991). There is also an effort in dance in Ireland to move on by featuring topics that other

European dance companies deal with, such as the cultural impact of technology, the meaning of the millennium shift, and archetypical themes of love and loss, or just abstract dance which explores new dance and movement space.

Long Memories: Dancing the Famine

When the Dublin dance company CoisCéim (Irish for footsteps) performs *Ballads*, the piece about the Great Famine, this is a moment of reflexivity and release.[3] As dance critic Carolyn Swift (1997) wrote of the performance: 'The Famine is a subject which could easily lose its emotion in mawkish cliché, but here the symbols and multi-purpose props, combined with highly imaginative choreography, results in excitement and catharsis'. Irish people in the audience, with different pasts, remember what they have learnt about the Famine, and what they know about their family at that time. Watching *Ballads* may also be a way to find out more about the Great Famine. This was actually what spurred David Bolger to make the piece in connection with the 150th anniversary of the Famine: 'At school we were taught very little about the Famine', he told me in an interview, but:

> it was a genocide. There were debates about how it should be commemorated. I suddenly realized that I have been brought up here – but I didn't know anything about it! How can you not be emotional about your own ancestors? I started to research this, read lots of books. My family and my parents never talked about it. My ancestors survived since I'm around … there is guilt.

In order to get into the right atmosphere, they started the rehearsal process on a dairy farm, Shawbrook,[4] for a week. David explained to me: 'We didn't want to rehearse on concrete. We didn't starve, though, that would have been detrimental. I used to be really ill when we were working on it, used to have this pain: the piece took us on!' In another interview (Theodores 2003: 49) David described how he stopped using music at the beginning of rehearsals: 'In *Ballads*, for example, I used just the sound of the countryside in rehearsals. I wanted to show that this Famine came from a very fertile place. I wanted to really try and get people to feel the land.'

David Bolger had made a name at this time as one of the principal choreographers in Ireland both nationally and internationally. He was acclaimed as a witty entertainer who made the audience, and no less importantly, critics, laugh. With his interest in vaudeville he had kept scoring comic hits. When he suddenly changed style completely and presented *Ballads* in 1997 with its harrowing story of destitution and death, his audience did not quite follow at first, and the reviews were mixed. A dance officer in Dublin told me that:

> There were some moments in *Ballads* that were criticized. This piece would try to represent psychic and racial suffering. To make entertainment you redance the suffering at the same time. That aroused some the furies. What is the fundamental human experience at the heart of that? It was only one interpretation. There was irony, as well.

The next time, at the revival in 2000, the audience was ready for the tragic topic of the piece. This time the critics raved, as they also did when the piece was on tour to Jacob's Pillow dance festival in Massachusetts in the United States. David had chosen *Ballads* for the American debut of his CoisCéim Dance Theatre.

As the first opening night and the set of subsequent performances took place in 1997, which was before I set out on my study, I had not seen *Ballads* live. But I had watched it on video and listened to many elaborate, if diverse, views on it from dancers, choreographers and critics. Because of this engagement with the topic of the dance piece, and the topic itself, *Ballads* was already one of the central dance productions of my study when I learnt about its revival. I thus saw to it that I was present at the opening night of the revival in order to watch it live. This would also give me opportunities to participate in the postperformance reception, and informal gatherings of dance people during the days before and after the opening night, and thus get to hear their discussions about the piece.

Ballads is divided into six episodes: the Prologue Harvest, Dusk, Hunger, Decadence, Flight and the Epilogue Dawn. As the piece opens, piles of old big books frame the dimly lit stage. The books contain the history, textual evidence of the Famine. The number of books, the weight of history, is overwhelming. A woman dancer reads one of the books alone on stage, as piercing sad cello music comes out, played by Diane O'Keefe on the side of the stage. The woman dancer throws the book on the floor and the pages starts falling out. (See front cover.) She rips out pages, and five other dancers pick up books from the piles and start ripping pages out as well, arranging them into rows on the stage floor, first perhaps as 'the road building carried out in reward for food' (Seaver 1998) and then as potato fields with neat furrows, also suggesting the white potato flower. But as the crops fail, the fields are messed up, and with more pages ripped out and flying and falling over the stage, the people who are left, turn and twist on the floor, tormented by hunger. There is a plank of wood on stage. It takes the form of a door leading into a cottage where it changes into a table, an empty table. Then it transforms into a wreckage of an emigrant ship struggling in a storm at sea with survivors clinging onto it, some of them thrown back on shore. The scene shifts and the shore turns into a strip of grass where starving people are searching in apathy for anything to eat. Other objects symbolizing the Famine are a pair of boots, the property of a landlord who turns up with his long coat and stern face in the revival (not in the original version), a bigger, darker figure than the others. Carolyn Swift (1997) captured the narrative and the shifting moods of the dance piece when she wrote: 'We see the pangs of hunger, the struggle for survival, the dishonesty of the desperate, the pain of parting, the wild rejoicing when hope is temporarily restored.'

Ballads was a very Irish event, a ritual commemoration, which became even more effective when it was repeated. The audience understood the second time. It knew what to expect and was prepared to consider the consequences of the Famine released by *Ballads*. The deep Irishness of *Ballads*, and the opportunity for reflexivity which it creates, is also evident in the programme where there is an essay titled 'Famine, Dance and Desecration' by writer Charlie O'Neill (2000: 3–5). This erudite little essay does not try to hide any disturbing details. With painstaking precision, O'Neill enumerates the causes of the Famine: 'The potato crop failure. Unfair land ownership. The landlord system. Unfair trade. Tenants in debt. Underdevelopment, dependency, political domination. Economic exploitation, cultural repression, lack of education and more.'

Reading the essay I was struck by the expression 'our Famine'. It comes in relation to sections on other famines in the world, but then 'our' instead of the 'Irish' famine accentuates the inclusive Irishness and reflexivity of this event.[5] An essay advertising a dance production in a programme is usually aiming at as broad a readership as possible. There is a considerable nonIrish population in Ireland, and with the expanding tourist industry, tourists find their way to dance theatre performances. But in this essay, O'Neill has an Irish readership in mind. O'Neill remembers the betrayal by the British: 'at the time of our famine there was an ample supply of food in the country. But while hungry people did not have the resources to buy it, those who controlled the food were exporting it to our colonial masters across the water. Our carers were dispensing the venom while selling off the antidote.' In the conclusion, O'Neill links his discussion on history with dance by saying that 'history is movement', and finishes with a reference to the trauma that the Famine is believed to have cut in the Irish psyche:

> This dance theatre is an attempt to touch an abstract, more feeling-based, understanding of a profound time in our history. Some would claim it's a time whose damage still scars our cultural psyche. But that scarring can heal. And lessons can be learned. I believe there's a sacredness in that. An ordinary 'change can happen' kind of sacredness.

In the Press release for the first opening, *Ballads* is advertised as a piece which 'sets out to explore defining emotional moments in the psyche of our people … David Bolger has developed *Ballads* out of a desire to come to terms with the emotional aspect of our identity'. This is a choreographer who says of himself 'what I am interested in is emotion in movement and the organisation of steps in that movement' (Theodores 2003: 46).

In 1999, before the revival of *Ballads*, I asked one of the dancers, Liz Roche, what it had been like to dance in the original production: 'It was an eye-opening experience. I've never felt particularly Irish, but then I felt very Irish. It's one of the pieces I really don't know what I think about it. David was very well aware that he was taking on something huge: everyone involved was frightened. People would cry on stage.' Liz also referred to the Famine as an Irish trauma: 'My father is a psychologist and he says the Irish are still recovering from that, the Famine. The whole irony about it was that there wasn't a Famine! There's been a huge confusion about what really happened.'

The conceptualization of the Famine as a trauma that could be healed by being repeated and remembered was especially prevalent in Irish intellectual and popular debate during the 150th anniversary. In his lyrical book about the Famine, in a short section titled 'The Trouble with Trauma (A Digression)', Stuart McLean (2004: 154–157) disputes the usefulness of this notion in relation to the Famine anniversary, seeing a risk of essentialism of 'a reified "national psyche"' which would be a way of 'tending to obscure the no less significant divergencies between the various protagonists involved in these acts of commemoration – states, academic institutions, individuals, groups'. McLean does not believe in the healing power, or any deeper understanding, that would come with recollections of the past. Dance and body theorists argue, however, that because of the multivocal quality of dance performances, they can offer opportunities to learn more about the past, as in relation to the Famine, while performances also unite people with different perspectives on the same issue. Like any good piece of art, in any genre, a dance performance can release emotions and uncover new connections and alternative interpretations on a personal, cultural and political level. As Michael Seaver (1998), in his capacity of dance correspondent for *Dance Europe*, specifies: 'The strength of Bolger's work is the immediacy of the images that he creates and his ability to suggest other resonances through these images. A dead body laid out on three piles of books immediately suggests a dolmen – a pre-Christian Celtic burial tomb.' Things have progressed in Ireland, 'change can happen', as O'Neill wrote in the programme for *Ballads*. But the awareness of being a part of a people that not that long ago was humiliated during devastating circumstances, is still there. The Famine happened too recently to be forgotten, let alone forgiven.

Making Memories: Selecting Stories

The fact that there is noone around anymore who has witnessed the Famine, leads to the question of how social memory of historical events in the past is constructed and conveyed. Father Pat Ahern, in Chapter 1, had an aural personal memory of crossroads dancing, he remembered listening to the music. When he combined this with his memories of stories he had heard about crossroads dancing, it became a part of a social memory. Dance tends otherwise to be associated with watching and thus primarily produce visual memory. Neil Jarman (1997) has discussed social memory in his important study of parades and visual display in Northern Ireland. Jarman argues that images such as murals or banners are put together in the same way as the practice of storytelling, with repetition and certain formulaic conventions intended to confirm rather than surprise even if there is a certain room for improvisation. It is significant that repetition, which actually is what makes us remember, tends to imply some kind of change (cf. Stokes 1997) whether through improvisation, mistake or any other elaboration. A common structural formula of storytelling and social memory is that the narrative can be deconstructed into distinct episodes. One of the central episodes of *Ballads* – a story within the story – portrays a single moment of happiness and hope: a new potato crop is growing and young lovers are dancing on the field. This is framed by traditional Irish steps and music, which contrasts with the modern dance steps and music in the rest of the piece.

My historical span in suggesting the Famine as embodied memory as being articulated in *Ballads* may appear wide, but Nicolas Argenti (in preparation) goes back to about the same time in his study of how the slave trade in the precolonial Cameroon grassfields is remembered in masked performances at the end of the twentieth century. Argenti traces the dance steps he sees in deep detail to the slave caravans: 'the slow shuffle of the masks and the perpetual hunger and exhaustion of the carriers. The stooped figure of the dancer gingerly balancing his unwieldy headdress, and the porter staggering under his headload.' Argenti argues that 'the bodily memories of these cataclysmic events are handed down transgenerationally in ways that are not open to discursive contemplation'. This embodied quality is then a way for young people to express their concerns and conflicts over the ongoing state formation in the Cameroon grassfields. Argenti is making the astute analytical point that severe violence and trauma can only be decoded with time.

Social memory has been explored in Northern Ireland by anthropologist William Kelleher (2003: 14, 56) in his study of the Troubles in the town he calls Ballyboign (see also Feldman 1991 on violence as embodied collective memory in Northern Ireland).[6] Kelleher suggests that the history is embodied in the practice of 'telling', which is the ability to 'tell' whether a stranger is a Catholic or a Protestant. This comes through in body posture such as the observations that Protestant men stand straight and are handsome, Catholic men slouch, Catholic women are prettier, and also in body movement along the street of the other side of the community. Kelleher shows how people he researched 'mapped their social world through their moving bodies. Those moves were acts of memorization, forms of practical consciousness, and they elicited narration.'

Contemporary Memories: The Troubles and Youth Emigration

When I was preparing this study, I knew I wanted to include both the Republic of Ireland and Northern Ireland. The reason was that, again, dance moves across the Irish border as dance theatre companies go on tour, and *Riverdance* performs in Belfast. Dance championships and traditional dancing take place all over the island. Dance people, dance followers and young people in the countryside travel, sometimes quite far, to see a performance. Contrary to most anthropological studies conducted in Northern Ireland, I was not planning to study the Troubles. With the voluminous literature, from different disciplinary angles, on this conflict already in existence, I did not think there was a need for yet another addition. According to my early explorations in the North, most people seemed to have very little, or nothing at all, to do with the sectarian violence on an everyday basis.

The Troubles flared up in its contemporary form through violence in connection with a civil rights march in Derry, in which Catholics and Protestants participated, in August 1968. The British Army arrived in August 1969, to deal with the riots that followed the Protestant Apprentice Boys parade. The political issues that were at stake, and still are, go all the way back to the seventeenth century, especially the Battle of the Boyne in 1690 when Protestant William of Orange, who was to become King, defeated Catholic King James II and his Irish followers, thereby formalizing a Protestant ascendancy. There was already a Protestant settlement, colonizers from Scotland, while the native population was Irish Catholic. The Troubles, and especially the massive annual celebrations of The 12th of July, commemorating the Boyne with hundreds of small and big parades, are about tradition, space and power, evoked by different interpretations of historical events. Who has the right to express what political–religious identity in what public space, and in what way? The most well-known example of this is probably the tensions around a Protestant parade (some of whom see themselves as 'loyalists', meaning loyal to the British crown) insisting on marching along the Garvaghy Road in a Catholic area of Portadown every year. The 'marching season' lasts between March and August and includes hundreds of parades all over Northern Ireland primarily organized by Protestant loyalist groups, but some initiated by Catholic republicans (who seek a united Ireland).[7]

It would not take long, however, before I began detecting signs of the Troubles in dance theatre. As these were presented quite differently from what is conveyed through the media image abroad, I found them intriguing to pursue: instead of harrowing reports of brutal murders and inner city areas shattered by bombs, there were stories about what happens after the violence, about long-term grief and loss, but also about sudden hope for peace, and about how incomprehensible this conflict may appear even to people in Ireland. David Bolger was quite open about it: 'It's really hard to understand what's going on in the North, it's too close to here. I don't think I could do something on it.' Yet he touched on the Troubles in *Ballads*, where there are hurling sticks, they play hurling, an Irish game. In *Ballads*, the hurling sticks are manipulated as guns, which is a reference to weapons being used in the Troubles. This I would not have realized without David bringing my attention to it.

At one point when I was watching dance videos with David's producer Bridget Webster in CoisCéim's studio in Dublin, we were scrutinizing *Reel Luck* from June 1995. Starting out with de Valera's vision of a land of humble and hardworking people (see Chapter 1), it moves on to acknowledging *Riverdance* in the Eurovision and ends with the then new peace in the North. Bridget talked about how this was the second production they ever did, that it had been performed at a dance festival and that it had premiered in Limerick to great acclaim. They had taken it on tour to Edinburgh and London, where it had continued to get very good reviews: 'This was just after the first ceasefire in the North. There was a sense of positivity. When the piece was performed in London, the ceasefire had been broken so there was a different atmosphere in the audience'.

When Irish people go abroad, especially to England, and the Troubles is in the news, they often have to deal with being associated with it. Michael Keegan Dolan, for example, who grew up in Dublin, told me that when he was in London to train at the Central School of Ballet there were a lot of IRA bombs, and he, like other Irish people, was seen as representing Ireland, and thus somehow also the Troubles (even though the violence assiciated with the Troubles usually takes place in Northern Ireland). This has continued since the 1970s when the Troubles began, and is expressed on a scale from well-meaning interest to racist accusations. It happens even though these Irish people clearly have nothing to do with the Troubles, dismiss it or, strange as it may seem from the outside, are unconcerned, not about the poignant point about safety, but about what side, or issue, may be 'right' at the moment. With the many factions that keep emerging and the constant criss-crossing, not only of retaliations but also of allegiances, twining political, public and private life together, as described by Donnan and McFarlane (1986), it may not be easy, or there may not be any reason, to take sides.

The relationships between Catholics and Protestants, sometimes taking the form of a divide, sometimes integration, surfaced and structured parts of, but far from all, dance and dance culture contexts in Northern Ireland. Instances of integration were either commented on, or just accepted as a matter of course. If children are often seen as symbols of a better future, this is particularly prevalent in Northern Ireland (cf. Lanclos 2003). As one of many implicit agendas to enhance future understanding between 'both sides of the community', choreographers and dance teachers were involved in school schemes, some in Education for Mutual Understanding (EMU) programs teaching Catholic and Protestant children to dance together.[8] This could be any dance form from traditional Irish dancing and set-dancing to salsa, dance theatre and ballet.

At the launch of the EarthQuake 2003 festival in Belfast, children performed. This is an annual dance festival in Northern Ireland hosted by Dance Northern Ireland (an organization which arranges dance classes, performances and community project). The launch took place the day before I arrived, but a ballet teacher from a small town in Northern Ireland gave me the following report: 'It was so like a snap shot of Northern Ireland: my little ones were doing butterflies. I had twelve dancers. Ballet is very Protestant. Irish dancing very Catholic, very nationalist. Ballet was on for forty seconds – which was what they had asked for – but Irish dance hugged the stage for twenty minutes!' In a situation of competition, which this was, where one side was given more space, and thus outshone the other – the sectarian divide surfaced. I believe this accentuation of the conflict in a competitive situation is typical for everyday life in Northern Ireland, as in any other place where there has been a longstanding tension between different ethnic, religious and/or political groups.

I kept noting during the course of my fieldwork that ballet was often linked to Protestants, even identified bluntly by choreographers as 'the art form of the colonizer' both in the North and the South. But I also observed ballet classes in Northern Ireland where the divide did not matter. One of them took place in Bangor, a coastal town, at a ballet school where Graham Drake teaches. When I asked him about the backgrounds of his pupils, he replied: 'I don't honestly know. Coming from England, I don't have the radar other people have here. There are predominantly Protestants in Bangor as an area, but we do have Catholics here too.'

Having lived abroad during long periods, and still travelling in Europe, the United States, Asia and Australia in her capacity of ballet teacher and examiner, Eileen Ferguson,[9] who originates from Northern Ireland, now runs a ballet school in a church hall in a destitute area in North Belfast. Tall and agile, she took me there in her car, one wet Friday afternoon in the spring. With the rain rattling on the car windows, we drove through the city traffic which was getting congested as people started leaving work. We reached the church hall, which looked austere to me. When the girls had lined up along the bar to do their warming up exercises, an elderly lady started to play the piano. The music sounded hard as it echoed back from the bare walls in the cold hall. The girls were around ten years old in different shapes and sizes. They were all wearing the standard navy-blue ballet leotards, and some wore pink tights with it. I watched two classes. Eileen was clearly a committed teacher, trusted and admired by her pupils. Contrary to much ballet teaching, especially in Britain (cf. Wulff 1998), she taught them in a basically encouraging tone, phrasing corrections very mildly, giving compliments to everyone. One of the older girls had won a scholarship to go to Scotland to train. It was obvious that the girls enjoyed their dancing, they moved eagerly, concentrated with the music. It was touching to see how they struggled to lift legs as high as possible and stand still in balance. Towards the end of the second class of slightly older pupils, they were in the middle of the big floor doing the famous Hungarian dance and the Tarantella from *Swan Lake*, the ballet of ballets, with fine flowing technique and captivating expression. I was impressed. Afterwards, Eileen told me that:

> The girls have mixed backgrounds, from both sides of the community. Some come from the coast. No distinctions are made, you can't tell. That's partly the reason to have this. Here we have segregated schools – whereas in ballet, religion doesn't come into it.[10] They're working together. In the arts it's not a problem, it certainly never comes across any problems because of the divide.

When I interviewed Marie Mannion who teaches dance and drama in St Louisa's Comprehensive College in West Belfast, she talked about this as a 'heightened political area':

> What my students choreograph, what they compose is coming from something very personal for them, many of my students come from West Belfast. They respond to their culture, it can be quite violent, you know. After one of the imprisonments, they did a piece based on political imprisonment, it was their need to do this, they had to do this.

But Marie Mannion also saw some images of integration in dance: 'It's beginning to happen. *Dance, Lexi, Dance!* the video, makes a point of saying Protestants don't do Irish dance, now they do!' Many people recommended I saw *Dance, Lexi, Dance!* which indeed is an illustration of recent integration among young people in the North. The film is about a Protestant girl who comes home to her widowed father and asks to be a traditional Irish dancer. He refuses as this is presented as a Catholic pursuit, which he does not know how to do. The girl starts dancing anyway. She gets to a competition – and wins!

The violence in the North was a topic John Scott, a renowned choreographer in Dublin, took on in his epic *Macalla* from 1994. The piece became Scott's real breakthrough. Trained as an actor and singer, and with a degree in English literature, Scott was attracted to choreography already in the late 1980s and set up his dance company, irish modern dance theatre, in 1991. *Macalla* is Irish for echo, that is, in this dance piece, an echo of history, mythology and violence. Scott's aim was to 'remember something that was lost, an echo, and put it back again. But there are still gaps in an echo!', he told me in an interview, and that also 'we wanted to have a funeral to the memory of those who have died in the violence. In the South we forget the North.'

Macalla was performed as an installation in the RHA Gallagher Gallery in Dublin. The dancers/actors moved between different rooms, down a staircase and out on a court yard. As to the choreographic process, he has said that:

> I started to work with Joanna Banks and I started to also work with some young student actors who had no movement experience whatsoever.[11] I found their physicality was so beautiful ... *Macalla* was a piece I did in four different spaces and it was the most political thing I ever did. I made it after the first Peace Treaty happened in Northern Ireland in 1994.

> I remember on New Year's Eve 1994 coming into 1995, the wall at the Shankill and the Falls Road, the gate. One of the gates was open and the two communities came together with candles ... I put that line into *Macalla* just as a group of people at a funeral coming towards each other and I thought it was the funeral for all of what happened in the North. It was a way of dealing with all that blood (Theodores 2003: 221, 225).

The Idea of Leaving

Contemporary memories in Irish dance theatre also focussed on the theme of youth emigration, and the whole idea of leaving – or staying while your friends go. Both John Scott and David Bolger talked about youth emigration during the past decades, and how people in their generation had started to move back recently. In *Back in Town* from 1997, David was inspired by the lyrics and music to the songs 'Dublin' and 'The Boys are Back in Town' by the late Phil Lynott, the black rock star from Dublin and his band Thin Lizzy. In the sad song 'Dublin', Phil Lynott sings about being on the boat going to England, watching Ireland disappearing. He depicts a journey starting with his friends coming down to the quay to say goodbye, and trying to cheer him up. They smoke and joke together. As the boat is leaving and he is on his own, he is overtaken by sorrow: he misses the girl he loves, his home city, yet takes some comfort in the fact that he is also leaving unemployment and the constraints of Catholicism. The other song Bolger worked with for the dance piece *Back in Town* was the mega hit 'The Boys Are Back in Town' from 1976. This song is about a joyous homecoming to Dublin: young men are pleased to be back with old friends and fun, and look forward to meeting girlfriends they could not forget. This is all conveyed on stage by dancers who perform vigorous teenagers immersed in summer club culture in the 1970s, but soon have to deal with 'hard edged decisions of emigration as the pressing problems of unemployment at home seals their fate' (www.coisceim.com).

The threat of people leaving is still there today. After the period of economic expansion which saw Ireland labelled the Celtic Tiger, there is now a certain recession, and many do leave, which produces strong emotions of homesickness, longing and displacement. In the spectrum of emotions that leaving Ireland produces, one is a feeling of guilt. John Scott told me, for example, about thinking of himself as 'a coward' for not daring to emigrate when his friends did, yet others are happy at home. Dance people in Dublin who have lost friends and family to other countries talk about how those who have left call them when they are homesick, but point out that these emigrants who sometimes think nostalgically about Ireland do not quite know what it is like to live there any longer. And those who return after many years abroad often seem to find life very different from a town in Australia or a big city in America. A woman in Dublin who lived for more than a decade in New York with her Irish husband until he died, went back and was initially very well taken care of by her family, but when she made it as a successful B&B proprietor they became less supportive. Talking to me about her independent lifestyle and Pakistani boyfriend, the woman said: 'I was closer to my family when I was living away'. It seems to be hard to get back in again into Irish family life and society, to be reaccepted as a part of peoples' everyday existence. It is as if Irish people who have lived abroad are seen as 'tainted' with foreignness. And some people leave again, either to their original emigrant country or to another country. In many cases, they themselves have changed, more than Irish society, while they have been away.

Still, those who stay in Ireland tend to travel, often on a global scale. John Scott identifies himself as 'a real traveller' on the basis of his annual tours with his company to France and the US, and a visit to Japan. The other end is represented by a young dance administrator in Belfast, who described how 'young people in the countryside, they tend to travel. I've travelled thirty miles to get to a venue'. Originating from a small village in the north of Northern Ireland, he had been to the Republic of Ireland, but as he said, 'I have never been abroad', meaning off the island.

Tour and Travel

Before I go into the geographical mobility of Irish dance in Europe and globally, I want to go back to the dancing masters who went around Ireland, North and South, in the past, teaching people of all classes to dance. Dancing masters are first mentioned in a contract from Cork originating in the eighteenth century (Brennan 1999: 45), but some of the people in my study remembered them, in particular Father Pat Ahern, who recalled a travelling master in Co. Kerry in the 1940s: 'I had come into contact with the dancing master, he came to teach us at the school. They would have disappeared at the turn of the century, but some were still around later. He came for six-eight weeks at the time.' This can thus be said to be an early geographical movement of dance in Ireland. Now media and new technologies have increased the opportunities for mobility considerably. *Riverdance*'s seven minute performance in the Eurovision Song Contest, which reached out to millions of television viewers, is a pertinent case in point.

In the current debate over fixity versus mobility in social life, mobility is on an upswing. John Urry (2000: 1–2) has even launched a new sociology beyond societies, a sociology where 'mobilities of peoples, objects, images, information and wastes' as well as 'imaginative travel' and 'virtuality' replace societies as the centre of sociological investigation. This manifesto builds on social analyses of cultures as travel and movement, often made possible though media and new technologies.[12]

Rapport and Dawson (1998: 27) importantly acknowledge how home and identity are formed through movement. As they suggest not only can one 'be at home in movement, but that movement can be one's very home.'

In an article titled 'Perpetual Motion', Irish writer Fintan O'Toole (1997b: 77) reflects on Irish culture saying that it is 'not just marked but actually defined by the perpetual motion of the people who bear it. Emigration and exile, the journeys to and from home, are the very heartbeat of Irish culture. To imagine Ireland is to imagine a journey.' Yet, O'Toole goes on, this journey has changed; for one thing, the motions have intensified. . In a larger analytical perspective, mobility clearly produces new connections and meanings of place, indeed new power structures. Now this mobility includes tourists, even indigenous tourists, as well as business people and students. With Ireland's economic boom in the late 1980s and early 1990s came an extensive tourist industry. Now there is an economic setback. However, Ireland continues to be a popular travel destination, and is still a player in the new global economic structure constituted in large part by tourism and travel.[13]

Considering dance theatre companies and *Riverdance* touring as a type of mobility, this can be discussed on an abstract analytical level in terms of global structures, yet it is obviously made by people who live on the road for months on end. Joanne Doyle, the leading woman dancer in the Liffey company of *Riverdance* talked to me in an interview about the experiential ethnographic level of this mobility, about the ups and downs of touring:

> It's very different. When you live in a place it's a much easier lifestyle than when you're on the road. When you live a normal life and you're able to cook which is a big thing for me. I miss my apartment, my friends, my parents when I'm living away from Ireland. The whole company is in the hotel. You cannot get away. I love it! But it's not a real life! I nearly cried Christmas Day, at the end of the tour. The only time you're happy is when you're on stage. Being on tour is like being married to everyone!

Riverdance keeps doing extensive foreign, even global tours, while Irish dance theatre companies mainly tour in Ireland. These companies are small, there are about five dancers at a time performing with each one of them, and about forty modern dancers altogether in Ireland that move between the different dance theatre companies. Dance theatre companies usually go on one short foreign tour each year, often performing at dance festivals. England and Scotland are the most common destinations, but they visit the United States and France, Scandinavia and Central Europe quite often, too. Some of the choreographers are involved in cultural exchange of dancers and choreographic projects with other countries.

The vast majority of dancers that travel to Ireland are Irish dancers: children and teenagers go in thousands with their dancing schools, teachers and mothers in order to compete in the annual championships, the World and the All Ireland Championships in Irish dancing (see Chapter 6). Some dancers go regularly to both of them, as well as to the 'Regional's' in Ireland, England and/or the United States. There is even an annual All Ireland Championship in Irish Dancing arranged in the United States, which is a qualifying competition for the major championship, the 'World's', in Ireland (this incidentally took place in Glasgow, Scotland in 2002). One of the winners at the 'All Ireland's' in 2002, Michelle Lawrence, who was sixteen years old, comes from Co. Tipperary. Her competing had taken her to Toronto, Boston and Amsterdam. She had been in Britain five times for championships and six times in Scotland. Starting competing as a very young child, not even four years old, Michelle had already won many competitions. Winning the 'All Ireland's', the solo step dancing for senior girls 16–17, however, clearly surpassed the previous victories. There had been worries that she would not be able to compete this time, her mother told me, because a bone had been dislocated in her foot. It was put back only a few days before the 'All Ireland's' – and then she went on to win!

Dance mobility, both the steps and the touring, can be stopped dramatically by injury. When I had just arrived at the 'All Ireland's' in Killarney, Co. Kerry, in 2002 and was walking into the auditorium, where the competition had already started, I noticed a nurse running past me. I understood that something had happened and when I came inside a young girl was carried out on a stretcher. She had hurt her hip while practising, I learnt later. Injuries happen in competitive Irish dancing as all other dance forms today.[14] Choreography in shows such as *Riverdance* allows for a less rigid posture than competitive dancing, but injuries still can occur. *Riverdance* has developed a healthy dancer programme to prevent injury and tours two masseurs and a physiotherapist to assist in this prevention, as well as to treat injuries that can occur. There are extra dancers travelling with *Riverdance*, so no dancer performs in every show and regular rotations allow for rest periods. Should a performer incur an injury while on stage, they can be withdrawn and attended by the medical personnel who are on duty for every show, and a replacement dancer is available to cover their place on the show.

The Moving Irish Body

In a sense the body is constantly in motion, more or less. For there is in fact movement also in a body which is fixed in a still pose, because of the heartbeat (Wulff 2003). As Susan A. Reed (1998) points out in a review article of dance and movements studies, in the expansion of the anthropology of the body, moving bodies have not really been taken into analytical consideration. Recent dance scholarship is, however, often phrased in terms of moving bodies in relation to the politics of culture, the construction of gender, ethnic and national identities.[15] There is also the branch of dance and movement studies which focuses on connections between urban milieux, that is, architecture and space, and everyday movement, such as walking and running as well as posture.

To the many uses of the concept of habitus (Bourdieu 1977) belongs the insight that the practice of dancing reveals dispositions, i.e. perceptions and actions that are being inscribed in a dancer's body. Such dispositions consequently have an impact on the dancing as well as on the social life of dancers, but also on dancers' movement patterns *outside* dancing (cf. Wulff 1998; Wainright and Turner 2003). Other dispositions affect nondancers, which made me ask John Scott: 'How do the Irish move'? Aware that the entire population of a nation does not move in one way, I was yet hoping he would tell me about some discernible Irish everyday movement, walking, posture, in short how the Irish movement habitus makes people move. In his capacity of a choreographer, he had indeed spent a lot of time observing movement: 'They stoop,' he said and: 'They don't move their hips. We're shy too, but very dramatic. But there is a reticence' (Wulff 2003). Although John Scott never said so, he made me think of men, rather than women. This gendered description came up also during an interview with a young man who worked as a dance officer in Belfast: 'We slouch, you stand and your shoulders hunch, your hands in your pockets. Especially men in bars. It's a lazy way of standing, a lazy way of sitting. It's funny to see a bunch of Irishmen, half the thing is how he's moving.' Some of the Irish choreographers distinguished between the movement patterns of people in the North and those in the South of Ireland, saying that in the North people move in a more restricted way than many people in the South , and that Catholics tend to move more softly than Protestants.

Dance scholar and choreographer, Diana Theodores (1996: 204) worked as a dance critic in Ireland in the 1980s. She has identified 'the *solitariness* of Irish dancing, with its historic resistance to physical touching'. There is admittedly an abundance of solo dancing in Ireland, which supports the joke made by Michael Keegan Dolan: 'Ireland, country responsible for the extinction of the *pas de deux*!' He enjoyed talking about the tendency to avoid physical contact in everyday life even among family members and said that, 'In Ireland, we've never been in touch with the body'. Keegan Dolan dislikes 'the Irish fear of touch' and 'a lack of sexuality', suggesting that this carries over to Irish everyday movement, and is caused by the Catholic Church. Telling me about liturgical dance, especially broadcast on television, Father Dermod McCarthy, who was in charge of Religious Programmes at RTÉ, confirmed that certain senior Church people 'are afraid of the body' and that they had indeed been critical of his broadcasts of 'dance on the altar', seeing it in terms of sexuality (Wulff 2003: 188–89; see also Mulrooney 2006).

Producing Place through Mobility

The sisters who were dancing their goodbyes to their departing aunt, in the prologue to this chapter, did a type of house dance. It took place at a 'spree'. This one was an American 'wake' that used to be held the night before someone was emigrating. Such sad occasions were even referred to as 'live wakes', Helen Brennan (1999: 104–5, 114) notes, since in the past people who were leaving Ireland in most cases never came back. This explains why the sisters did not want to let go of their aunt: they would never see her again.

Dance and dance culture have been connected to travel, displacement and mobility for a long time in Ireland. This mobility has increased recently and accelerated into webs of regional, national and global movements, enhanced and connected by media and new technology. In this chapter I have investigated the meaning of embodied memories in motions in Irish dance, in particular how dance performances, dance classes and the culture around them have spoken about topics such as the Famine in terms of a long memory, and the Troubles and youth unemployment in terms of contemporary memories. The views, voices and stories I have quoted here reveal that history and popular or social memory weave into each other. It is not always relevant to separate 'history' as an academic endeavour or ideological project of nation-building from popular and collective memory of historical events. The lack of knowledge, and the silence, about the Famine was a recurring theme around the dance piece *Ballads*. This was the case despite the vast academic Famine studies, which does not seem to have reached into all social science debate. I was dismayed during the course of my fieldwork, when I met leading American and European scholars who had no idea about the magnitude of the Irish Famine.

A fundamental distinction to make, however, on the basis of dance performances, dance classes and the culture around it we have seen here, is the one between historical events that took place centuries ago on one hand and recent historical events that people in my study remember at first hand. The nature of these types of memory is by necessity different, even though both may have passed through official academic and political reformulations. But lived history, in its individual forms, should be recognized as crucial parts to consider in any analysis of the past (see also McWilliams 2001). Such individual, personal memories can shed new light on larger historical processes.

Akhil Gupta and James Ferguson (1992) were among the first to formulate the need for attention to the role of mobility in anthropological studies of place. In a wider perspective, mobility clearly produces new connections and meanings of place, indeed new power structures. This certainly relates to how Ireland is produced as a place, both in the dance through steps and stories, and in dance's mobility across Ireland and the world.

Notes

1. According to the FORTE report (1996: 50) 'there are estimated to be 62 million people of Irish descent scattered around the globe. 18% of the US population claim Irish ancestry'. These demographical figures are thus self-identifications and likely to vary when it comes to number and quality of family links back to Ireland.
2. See Lloyd (1993, 1999), Kiberd (1996), Gibbons (1996), Walker (1996), Foster (2002) among many others.
3. The headline of this section was inspired by a conversation I had with legendary broadcaster and writer Seán Mac Réamoinn on the preoccupation with the past in Ireland. He summarized this in the catchy phrase: 'The Irish have a long memory'.
4. Shawbrook is a working dairy farm in Legan, Co. Longford where some of the buildings have been converted into a ballet studio, a theatre and dormitory accommodation. Apart from ballet teaching, the studio is used for an international residential dance summer school and choreographic composer workshops.
5. There was a special performance of *Ballads* two days before the first opening night in 1997. This was a Gala Benefit Night. The proceeds of the performance went to Trócaire in support of famine relief in North Korea.

6. See McCarthy's (2005) edited volume for contributions from geography, history and archaeology on memory and identity in Ireland.
7. See Walker (1996), Jarman (1997), Bryan (2000). See also Falk and Wulff (2003).
8. Some of these choreographers grew up in Northern Ireland, others in the Republic of Ireland, there are both Protestants and Catholics, men and women, among them.
9. This ballet teacher held a RAD (Royal Academy of Dancing) Diploma linked to Durham University. The RAD is a British organization with representatives mainly in the Commonwealth countries. Ferguson was thus not only a ballet teacher, but also a senior examiner of ballet and travelled widely to teach and examine ballet pupils and teachers (see also Wulff 1998).
10. Just to clarify, there are now some integrated schools in Northern Ireland. See for example, Lanclos' (2003) study on how children in Belfast negotiate age, gender and sectarian identity through skipping rhymes, clapping games and dirty jokes in the playgrounds in two Catholic, two Protestant/state and one integrated school (see also Wulff 2005b).
11. Joanna Banks, an ex-dancer from England and the Royal Ballet who had lived in Dublin for many years, was the Principal of The College of Dance in Dublin, an institution for dance training, during my fieldwork.
12. See Hannerz (1996), Appadurai (1996), Clifford (1997a,b), Rojek and Urry (2000), Löfgren (2002), Garsten and Wulff (2003) and Bruner (2004) among others. See also Wulff (1998) on ballet dancers and especially their touring culture, and Hannerz (2004a) on foreign correspondents. There are chapters on movement in Eyerman (1999) and Tsing 2004.
13. Manuel Castells (1996), among others, has drawn attention to this.
14. See Wulff (1998) on the culture of injury and pain among ballet dancers, as well as modern stage dancers.
15. Among the many works making minor or major analytical points about the moving body in dance scholarship are Hanna (1988), Cowan (1990), Williams (2003[1991]), Ness (1992), Farnell (1994), Foster (1995, 1996), Burt (1995), Novack (1995), Lewis (1995), Browning (1995), Franko (1995), Morris (1996), Cooper Albright (1997), Ajayi (1998), Reed (1998), Banes (1998), Sklar (2001), Wulff (1998, 2001, 2003), Wainright and Turner (2003), and Neveu Kringelbach 2005.

Chapter 4

The Link to the Land

Wie were a colonized country, an occupied country. What happens is that land becomes important for survival. The English took land and left the poorer land to the Irish. If you had no land, you had no status in the community, that has carried through: people have a very deep desire to own property.

These are the words of Kathy McArdle, a young manager at the Project Arts Centre, a theatre and exhibition space in Dublin. I met her in September 2000 after *The Flowerbed*, a dance theatre production by Michael Keegan-Dolan, had premiered at the Project Arts Centre.

The land, in the form of a green lawn, is the focus of the action in *The Flowerbed*. Dealing with territoriality in the suburbs, this Romeo and Juliet parody unfolds through fights over the lawn between two neighbouring families whose children fall in love with each other. The lawn symbolizes the land, the nation. A male dancer keeps mowing the lawn, laying down on the grass. 'He is fucking the grass, making love to his grass', Michael remarked to me. 'He is making love to Ireland?' I suggested. 'You said it', he admitted looking serious now, his cheeky expression gone from his face. Hilariously entertaining, *The Flowerbed* was yet inspired by the dark memory of territorial conflicts over a piece of bog land, to which Michael's family used to have the cutting rights. Every time Michael came there with his father, the sticks surrounding their piece of land had been moved.

This chapter highlights the importance of land in the production of Ireland as a place and a plurality of places in dance. As has already become clear, the meaning of place in Ireland is highly charged: there is a lot of negotiation over national identity, politics and the role of religion in relation to place. The controversy over dancing at the crossroads, which I begin this book with, is an example par excellence. To place belongs the idea of home, and the central meaning home has in Irish culture. Notions of land, place and home are all expressed in dance, especially through stories in dance theatre. But the closest connection to the land is when entire dance productions or sections of them draw on Irish occupational songs and on old mime dances. They are built on the rhythmic movements, the beat, of different work on a farm, such as planting potatoes with a stick, milking and making butter in a churn. These old songs, work songs, as they are also called, helped make the work easier: certain work would take eight songs to finish. Work songs would drive the process in hand rather than be driven by it.

Tombs, choreographed in 1998 by Robert O'Connor and Loretta Yurick for their Dance Theatre of Ireland, is another good example of the link to the Irish land. This dance production was inspired by Newgrange, Co. Meath, the site of a megalithic monument believed to be 'burial tombs, sacred temples or astronomical observatories' dating from around 3200 bc.[1] At the winter solstice in December, a ray of sunshine pushes into the tomb passage and a chamber, that are thus lit up for a few minutes at dawn over a period of five days. This spectacular scenery and the fact that not all that much is known about the monument or the people who built it has made Newgrange a source of Irish mythology and as such associated with Oengus, the god of love, who was supposed to have resided there. In *Tombs*, Robert and Loretta work with 'the mystical and the modern, trying to understand modern life through the cosmology connected with Newgrange, especially the possible meaning of the light. Newgrange is a calendar device which links people with the solar system, life with spiritual life and an opportunity to meet night and day', Robert told me. The spiral design, often appearing as three joint spirals, which has become a staple motif of Celtic design (even though it is in fact much older), originates at Newgrange. It was a prominent part of the *Riverdance* set, and it is also in the *Tombs* set. These spirals are reflected in the choreography as circular, spiral movements both in *Riverdance* and in *Tombs*. This image of anchoring Irish dance pattern in the Newgrange spirals, making them spin through dance movement as it were, is also used by Irish author Éilís Ní Dhuibhne (1999a: 47, 48) in her exquisitely structured novel *The Dancers Dancing*. It is a rhythmical rendering of a group of adolescent girls that spend the summer of 1972 learning Irish in the Gaeltachts. Just like the Irish language movement which the Gaelic League set forth almost a century before, these classes in the Irish language are combined with learning to dance at a céilí:

> The curtains are down, the large room glows in the evening sun. The children file into the schoolhouse and sit on the benches, now placed along the walls, under the cracked blue maps and posters of smiling families of outmoded appearance and unusual faded colours. Headmaster Joe takes up position beside the record-player and announces the dances.

> Slowly, awkward as elephants, they walk their way through the patterns, which to the uninitiated seem unbelievably complicated ... The legs move a bit faster and to anyone viewing them from above – only one person is, Headmaster Joe – the patterns begin to take a loose shape. They are like the patterns on the crochet tablecloths sold in the souvenir shops in Tubber, or – he wipes his forehead – the swirls cut into the stones at Newgrange.

Because of the legacy of colonialism in the Republic of Ireland in combination with the constant threat of people leaving though emigration, the emigration itself, and exile experiences that imbue Irish society, I will argue that the link to the Irish land is stronger than in many other places. Traces of colonial conflicts as well as internal disagreement and struggle over land rights have probably added to the complexity of this link. It goes back to the early colonization of Ireland and the British settlements on plantations and estates in the sixteenth and seventeenth centuries. Penal Laws first established in the seventeenth century would enforce long-term limitations for Catholics not only on practising their religion, but also on owning land. In the aftermath of the Famine, landlords and tenants agreed to a system where tenants were able to leave rented farms to their own inheritors. This was confirmed in the Land Act of 1870. A few years later, an agricultural decline put landlords under financial strain which made many of them turn to the eviction of poor tenants. By joining forces in the national Land League, tenants were able to secure their leases, as also with subsequent land acts (Power and Whelan 1990; Fitzpatrick 1989). Yet tensions over land rights have remained, although changing to a different scale and nature.

Place and Power: *Territorial Claims*

Mary Nunan, well-established choreographer and dancer, discussed the contacts between the Republic of Ireland and Northern Ireland in *Territorial Claims* from 1992. It could also be seen as one interpretation of the relationship between Catholics and Protestants in the North. *Territorial Claims* brings up conflicts over territory and rights, symbolized by moving tables and splitting and throwing papers and having a dancer stamping on them.

Recalling the trajectory of her career, Mary told me that she had some introduction to Irish dance, which awakened her interest in movement, in physical education in school. Physical education was a big, new thing in Ireland at the time. One of her teachers had taught a bit of folkdancing – and 'I really liked it!'. She graduated with a degree in physical education, and started taking Graham technique classes[2] in modern dance in Dublin. Joan Davies came and taught a class one evening. She opend a studio for a year where Mary went in the evenings before moving on to New York and further studies. There was the Judson Church for postmodern dance performances, famous for having 'liberated so many people'. Mary went to the Graham school, but found it very intimidating. There was a teacher who taught Hawkins dance technique and suddenly Mary was aligned to a whole choreographic technique. She came back to Dublin because of an offer to teach for a year in Limerick and was excited to join Dublin Contemporary Dance Theatre in 1980 mainly because of Joan Davies: 'As a young dancer you can be seduced by form. I don't share her views on everything – but at least she made me articulate them.' Mary was to spend five years with that company, a repertory company. The company brought in guest choreographers and they could choreograph their own work. At the end of that time Mary decided it was time to quit. She went ahead to work as a choreographer-in-residence in 1986 thinking it would be for a year. In 1988 she founded Daghdha Dance Company, at first on only Ir£6,000, but later in 1999 they received Ir£130,000 from the Arts Council.[3] They have a lot of space and facilities at Limerick University where they are still based. Mary talks about her choreography in terms of:

I tend to work with Irish themes, certainly, my first solo *Company* used Samuel Beckett. I spoke and danced. I work with literary themes, at least I did in the beginning. *Territorial Claims* changed our reputation internationally: it has traditional Irish dance at its core, the situation in Ireland.[4] It's about how the hair stands at the back of your neck – can that change instantly into people killing each other? It evoked a huge interest at the Berlin Festival. We didn't realize its power in that sense.

Territorial Claims opens with two tables next to each other on stage. A couple in calf-long coats, full trousers and hard shoes start doing Irish dancing steps in slow motion to a man's rhythmical humming of a traditional tune. Meanwhile a male dancer is arranging a massive amount of papers in neat piles on the tables, and the couple dance faster and finally reach into the customary speed and step sound of Irish dancing. They move across the floor and up on the table where they dance a hornpipe until they are pushed off the table. The other man separates the tables and corners the woman dancer behind it against the wall. She continues her Irish dancing against the wall locked in behind the table until she is released and the table goes back to the middle of the floor – but now apart from the other table. The couple continues dancing, on, around and under the table. One of them does a solo on top of the table but is soon forced to lie down, chained to the table by their partner. There are two couples now, one on each table. They start pulling each other down to suggestive drumming, alternating with helping each other to get up again. Suddenly all four start crossing themselves energetically. One dancer is still standing on top of one of the tables, he moves his arms straight out from his body so as to form a cross, or perhaps embody the image of the suffering of the crucifixion of Jesus Christ. The delicate sound of a jew's harp enters the drumming. In the background, a dancer is working on the piles of papers, he pushes down the dancer from the table, and starts spreading the papers on both tables. Down on the floor he builds piles of papers around him, like walls of a house. The Irish dancing couple destroy the paper structure by dancing on it.

It is obvious to interpret the two tables that sometimes are placed next to each other, sometimes separately, as illustration of political unity versus distance between the Republic of Ireland and Northern Ireland, that are adjacent geographically on the island. But the fact that the many papers symbolize endless, painstaking negotiations, meetings and agreements for peace that keep being broken, which Mary pointed out to me, may be less obvious at least for an outsider to the politics of Northern Ireland.

Bog Lands: Fuel for Identity and Imagination

The vast areas of peat bog in the midlands, the uplands and the west coast of Ireland have been a source of inspiration for a number of dance productions.[5] Here I will focus on *Morphic Fields* by Cathy O'Kennedy. But first we need to find out what exactly a bog is? In the book chapter 'Céide Fields: Natural Histories of a Buried Landscape', Stuart McLean's (2003: 48, 51, see also 2004) main aim is to join the natural and historical sciences through a suggestive study of bog lands in Ireland. McLean describes peat bogs as a substance composed of:

two layers: a thin upper layer, consisting of a soft carpet of living vegetation, mostly sphagnum mosses, and underlying it, a much thicker layer of peat, made up of the compacted remains of plants and animals, accumulated over hundreds or thousands of years. Water passes rapidly through the upper layer, but is retained by the lower, through which it moves at a much slower rate.

Discussing the elusive materiality of bogs, and this porous land which would not take colonization, settlement or transport, yet has swallowed, and because of its special acids, preserved, houses, dead bodies and artifacts, McLean brings up the impact of wet and cold weather on large areas that had been cleared of forest, with periods of warmer climate in between. The custom of cutting the turf for fuel goes back to colonialism when it could be included in leases for tenants. In the 1930s, turf cutting on the coast, south of Ballycastle, revealed a major site of homesteads and graves under the bog, which was excavated by archaeologists and now is open to visitors as Céide Fields. McLean compares the Irish bog lands to 'other wilderness spaces in Western Europe' that also have been connected with supernatural beings and powers. There have been reports of fairy armies and the tantalizing *pooka* (a trickster) on the bogs in Ireland. Now peat is still cut by local farmers, arranged in stacks and left to dry in the fields, while machines keep covering enormous areas, cutting also to produce commercial peat briquettes that are for sale all over Ireland. Peat is important for Ireland's electricity supply, but it is also used for setting turf fires at home.

Having seen fields full of peat stacks while going across Ireland by car, and found the substance of bogs and its stories fascinating, it was not until I was warmed by a turf fire one cold night that I really understood the cultural meaning, some of it at least, of turf, and bog lands, for Irish people. This happened when I was staying with choreographer Cathy O'Kennedy and her partner, Michael Seaver, the dance writer, in their old house in Kildare, outside Dublin. Some of the radiators did not work, but in my bedroom was a small, lively fire fed by turf. As the warmth slowly spread in the room, the low windows got all moist. Lying in bed next to the turf fire, I enjoyed its dry, soothing smell. This bodily experience made me feel enveloped in the glow of a turf fire, just like those that have warmed Irish people for a long time.

As described in Chapter 1, I was spending a lot of time in dance critic Carolyn Swift's little study in Dublin, the house at the back of her garden, reading though the many files in her archives. Looking up, now and then, I could not help noticing what Carolyn had put on her walls. There were the usual framed photographs of dancers signed by them thanking her for friendship and support, commonplace in the ballet and dance world, next to posters announcing dance festivals and performances. Behind my back, I discovered a small certificate saying:

Save Cloghernagun Boog Campaign 1996
This certificate recognises the contribution made by
Carolyn Swift
to the work of the Irish Peatland Conservation Council by sponsoring TWO
acre(s) of threatened bog.
Peter Foss
Chairman, IPCC.

The Irish Peatland Conservation Council, founded in 1982, and its agenda to preserve Irish bog lands, are mentioned by McLean (2003). This is important, according to the IPCC, not only because the Irish bog lands are unparalleled in Western Europe, but also because they are under threat of extinction, both by machine and traditional cutting by hand. In line with European Union environment regulations, the Irish government has thus indicated some bog lands as conservation areas. This has met with criticism from groups that point to the need for bogs as fuel. Irish farmers have protested against the schemes to restrict turf cutting. In their case, it is a matter of livelihood.

This all, from imaginations about supernatural beings, the elusive materiality of the bogs, to the longstanding use of turf as fuel and not least the debate about what to do with the bog lands now, especially with the perceived risk of their extinction, makes the bogs a crucial component of Irish identity.

Morphic Fields

So called site-specific dance can take place in forests, underground caves, fields, subway stops, anywhere a committed audience can be taken to watch it, or happen to pass by. It is not uncommon in international dance theatre. John Scott did a site-specific dance piece titled *Last Supper* at the legendary Trocadero Restaurant in Dublin. The audience was invited to sit at tables with the dancers who performed at and on the tables. The piece was one of the highpoints of the first International Dance Festival Ireland in May 2002 and very well received in *irish theatre magazine* in a review of the Festival by Christine Madden (2002: 16–7):

> Nowhere was incongruency more prevalent than in Irish Modern Dance Theatre's *Last Supper*, which proved you don't have to be a child to have fun in play. John Scott set this ticklish piece, a dinner's evening from hell, in the Trocadero restaurant in Dublin. Amongst the audience members seated at tables in a smallish room, the eight dancers lay in wait until the piped-in Sinatra went wonky – their cue to let loose. The performers behaved badly, drawing rings on themselves, blowing through straws into glasses of water until they bubbled over; Scott stuffed an entire cloth napkin into his mouth. They walked over people seated on the benches; slammed their hands on the table, jolting glasses and slopping wine about. It was like eating in a posh restaurant with the entire cast of *One Flew Over the Cuckoo's Nest*. The audience were captive, and torn by conflicting impulses either to act 'normal' or to stare and laugh, and perhaps even take part. As inhibitions broke down, the piece became hugely entertaining.

A year earlier, Cathy O'Kennedy had told me about her dance production, *Morphic Fields*: 'I wanted to perform on the bog. I was struck by a sense of place. I didn't want any music, just silence, and just chose the music the night before'. As it turned out, *Morphic Fields* was performed at the Samuel Beckett Centre, a theatre at Trinity College, in June 1999 in Dublin. It featured two duets: one woman dancer, Lucy

Dundon, danced with one male dancer at a time with the bog landscape on a video screen. Afterwards, Cathy talked to Diana Theodores in terms of how:

> The inspiration for it was an abandoned place in Kildare out on the bog. It was originally a work camp for the people from the west of Ireland, who used to come and dig the bogs in the summer in the 1960s and 1970s before the bog was merchanised … It has an extraordinary sense about it. I felt this sense of place and a people who had been in that place, and almost of what they had done (Theodores 2003: 181–82).

They spent all their time working. 'There was no social life. They came here, they got up in the morning, they dug the bog, they came back. They did this all summer long … I was talking to somebody about it and they said, "Oh, that's a morphic field". The physical equivalent of Jungian theory of the collective consciousness' (Theodores 2003: 182). This non-verbal collective physicality, which defined the bog digging, is of course useful to transfer to dance. Cathy pointed out to me that the bog was owned by the state, that it was used to fuel houses before electricity and that it had to be cut for the power stations. And 'then came the machines in the 1970s that dig the bog quicker than people do'. So it was a unique bog landscape near her house that had first given her the idea for *Morphic Fields*, but the song 'I'm a bogman', with its irony about being proud over the bog lands now and in the past, had also (with typical Irish self-irony) been included as an aspect of the choreography. Still, Cathy was hoping to be able to do *Morphic Fields* as a site specific piece at some other point: 'One day the dance should actually happen in one of those huts and the audience should be on the outside, so you could actually walk around and look into the dance from the windows' (Theodores 2003: 182). This could be meant to evoke the memory of priests looking in through the windows of the cottages in the past, checking that people were not dancing, but, so the story goes, only seeing the upper bodies being still, as that dancing took place in the feet only (see Chapters 1 and 6). But in this case, the audience was supposed to see the dancing, which like most contemporary dance theatre engages the whole bodies of the dancers.

A New Linkage: *Giselle* in Ireland

In 1841 the Romantic ballet *Giselle* had its world premiere at the Paris Opera. Articulated through delicate dancing, this dramatic love story about death and spirituality was to become an acme of the classical ballet repertory. Not really because of the story in itself, which was rather archetypical, but because of the soft, lyrical music and the choreography, especially after Marius Petipa had stylized it in St Petersburg. Like other outstanding ballet productions, most notably *Swan Lake* and *The Nutcracker*, *Giselle* has also appeared in burlesque versions in dance theatre such as by Swedish choreographer Mats Ek. All *Giselles* follow the same story, however, which starts with a meeting of the peasant girl, Giselle, and Prince Albrecht, who are in love with each other. Villagers return from the fields to celebrate the harvest. The Duke arrives with his daughter, Bathilde. She is Albrecht's fiancée. This is revealed at a party that night.

Giselle is overtaken by grief and loses her mind. She stabs herself to death in a famous 'mad scene'. In the second act, the so called *willis*, spirits of young women who have been abandoned before their wedding, come out as night falls. They entice Giselle to rise from her grave. When Albrecht approaches, the willis disappear. Giselle comforts Albrecht who is in deep sorrow over her death. With the morning light Giselle has to go back into her grave. They say a final farewell knowing that they will never meet again (Balanchine and Mason 1989).

With his characteristic wit and talent for theatricality, Michael Keegan Dolan presented his radical revision of *Giselle* at the Dublin Theatre Festival in 2003.[6] It was extremely well received, also on tours to Edinburgh and at the Barbican Theatre in London. Like his other dance productions, *Giselle* is not only a funny parody, it also features fine duets of affection. This range of feelings and moods makes for a very strong performance. Michael connected the classic story to the Irish land: 'I am taking the bones of the story of *Giselle*, which is a very simple story – girl gets betrayed, girl dies, guy goes to graveyard, gets haunted, you know, and what I've done is that I have located it in the midlands of Ireland' (Theodores 2003: 119). This Giselle is asthmatic, but '"there is still a prince"', Michael asserts, '"OK, so he's not a prince. He's really a Slovakian bisexual line-dancing teacher"', (O'Mahony 2005).

On the web site of his company the Fabulous Beast Dance Theatre,[7] this *Giselle* is introduced as:

> This piece examined some of the universal human conditions, which are exasperated by living in a small town in the centre of Ireland. Giselle is set in Ballyfeeny, where the cloud is always low and where people keep secrets for very good reasons.[8] The dark brutal lives of the town inhabitants are temporarily broken by the unlikely gaudy glamour of the weekly line dancing class. This is especially true for Giselle McCreedy, an innocent trapped by parochialism and ultimately betrayed by the false promise of escape. Despite the dark backdrop of their lives, the power of forgiveness, the precedence of sincerity, and the resilience of the human spirit, ultimately win out.

In an interview with Diana Theodores (2003: 27, 119) Michael says that:

> The thing about *Giselle* that has always bothered me is the representation of a rural ideal, very popular in the romantic period, peasants running around in tights, maidens dancing in circles. It's a massive area, I could talk about it for hours. There is a connection here between how we like to see ourselves and how we really are, how we like to sell the concept of rural Ireland to the tourists and the reality of rural Ireland, which very much has two sides, the green hills, the rainbows, but also the violence, the darkness. Everything has two sides.

Michael also talks about the inward looking nature of living in the very centre of an island. The world he invents for *Giselle* 'is a place where it rains every day, where it is mucky, where things change incredibly slowly, where people are terrified of change'.

Later though, he specifies for Theodores: 'But I also look at the midlands as being the heart of Ireland'. Highly verbal with an intellectual inclination, Michael talked to me with great passion about how the 'English were in Ireland' and that 'we have totally neglected our culture'. Growing up in a well-educated family, he had started studying at Trinity College in order to become a barrister, but, he said in my interview with him: 'I left Trinity, went on a plane to London and ballet school! My father had a nervous breakdown – he's coming to the performance on Wednesday. He has recovered now'.

It is likely that the fact that Michael's grandfather was shot in the uprising against the English in 1916 has ignited Michael's engagement in Irish themes in his work. 'I'm on a mission, I'm doing specific things', he told me, and: 'I try to be holistic, didactic, try to heal people'. Talking about comedy as 'a glue', and that people still want to be entertained he yet stressed, 'Ireland is a lot darker and bloodier than people know'. When I first met Michael in 2000, he was still living abroad, mostly in London, and travelling to the United States and Germany for his choreographic work in opera. But he kept going back to Ireland to mount award-winning productions on his Fabulous Beast Dance Theatre. Eventually he did buy a field in the very midlands with an old schoolhouse close to a bog land, where he now lives. Like many Irish expatriates – he too has moved back home to Ireland.

'Home is the Hub'

'Have you noticed here in Ireland', young ballet dancer and teacher Susan McCarthy asked me, 'Everyone is obsessed with getting their own houses, owning property? I think it's because we were occupied'. She talked at great length about how 'for my friends this is a huge thing, owning property. But how are we going to afford buying a house?' Combining university studies with teaching ballet, she had both an artistic and an academic ability as well as ambition while her woman friends, they 'are only thinking about getting married, nothing else, not about education'. As to the obsession with getting your own house, and home, she did consent that 'the home is the hub of activity that everything starts from'.

Looking back at the Public Dance Hall Act from 1935, which prohibited, but did not manage to stop, dancing in homes (or any other dance forms), it is especially interesting to reconsider this issue in a contemporary perspective as it epitomizes the enduring significance of the idea of home in Ireland, where it is formed partly by cherished memories of house and barn dancing in the past, partly by the continuing plight of emigration which, notes Fintan O'Toole (1997a: 81, 86) 'has been the overwhelming fact of Irish life for the last 150 years'. Since 'home comes into focus only when one is away from home', and 'it is particularly true of Irish culture that the imagination itself is inextricable from the idea of home, usually made powerful by the act of leaving it.' Therefore, O'Toole (1997a: 86–87) goes on to say: 'in the network of recollection and imagination – remembering the past and inventing the future – that makes a culture, there's no place like home'.

As I mentioned in Chapter 1, Helen Brennan (1999: 128) accounts for circumstances around dances held in homes and barns just after the Public Dance Hall Act had been introduced in 1935. There was, for instance, the practice of poor families arranging dances with admission fees, not only as an entertainment, but primarily as an addition to their earnings. With the new Act, this became illegal, as was the widespread custom by farmers of holding a dance without a license 'for the workers who had helped him save his crops' such as turf and potatoes. Brennan (1999: 129–31) also renders the story of a widow who used to invite neighbours and other people to dances in her house as a token of gratitude for giving her a hand with the farm. This was disclosed and brought to court as a sergeant happened to pass by her house late one night and:

> saw a lot of bicycles and heard music. In the kitchen there were about thirty persons. Some present had come from long distances, as far as Kilmihil, some twelve miles away. A set was in progess, dancing to the music of a flute played by a young chap who was sitting in the corner. There was no one at the door and no charge.

The widow was acquitted, probably because her dances were not arranged in order to earn money.

Dancing in Irish homes goes a long way back, such as accounts from 1836 of how dances were 'held in new houses to tramp down the clay floor'.[9] And there is the old tradition 'to céilí', which 'still goes on in rural areas among the old folk'. But it used to be more common that 'certain people would come "ceiling" a certain night, Thursday night for instance, and also with musicians', I was told by Chris Ball, an arts officer.

There is also the call in set dancing 'Around the house and mind the dresser!' which goes back to the practice of dancing at home. In set dancing, there is a movement termed 'around the house' for 'the anti-clockwise swirling of the four couples in a dynamic circular motion'. Sometimes 'and mind the dresser!' is added as a warning not to run into other dancers, to keep the pattern (Ó Súilleabháin 1998: 76; Quinn 1997). Michael Roberts, a set-dancer, told me that the saying originates 'in the past when they did house dances, they cleared the floor, moved all the furniture except the dresser with all the plates and cups. It was too heavy to move. And then when the dancing started they danced around the house but had to mind the dresser!'

A few times I heard witty descriptions of how in the past, the houses were so small they used to do the half-sets instead of sets! So they went out and danced in the yard, in order to get more space. Dancing in the yard is illustrated in an arresting scene in the film *Dancing at Lughnasa* directed by Pat O'Connor from Brian Friel's play. It was David Bolger who choreographed the dance sections in the film, which is narrated as a nostalgic memory of the summer of 1936 by the son of one of five unmarried sisters who share a cottage in a small Donegal community, hardly able to make ends meet. This summer their older brother returns, after having worked as a missionary priest in Uganda, and the father of the boy makes a surprise visit. It is the end of August, early September, which means harvest time, and the celebrations of an old pagan ritual at Lughnasa with drumming and drinking. In the low kitchen, the sisters hear an inviting Irish tune on the crackling radio, and one by one, they break out in joyous dancing. As their movements grow faster and bigger they open the door to the yard and get out there for a euphoric climax of togetherness. 'From then on', David said to me, 'they know that adult life is going askew: dancing in the yard, togetherness, touching each other. From then on everything goes downhill!' The brother dies of a heart attack, the father of the boy joins the International Brigade to fight against Franco in Spain, the older sister loses her job as a school teacher and two of the sisters leave for the streets of London, never to return.

The fact that the dance scene in *Dancing at Lughnasa* has caught the attention of a number of academics as well as writers on social and cultural life in Ireland, must mean that it touches an Irish nerve. In an analysis by Luke Gibbons (2002: 93) of the play *Dancing at Lughnasa*, music on the radio, both Irish traditional music and American popular music, in combination with the pagan drumming at Lughnasa, are suggested to unleash the sisters' 'restricted inner worlds' in 'an imaginary space' of intense bodily expression. While Gibbons relates the different types of music, and thus the sisters, to metropolitan centres far away, Barbara O'Connor (2003a) emphasizes the impact of the Irish tune on the sisters. It is the Irish rhythms that make them drop their household chores and throw themselves into 'wild and frantic dancing', which she sees as 'a gesture of resistance' to the patriarchal order. Fintan O'Toole's (1997b) description of the dance scene is one where the sisters' deep sense of desperation is pounded out in a parody of a reel to a céilí band playing *The Mason's Apron* on the radio.

Talking about his choreographic work with the film, David told me that he finds 'this a beautiful subject, very passionate without being sentimental'. Like many of my informants, he referred back to colonialism when he interpreted the film for me: 'they could dance in the kitchen alright, but not go out in the yard. It was – because of colonialism'. But they did anyway, and they still 'sometimes break out in spontaneous dancing in the kitchen in the country'. Having worked with actors before who were not dancers, David had to devote quite some time to teach these women 'a very crash course in Irish dancing, as most of them were not from this culture' and had not been 'brought up on a diet of traditional music'.

A famous feature of the idea of home in Ireland is hospitality. In the essay titled 'The Irish'. Éilís Ní Dhuibhne (1999b: 59) explains Irish hospitality with a lingering 'natural neighbourliness of the traditional rural communities' where people depended on each other, but also as a part of Christian charity, as well as a a general helpfulness. But the warm welcome for foreigners tend to be directed to tourists who come for short visits, rather than to refugees or immigrants who are hoping to settle in Ireland. Instead they may be the targets of hostility. I did notice, however, that foreign settlers without Irish in-laws could feel left out of the hospitality after some time while Irish expatriates of course were welcomed back at least initially, especially if they were of a generation that was born in Ireland.

Dancing on the Radio

When I was doing fieldwork I leant about a radio series called *Take the Floor* which was broadcast in Ireland in the 1950s.[10] It made people dance in homes, thereby doing what could be referred to as house dance. *Take the Floor* was remembered as a wonderful entertainment by, among others, Father Dermod McCarthy. He wrote to me about this special treat in an email:

> I remember it well and it was a very popular show. It was a mixture of songs, instrumental music, and jokes by a wise-cracking presenter/comedian named Din Joe (stage name!) who was in reality the owner of a large garage and car sales business in Dublin. Now and then the traditional Irish music band would start to play music for a particular Irish folk dance, the participants (the programme was always recorded or broadcast live from a parish hall or some other venue where dance was possible and a crowd invited) would choose their partners, and Din Joe could be clearly heard calling out the instructions for the movements over the sounds of music and dancing feet. It was great fun. Sometimes listeners were encouraged to turn up the volume, push back the chairs in their kitchens at home and try out the dance themselves! We even did it once or twice in my home. It was a different world then!

About a month later Father Dermod specified his earlier story:

> As I re-read my mail describing the programme to you, it brought a smile on my face as I remembered the scene in our medium-sized kitchen at home in County Leitrim as my brothers, sister and whatever friends of hers happened to be there swung each other around the room to Din Joe's instructions on the radio at top volume, with my mother calling out warnings not to hit the china-cabinet or fall across and break the chairs! The dances were most often the 'Siege of Ennis' (two couples opposite two couples), 'The Walls of Limerick' (one couple facing another couple) or 'The Haymaker's Jig' (five men facing five women), or one of the Set-dances associated with different regions in Ireland. Happy days! By the way, Din Joe's real name was Denis Fitzgibbon.

Urging the readers of her book, not only to read about dance, but to go and watch traditional dancers and then ask for a lesson 'to find your dancing feet', Helen Brennan (1999: 72) quotes Din Joe's infectious call, '"Take the floor, big, little and small!"'

Looking at the Irish Landscape

The physical shape and location of a place plays a great part in how it is perceived. The fact that Ireland is an island is an important feature in the construction of Ireland as a place. In her study of crannogs, manmade islands in Ireland, archaeologist Christina Fredengren (2002: 109) says:

islands have a special effect on us structuring our experiences in particular ways. An island seen from the shore, like a mountaintop seen from below, invokes a tension in the landscape, creating the dichotomy of being here in body while one's thoughts are elsewhere. Islands – and to some extent also mountains – create a longing, a tension in the landscape by dramatising the spatial difference between here and there.

John Gillis (2001: 40) brings in the quality of remoteness of islands into this discussion, suggesting that this is what makes islands, yet he points out that remoteness does not necessarily imply physical distance, it can also be achieved through 'travel through time'. As Gillis specifies, remote places such as islands tend to be connected with pastness whether this in accordance with their history or not. Travelling to an island might be experienced as a trip back in time, not least if you are an Irish expatriate going back to visit your grandparents' country of origin. Still, this pastness, especially when it risks being conflated with ideas of backwardness, is not always appreciated among Irish people living in Ireland. This I noticed from time to time both in the Republic of Ireland and Northern Ireland in relation to Irish return migration, tourism, as well as academic research. A romantic representation of Ireland in tourism marketing has been critiqued by Irish scholars such as Barbara O'Connor (1993: 70) who, in a discussion of tourist imagery and national identity in Ireland, notes how images on postcards and tourist brochures depict men in leisurely conversation on a country road and people cutting the turf. O'Connor observes how Ireland is 'represented as a pre-modern society', and Irish people as quaint and the 'other', in tourist marketing. For Irish people this representation has blended with the lingering memory of colonialism, she argues, and has thus had a negative effect on how they value themselves. The construction of Ireland as a tourist site is thus also contested.

The visual perspective of Ireland as an island is created on arrival or departing, whether by plane or boat. Then the traveller is reminded that Ireland is located out there between the Irish Sea and the Atlantic, closer to other islands, the British Isles, rather than a mainland. Watching Ireland, like any island, rising through the sea while flying in to it, is remarkable every time. Suddenly Ireland is there, in such scope and detail: the long winding beaches holding back the buildings of Dublin and the low land of farms and fields reaching towards the horizon. Éilís Ní Dhuibhne (1999a: 1) takes us on a flight across the map of Ireland:

Imagine you are in an airplane, flying at twenty thousand feet. The landscape spreads beneath like a chequered tablecloth thrown across a languid body. From this vantage point, no curve is apparent. It is flat earth – pan flat, plan flat, platter flat to the edges, its green and gold patches stained at intervals by lumps of mountain, brownish purple clots of varicose vein in the smooth skin of land. Patterns of field, rough squares and rectangles, are hatched in with grey stone. The white spots, sometimes slipping disconcertingly out of focus, are sheep.

What looks like a neatly arranged world down there, from this perspective of vertiginous breadth and depth, does of course not show everything on the ground: 'What you can't see is what it is better not to see: the sap and the clay and the weeds and the mess', Ní Dhuibhne (1999a: 2–3) enumerates and continues her poetic stream of consciousness using telegraphic images, from 'heart and kitchen and sewer' to 'weep and laugh'. By then we have landed in Irish culture and find ourselves in the 'in between, that is the truth and that is the story'. In her introduction to the volume *Theorizing Ireland*, Claire Connolly (2003: 2) invokes this particular zooming in on Ireland by Éilís Ní Dhubhne as a way to understand Ireland by 'the move from elegant abstraction into the specifics of culture'.

Landscapes are not only settings and scenes to enter and look at, argues European ethnologist Orvar Löfgren (2000: 30–1, 34), but landscapes are in fact 'produced by movement, both of the senses and of the body'. Such movement pertains to the mind during the contemplation of a picturesque scene, or the body as it travels through a landscape. Löfgren also writes about one particular kind of power struggles over place: conflicting values over the same piece of land between farmers and tourists. Who 'owns' the view? Those who work the land or those who just look at it in passing when on holiday?[11]

A Legend of the Land: *Bridie*

A symbol of Christian charity, Saint Brigid is celebrated on 1 February in Ireland (cf. Ó Catháin 1995).[12] At the Saint Brigid Festival in 2001 there was a ceremony led by a minister who gave a speech in Saint Brigid's Cathedral by Saint Brigid's Well in Kildare Town (one of the centres for the Brigid celebrations). The ceremony included a dance solo titled *Bridie*, choreographed by Cathy O'Kennedy, and it drew a crowd of people, also visitors from America. The site specific solo was a restaging of the story of Saint Brigid. Cathy told me her story of Saint Brigid, which starts with how young Brigid was taking her vows to Saint Patrick to become a nun. But he read the wrong sermon – he read the sermon which ordained men for priesthood! This seems to have given Brigid extra power and she founded a double monastery for both women and men, as well as other convents across Ireland. Then, Cathy came to how Brigid asked the bishop for land: 'He said she could have as much as her cloth could cover. She took it off – and it grew – and she founded her convent where the cathedral is now, on the site where the convent used to be'. (This is also reflected in a traditional dance called 'The Weaving of Saint Brigid's Cloak' which I saw at the All-Ireland's in Killarney the year after.) The story of Saint Brigid is an instance of how a pagan Celtic tradition blends with Christianity, or as Cathy expressed it, 'Saint Brigid is the pagan version of pre-Christian tradition, the Celtic tradition. Within the Irish tradition she is a healer associated with heart and home, associated with water and wells'. And, so the story moves on, snowdrops signify Bridget's footsteps: wherever she had walked there would be snowdrops. They come out at the time of Saint Brigid's Day in February.

The dance solo *Bridie* was put together as a journey, like a pilgrimage, looking for Saint Brigid. The dancer, Lucy Dundon, small and red haired with fair skin, was the ideal embodiment of this very Irish saint. 'She's [Lucy is] my inspiration, it explains through her body the idea of the pagan, the saint', Cathy said. Wrapped up very close in a long blue cloth which unwrapped as she danced, Lucy moved delicately on the cold floor in the cathedral to loud modern music by Witold Lutoslawski, a Polish composer.

If the link to the land is close in Ireland both physically and as a state of mind, so is the link to religion, in many ways, especially Catholicism, as a guiding principle in moral issues in the Republic of Ireland. Even though beliefs and practices certainly differ, not least generationally, I encountered interesting instances of residue of religion even among people who claimed, at least contextually, to have left such concern behind. Like Cathy, they had often been raised in a strict, forbidding religiosity. On top of that, Cathy was well aware of the condemnation of dancing by the Catholic Church in the past. In a newspaper, she had found one of the letters from the 1920s reprinted where bishops ordered their priests to read at mass. The priests were famously summoned to preach against the 'evils of dancing', not least since dancing was alleged to be detrimental to the faith.[13] But Saint Brigid was different. She had come to Cathy in a dream offering the structure of the dance. 'For me', Cathy said, 'Brigid is all around me, I just have to put up my hand, when I need something. She can find it for me'.

With this site-specific dance piece about a woman saint, the gender aspect is added to the link to the Irish land. Here is a woman saint who is more prominent than other women saints because she had the male sermon read to her. Yet she makes use of her position by increasing her female virtues of charity and generosity.

The Irish Land, Dance and Displacement

Looking at the Irish landscape through dance reveals political and religious power struggles in a changing society, but also a cheeky resistance: people danced at crossroads and in their houses despite prohibitions. The voices and visions from the Irish dancing community I have quoted here, confirm that the attachment to the Irish land is firm, not least because of the lingering impact of colonialism. This chapter has tied in with the study of landscape 'as attachments to land, conflicts over land, the use of images of the past in the social construction of identities, and variant views of history, development and change' as recently summarized by Stewart and Strathern (2003: 10).[14] The dance production, *Territorial Claims*, exemplified conflicting politics between the Republic of Ireland and Northern Ireland expressed through differences between Catholics and Protestants. Bog lands in and around dance symbolized power and identity negotiations, sometimes in the form of supernatural beliefs, but also as a threatened environment supported by the historical specificity of this very Irish type of land. When Michael Keegan Dolan replants the ethereal classical ballet *Giselle* in the Irish midlands, the heart of Ireland, this is a new linkage to the Irish land which identifies a contemporary complexity of belonging and entrapment. In a place where your land has been occupied, the idea of home has a special meaning, thus home is often celebrated in Irish culture. I never saw dancing in homes during my fieldwork, but I heard many stories about such practice ranging from ways of hiding dancing in the past to sudden surges of dancing in the kitchen and out in the yard. A testimony of this is the rapturous dance scene in *Dancing at*

Lughnasa discussed in terms of release, resistance and desperation by different Irish observers. In a little email ethnography we get to hear about a truly happy practice of dancing to the radio at home in the 1950s. Looking at the Irish dance landscape is of course a very varied exercise depending on the vantage point. The view from mainstream Britain is not the same as from the Irish diaspora in the United States. While the process of looking at Ireland from overseas thus provides a number of different perspectives, looking out from Ireland is yet another view with its special experience of remoteness. Looking down on Ireland from an aeroplane, as in Éilís Ní Dhubhne's cameo of Ireland's map, she discusses the meaning of the shape of an island, and its hidden story. In the next chapter, the widespread practice of eloquent storytelling in Ireland will be discussed in terms of the fact that Ireland is an island, among other circumstances.

Reflecting on the map of Ireland from another perspective, Fintan O'Toole (1999) puts forward the idea that emigration has merely separated the people and the land, they do not share the same boundary anymore, yet the Irish map can be seen as a lie. According to O'Toole the lie of the land (in two senses!) is that for more than 150 years, a lot of Irish history has taken place outside Ireland, yet constantly looking back. Löfgren's (2000: 18) discussion of 'the ways in which landscape experiences are emotionalised' fits well into dance in Ireland. Both the Irish in Ireland and the Irish diaspora express strong national emotions for Ireland as a place. As people and events are engraved in places and landscape, those who have left are remembered through empty spaces in the land. The Irish dance landscape has extended abroad since emigration started. Viewing landscape as process, Eric Hirsch (1995: 22) 'relates a "foreground" everyday social life ..."to a background" of potential social existence. This could be applied to the Irish diaspora living their everyday social life in a foreground far away from Ireland, but keeping Ireland as a background of potential social existence to which one may return.'

Together with Seán Curran from New York, John Scott made *That Place, Those People* for the Belfast Festival in 1998. The dance production draws on Seán Curran's experience of forming his identity with emigrant parents who left for the United States in the 1950s. Themes of emigration and homesickness are included in the narrative of *Riverdance*. Young Irish dancers who practice competitive dancing in the diaspora also reach out to the old homeland.

Writing about the 1980s in the west of Ireland, John Waters (1991: 83) contrasts everyday life there with the views about Ireland which were expressed by people in talk shows on the radio during that time. These people identified a loyalty to the land with a sense of The Past. They were looking down on 'de Valera's dancing-at-the-crossroads vision of a people content with hard work and simple pleasures'. Instead they argued for a Modern Ireland, an urban, industrialized class society, which the people in the west of the country did not recognize. 'An attachment to the land, they averred, was no longer a defining feature of what it was to be Irish'. This stance is likely to change yet again, however, just as the meaning of the link to the Irish land keeps being reformulated. Through diversity and divisions in Irish culture, both in Ireland and abroad, runs a shared link back to the land.

Notes

1. See www.knowth.com/newgrange.htm for visitor information about this UNESCO World Heritage Site, which attracts 200,000 visitors annually. Admission to the special solstice event is by lottery. In 2003, 20,000 people applied for the fifty tickets that were available. The website does not mention the eventuality of cloudy weather on these five December days. Apart from this dance production, I did hear about the wonder at Newgrange in other contexts during my fieldwork. An elderly lady was said to be in line to get a ticket years ahead for her little grandchild to see the solstice when she was older. See also Mac Uistin (1999).

2. Graham technique, one of the first modern dance styles, was developed by Martha Graham.

3. Mary Nunan remained as Artistic Director of Daghdha Dance Company until she resigned in 1999 and Yosiko Chuma took over. Since 2004, Michael Klien has been Artistic Director.

4. *Territorial Claims* was the first ever project in Ireland in which a film director, Donal Haughey, and a choreographer collaborated in order to make a screen adaptation of a dance theatre work. The video premiered at the Cork Film Festival in 1997 and was presented at the International Dance for Camera Festival in the Lincoln Centre, New York in 1997.

5. *Bog Feature*, choreographed by Nic Bryson from Belfast, first premiered at the Belfast Festival in 2002. It was later performed at The Firkin Crane in Cork, one of Ireland's venues for contemporary dance performance. This short piece was presented in the program leaflet as: 'I want to capture something of the importance of Bogland in Ireland's history, to physicalise the affect on the human spirit of spending time there ... an environment where even decay is grinding to a halt ... also to reflect on reasons to prefer to be in the city or even beyond these shores'.

6. During the time of my fieldwork, another dance production also titled *Giselle*, but with the subtitle *The Presence of the Past*, premiered in June 2000 in Dublin. This contemporary dance theatre version was choreographed by Cathy O'Kennedy who told me that: 'A lot of the dancers said they felt a part of the performance. It was a very emotional piece for me, also for a number of the dancers, about love. We are who we are because of the past. There is a collective past in terms of family, women with their children. *Giselle* is my favourite ballet. This one is twenty minutes, about hope. It was about hopeful loss as a strengthening experience, a place to move on, there is a redeeming factor'. A classical production of *Giselle* is on the repertory of Cork City Ballet, a small ballet company in Ireland. A classical *Giselle* was also scheduled for Ballet Ireland, the major ballet company, for April 2003, with a subsequent tour around Ireland and the United Kingdom, but they had to cancel all this because of an unexpected decision by the Arts Council to cut their funding by more than eightly per cent, see Chapter 5.

7. See www.thefabulousbeast.net.

8. Ballyfeeny is a fictional name of this town.

9. See Armagh and Down Parliamentary papers (1836), Irish Folklore Collections, University College Dublin, XXXII, 63–4.

10. It was Séamus Ó Síocháin, anthropologist at National University of Ireland at Maynooth, who first drew my attention to this seemingly contradictory phenomenon. Although Irish dancing with its distinct step sound is unusually suitable for listening to, the visual aspect of dancing is admittedly crucial in most dance contexts. Dancing on the radio was also the topic of a new series, Nice Moves, hosted by Deirdre Mulrooney, broadcast in Ireland in 2004.

11. This raises wider questions about ownerships and land rights such as the growing problem of intellectual property – often in relation to music and dance – that 'belongs'

to the land, according to local beliefs, elsewhere, among First Nation people in North America and Australia.

12. The life of Colmcille, another Irish saint, was made into dance theatre by Adrienne Brown in 2000 and performed by her New Balance Dance Company.

13. See Irish Ecclesiastical Record (1926) and Brennan (1999).

14. See also Bender (1993) and Hirsch and O'Hanlon (1995).

Chapter 5

Storytelling Dance

Comedy is sometimes used in Irish dance theatre in an effort to help heal the hurt of history. This is also said to be the incentive behind Flann O'Brien's (1988: 46, 53, 59) popular satire of the Irish peasant novel, originally published in Gaelic in 1942. Born as Brian O'Nolan in 1911, the author spent his childhood under colonization.[1] The novel makes relentless fun of the Gaeltachts, and as the translator Power (1988: 6) points out, of Irish life generally: 'the key-words in this work are surely "downpour", "eternity" and "potatoes" set against a background of squalor and poverty'.[2] One of the chapters includes a description of dancing at a feis, a competition, in the countryside:

> The morning of the feis was cold and stormy without halt or respite from the nocturnal downpour. We had all arisen at cockcrow and partaken of potatoes before daybreak. During the night the Gaelic paupers had been assembling in Corkadoragha from every quarter of the Gaelacht and, upon my soul, ragged and hungry was the group we saw before us when we arose.
>
> The Dublin gentlemen said that no Gaelic dance was as Gaelic as the Long Dance, that it was Gaelic according to its length and truly Gaelic whenever it was truly long. Whatever the length of time needed for the longest Long Dance, it is certain that it was trivial in comparison with the task we had in Corkadoragha on that day. The dance continued until the dancers drove their lives out through the soles of their feet and eight died during the course of the feis. Due to both the fatigue caused by the revels and the truly Gaelic famine that was ours always, they could not be succoured when they fell on the rocky dancing floor and, upon my soul, short was their tarrying on this particular area because they wended their way to eternity without more ado.

Here is evidence of central Irish concerns, which I discuss particularly in Chapters 2 and 6 in relation to dance. With his strong engagement in Gaelic language and culture, it is likely that O'Brien hints at the Gaelic League's cultivation of Irish dances and other cultural expressions, primarily the Gaelic language. This surfaces through the notion 'truly Gaelic' about the Long Dance. The way 'truly' is repeated could be seen as a reference to continuous debates about the authenticity of Irish customs, represented by Irish dance and music and ideas about to what extent they are really Gaelic, Irish and traditional, as well as the importance of emphasizing Gaelic culture in a colonial context. Historical hardships of life in Ireland are portrayed in the image of dancers dancing until they died of exhaustion. Hunger and exhaustion lead over to the Famine, which also is said to be 'truly Gaelic', while 'that was ours always' may be a way to say that the Famine has had a major impact for a long time, and that this Famine was different from other famines in its cruelty and consequences. A quality of Irish storytelling is the long accounts that go on and on, typically repeating certain contents in a slightly different phrasing in order to reinforce them. O'Brien makes use of this rhetorical technique when bringing up the Long Dance (!) of all examples of traditional Irish dances, yet 'that it was Gaelic according to its length' is what we actually need to know. When he continues by saying that 'and truly Gaelic whenever it was truly long' we realize that he is using the dance to ridicule both the debate about Gaelic culture and tradition on one hand and the long, winding shape of stories in Ireland.

In the highly verbal culture of Ireland with its renowned traditions of literature and drama, the nonverbal art of dance offers alternative expressions of meaning and debate. 'Talking with your feet' is a common designation for dance in general. In Ireland there is also the poetic version, 'song of feet', especially about traditional dance. Following the findings of anthropologists of dance, that dance has an ability to articulate what cannot be made as clear through other modalities (Kaeppler 1978; Reed 1998; Wulff 2001), this chapter will examine storytelling and Irishness in Irish dance theatre, which also relates to funding policy. The Irishness I keep tracing in Irish dance throughout this book does not have to be about Irish themes – but might as well be found in the theatricality, in an exuberant storytelling about archetypical and contemporary human themes such as love, gender, friendship, family, the internet or world politics. Diana Theodores (2003: 28) identifies 'strong drives towards narrative and language' in Irish dance, yet sees a parallel orientation towards 'pure dance' in Ireland. So do I: Irish choreographers make abstract steps as well as more elaborate story dance. But I want to make a special point about the context of 'pure' or 'abstract' dance.

In dance scholarship, abstract dance and movement on the one hand, and story dance on the other, tend to be analysed as separate dance forms: story dance tells stories, abstract dance does not – as if abstract steps came from nowhere and were devoid of social context. Abstract dance steps in contemporary or modern dance in the Euro-American dance world, as well as ballet (refined by George Balanchine into the American speedy ballet style), go back to the modernist movement in the arts, especially abstract painting (Guilbault 1983; Wulff 1998). In my ethnographic experience, even abstract steps convey stories about their people and societies, although in different and sometimes more subtle ways than more theatrical story dance. The narrative is not necessarily linear, with a beginning followed by a middle and concluded by an end, but can take other forms. Abstract dance often consists of a number of separate episodic scenes of moods woven together by an all-embracing theme. Currents in other art, media and new technology forms, as well as training background, go into contemporary Irish dance theatre. Styles of abstract dance in Ireland communicate dance and life experience of Irish choreographers – some of which is Irish, others of which reflect more general concerns – and how they position themselves in the national and the transnational world of dance theatre.

My observations of storytelling as a distinguishing feature of Irish dance theatre kept being confirmed time after time by choreographers, critics and dance and theatre people without me having directed them towards this topic. David Grant, theatre director in Belfast, thus told me that: 'Ours is a verbal culture. I like dance with a story'. Seona MacReamoinn (2002: 32), dance critic, argues: 'The notion of 'theatre dance', by direction or aspiration, seems to be applied to many dance companies in Ireland. This is an intriguing, curious detail – perhaps evidence of our highly verbal culture.' Michael Keegan Dolan has described how 'my primary instinct is storytelling' and 'It's just part of me. Language is functional. It all has to be functional for movement to be functional – it has to create a character, it has to create a feeling, it has to lend itself to some other bigger thing, it can't be purely movement', (O'Mahony 2005). Young choreographer Jane Kellaghan finds herself doing stories: 'Even if I never gave my movement a story it seemed to end up having one' (Theodores 2003: 175). And David Bolger confirms that he is basically guided by his urge to be 'telling stories as a choreographer' (Theodores 2003: 28). While for Mary Nunan in Limerick, a spiritual connection, 'a deeper, internal connection to movement' defines her quest 'and not necessarily storytelling', she admits that: 'When I am making dance I always have a story, and it really annoys the hell out of me. I find it hard to just feel movement as movement, which is what I am really trying to do and I think now I'm beginning to get to the bag end of that' (Theodores 2003: 200).

Anthropologists of dance, as well as dance people in the Euro-American dance world (cf. Wulff 1998), perceive dance as having an ability to convey 'social and cultural circumstances that cannot be sufficiently expressed in any other way' (Wulff 2001: 3209). This does not mean that dance reveals what is completely unknown, or out of culture as it were, but rather that different dance forms ranging from folk and ethnic dance to dance theatre and dance shows, talk about, remind us about, discuss, confirm, and predict cultural and social matters.[3] Dance theatre choreographers often describe their work in terms of 'exploring' a particular topic, as David Bolger did in relation to the Famine when he was making *Ballads*. That was an opportunity to talk about a difficult topic which had been silenced in Ireland. Dance theatre can also provide spaces to discuss well-known, or not so known, topics in a new, different way, perhaps looking into the future. Having said this, I need to clarify that I am aware that a text about dance, such as this one, is in a different modality than live dance. Some mood and movement details get lost in the translation to text, while other aspects are gained through academic analysis. There are moreover instances when a text, not only dance reviews, can have an impact on the live performance in a kind of feedback conversation, a dialogue, between choreographer and writer.

Spinning Stories

Éilís Ní Dhuibhne (1999b: 53) identifies loquacity as a central characteristic of the Irish, and that a:

> high opinion of the Irish gift for writing and talking is shared by many, especially the Irish themselves. That the Irish are verbally gifted is a *sine qua non* of the image we sell to tourists, but it is probably based on truth. Ireland has produced a high proportion of internationally renowned writers, such as the verbally generous James Joyce and the verbally frugal Samuel Beckett.[4] It is commonly believed that there are more writers per capita in Ireland than in other countries.

Lawrence Taylor (1992: 153) also attests to the prominence of language as expressive culture in Ireland, ranging 'from the oral narrative that still characterizes much local Irish life to one of the most vibrant literary traditions in Europe'. Not only those who are involved in writing literature or plays, Ní Dhuibhne confirms, but Irish people generally, 'are talkative'. Creative wit, especially, is much appreciated. Here Ní Dhuibhne draws up a gender boundary when she argues that Irish men are wittier than Irish women, better at telling jokes, and that their conversation is full of funny comments and anecdotes. This comes to the fore when they are drinking. Then Irish men excel in being friendly, witty and chatty. They have had a lot of practice since puberty, which is the age when boys start to learn this skill partly by competing with each other. As they acquire a repertoire of entertaining phrases and stories, it is not uncommon that joking turns into a lifestyle. The Irish enjoy making fun of other people, Ní Dhuibhne (1999b: 54) points out, for speaking and behaving in a different, exaggerated way, by boasting for example. Such ridicule is not presented in front of people, but they are typically 'laughed at behind their backs'. But Ní Dhuibhne hastens to add the significant piece of information that 'the Irish like to laugh at themselves, at their sorrows.' This is where Flann O'Brien's witty account of dancing at a feis comes in.

The urge to lighten things up is also obvious in Irish plays, 'the literary form which is most closely modelled on conversation', Ní Dhuibhne (1999b: 54) continues. This is why Irish plays tend to be tragicomedies, rather than pure comedies or tragedies. By now I can see how a fusion of creative wit and dark drama forms a vital vein running through Irish culture. These two sides seem to belong together, they also coexist in many dance theatre pieces. Ní Dhuibhne (1999b: 54) writes about 'a moroseness which lurks not far beneath the skin of many Irishmen' that needs to be balanced with funny conversation. The importance of having a good time is of course illustrated by the Irish expression for this: 'the craic was good'.

The widespread practice of storytelling goes a long way back in Ireland, as evident in literary scholar Georges Denis Zimmermann's (2001) fascinating *The Irish Storyteller*, which draws on Irish literature in English and is framed by a folklore perspective. This big book takes a wide approach, from elite storytelling to popular traditions, both in oral account and fiction across the centuries. As Ó Giollain

(2000) remarks, there is now a revival in storytelling taking place at international festivals and special sessions in pubs. Traditional illiterate storytellers were discovered and introduced to wider audiences by the Gaelic League, and thus included in the nation-building project, also by supplying an immense amount of stories to the Irish Folklore Collections at the Department of Irish Folklore, University College, Dublin.[5] Angela Bourke (2003: 33-34) acknowledges the prestigious position of oral storytellers in rural Irish society, in particular in Irish-speaking areas, until quite recently. Not only an entertainer, 'the skilled story-teller was valued as outstandingly wise, thoughtful, and knowledgeable'. The long format of Irish stories also comes up in Bourke's (2003: 27, 28, 30, see also Bourke 1999) spell-binding essay 'The Virtual Reality of Irish Fairy Legend'. Even Irish fairy legends that are short in form 'connect with one another in reticulated systems that are both elegant and economical', explains Bourke. Disputing notions of fairy legends as 'less valuable, less important, than other kinds of narrative, notably the long, episodic hero-tales and the international folktales' both in their story-telling contexts and by collectors and scholars, Bourke contends the significance of fairy legends. With the support of folklorist Bo Almqvist (1991), she argues that the frequency of fairy legends makes them a subject for scholarly scrutiny. In fairy legends, humans meet other beings referred to as 'good people', 'little people' or 'fairies'. Setting out in the ordinary, in everyday life or on journeys, something extraordinary suddenly happens, whether good or bad. The legends usually move back to the ordinary in the end. How come listeners believe in these stories, if only contextually? 'People can both believe in them and disbelieve', says Bourke. According to metanarratives of folklore, certain stories get listeners to suspend their disbelief, but as Bourke notes, the story-teller must have a capacity 'to reconcile the impossible with the unexceptional'. It is the betwixt-and-between traits of fairy legends that make them appealing. Just like dance theatre, fairy legends are oblique, ambiguous and thus multivocal. When Bourke notes that Irish poets from W.B. Yeats to Nuala Ní Dhomhnaill have drawn on fairy legends, she thereby shows how this oral tradition turns into a written fictional tradition, at least as one of its trajectories, besides the folklore publications.

Developing Dance Theatre and Ballet

Ballet originates in the fourteenth century in what would become northern Italy. With noble families getting wealthy came an indulgence in Renaissance pastimes such as social dance: a pre-classical dance which was a combination of peasant folk dancing and court processions was very popular. In the sixteenth century, the first ballet production, *Ballet Comique de la Reine*, was presented to an audience at the court in Paris. In the following century, King Louis XIV provided ballet with a professional base by organizing training academies and theatres. Already in the eighteenth century ballet companies were to be found in many countries around Europe. In line with the Romantic period in the arts, classical ballet was set in the ethereal form it still features, with precise steps, point shoes and bell-shaped tutus, in 1832 after a premiere of the production *La Sylphide* in Paris. During the first years of the twentieth century, the impresario Sergei Diaghilev established the Ballets

Russes, a company which gave annual seasons in Paris and went on long tours to places such as London and New York. Dancers and choreographers with the Ballets Russes were to disperse and build ballet into a prominent art form on different continents. One of the dancers, Ninette de Valois, would establish the Royal Ballet in London. It is noteworthy that the doyenne of the Royal Ballet, this ballet company which to a great extent keeps cultivating an exclusive and somewhat aloof Englishness, was actually Irish! Anglo-Irish, to be exact. Born Edris Stannus, de Valois (who lived for more than a century, and was much loved and highly respected at the Royal Ballet, I noticed during my fieldwork there (see Wulff 1998, 2002). De Valois described vividly in her memoir how she learnt a jig as a child and always had a deep affection for Ireland (de Valois 1959; Cass 1993; Wulff 1998, 2002).

The Ballets Russes also represents a turning point in the history of ballet: its choreography and the way some of it was executed were early signs of a break with ballet. In conjunction with the modernist movement in the arts, this would develop into modern dance, now often referred to as contemporary dance, and later dance theatre, first in the United States, and moving from there to Germany. Isadora Duncan was a great inspiration for the early modern dancers, many of whom were independent women such as Martha Graham and Mary Wigman. They worked out seminal choreographic styles 'expressive and barefooted, with large swinging motions, occasionally using verbal utterances' (Wulff 1998: 44). A further change of direction of modern dance was initiated by choreographer Merce Cunningham and composer John Cage in New York in the 1940s. They included sections of silence alternating with outbursts of loud music and shrieks in their dance productions.

Wishing Time

In November 1999, John Scott made the piece *Wishing Time* for his irish modern dance theatre. I came for two rehearsals and the opening night at the small SFX City Theatre in Dublin. Talking about the production process, John told me that he had been working with Merce Cunningham's system of choreographic chance where tossing coins and throwing dice are used for making decision about order, repetition, change and inclusion of preexisting dance sections (cf. Foster 1986 among others). John had divided the stage in squares where he moved around the steps according to the results of his dice throwing.

Getting to the seats in the dark auditorium, the audience crossed the floor, which was the stage, and climbed up on the other side of it. This was the alternative experimental dance theatre scene in Dublin where critics from Irish newspapers as well as international dance magazines mixed with young artists and writers, design and drama students, family and friends of irish modern dance theatre and other Dublin dance people. The atmosphere in the foyer before the performance, and later at the wine reception behind the backdrop in the still dark auditorium, was young and 'artsy', inclusive, almost intimate, yet with elements of competition between choreographers also because of the presence of critics and Arts Council officers. The Irish dance theatre world is a relatively small, interconnected one, where everyone is bound to get to know everyone else quickly. Dancers, choreographers, musicians and critics meet in many contexts, some of them working in more than one capacity, such as the critic who also writes music for dance companies (Wulff 2004).[6]

For *Wishing Time*, the stage is set with a tin wall to the right and a backdrop of silver foil bands. Two spotlights are placed in the middle of the stage with a female dancer laying beside each of them. The piece starts with their bodies contracting in quick movements of painful cramps accompanied to the sound of Cagian loud tape music and their own shrieks. Two other female dancers enter, followed by two men. The four dancers pull the two women up from the floor then run to the tin wall and throw themselves repeatedly against it while shrieking, stamping and then dancing against it. The dancers are all dressed in velour shorts and tops in grey, navy, wine or red. The choreography is characterized by the dancers running, throwing themselves headlong on the floor hurting themselves, throwing themselves towards each other, jumping and catching each other. Pain is reflected in facial grimaces. There are duets between two men, two women and a man and a woman. The loud tape music now and then shifts into silent sections that are interrupted by more shrieks, hysterical laughs, even giggles. Towards the end, the mood changes and becomes ethereal, peaceful. There is a soothing, delicate sound of water falling.

Wishing Time would be categorized as abstract dance in most dance scholarship. Yet there is a kind of narrative, in the sense that there is a development of state of mind and mood. The subtitle *Notes from an Unfinished Heart* may provide a lead in the story of this piece which seems to deal with love moving into brutal confrontation replaced by a a new serene situation.

Dance Theatre in Ireland

As I indicated in Chapter 1, William Butler Yeats had a special interest in dance which comes through in allusions to dance in his poems. Dance theatre can even be said to have been introduced to Dublin by Yeats in the late 1920s when he started using dance in the narrative of some of his plays, so called dance plays that he directed for the Abbey Theatre as a part of the nationalist cultural movement. Yeats was trying to articulate an Irish choreography 'based on the patterns and rhythms of traditional Irish dancing', as Fintan O'Toole (2003: 11) noted in his capacity of Dublin theatre critic. It is quite possible that Yeats was envisioning a dance movement in Ireland, similar to the Irish literary movement with its modernist character which accommodated currents from abroad as well as indigenous expressions. In order to accomplish this he established the partnership with Ninette de Valois. She was already in London when Yeats asked her to join him at the Abbey Theatre. He needed her assistance in the restaging of his *Four Plays for Dancers*, which was the first in a succession of dance plays that Yeats and de Valois would stage together during the next eight years, with de Valois dancing in some of them. In 1927, de Valois set up the Abbey School of Ballet, which has been documented in a fine piece of work by Victoria O'Brien (2002: 46). The Abbey School of Ballet closed down when de Valois went back full time to the Vic-Wells Ballet in London, but it had by then 'created an enduring practice of dance performances in Ireland'.[7]

There were some modern stage dance activities in Dublin in the 1940s: influenced by Mary Wigman's expressionist dance, Erina Brady ran her Irish School of Dance Art in Harcourt Street. She also organized performances and barefoot recitals, and did choreographies for theatre plays, until she eventually left Ireland (Robinson 1999). Meanwhile in Cork, Joan Denise Moriarty founded an amateur ballet company in the 1940s, and in the 1970s the professional Irish National Ballet. It folded almost two decades later in the aftermath of the Arts Council removing funding at the advice of Peter Brinson (1985) (see Chapter 1). There was an attempt by the Arts Council to merge Moriarty's company with a ballet company lead by Patricia Ryan-Collins in Dublin, but the partnership did not work out. Patricia Ryan-Collins had been taken to Ireland from England in her teens by her mother when the Second World War broke out. Having started ballet training early, Ryan-Collins eventually set up her own small ballet company, and was able to provide dancers for opera and theatre productions in Dublin, even the Royal Ballet in London.

The story of Patricia Ryan-Collins' life and work is, like many such stories in the ballet world, one of determination, cultural creativity and world politics. Since this is taking place in Ireland, religion also comes into the picture. 'I'm going to be big over Russian dancers!' Ryan-Collins exclaimed when I was interviewing her. There was not a Russian embassy in Dublin at the time she started her company, so she went over to London in the late 1950s to ask for Russian dancers to come to Dublin. And when they arrived, someone from the Irish army was called in to translate. 'It was like a spy game!' Then the Legion of Mary (an apostolic organization of lay Catholics) started protesting outside the theatre where they were dancing, the Olympia. There were parades and people carrying placards saying 'Send back these Godless people!' and referring to the fact that 'Russians have no religion'. No wonder Ryan-Collins was pleased to tell me that: 'The performances were sold out. There were crowds, cheers. They went wild!' But the Legion of Mary insisted that the two Russian dancers, the Russian cultural attaché, the Irish interpreter and Ryan-Collins all went to an event where they took out religious scrolls and did prayers. This was followed by 'a lot of Irish dancing!'[8]

Joan Denise Moriarty mounted classical as well as modern dance productions, and choreographed ballets based on themes from Irish mythology, danced to Irish traditional music. Some of this music was written by Seán Ó Riada, such as the music to the ballet *Playboy of the Western World* which Moriarty adapted in 1978 from John Millington Synge's play.[9] Accompanied by live music by the Chieftains, the ballet version was a highpoint in the company's repertory, which toured widely abroad. It was also broadcast by the RTÉ. In Ruth Fleischmann's (1998) edited biography of Joan Denise Moriarty, Carolyn Swift (1998: 220) writes about Moriarty's longstanding endeavour to 'develop Irish dancing into a performance art which would tell a story, rather than merely demonstrate a skill'. Like other dance people and academics I talked to in Ireland, she compared *The Playboy of the Western World* with *Riverdance*: both dance productions tell Irish tales, but unlike other commentators Swift did not make a point of the fact that they both attained 'commercial triumph' and that both brought Irish dancing to the diaspora in London and New York. As a critic, Swift (1998: 223) was a *Riverdance* fan, but not really impressed with *The Playboy of the Western World*, seeing how 'the folk-ballet had vivacity and charm to match the music, but artistically it was only partially successful'.

In Belfast, Helen Lewis set up the Belfast Modern Dance Group in the late 1960s. A holocaust survivor, she had come to Belfast in 1947 from Czechoslovakia with her husband, whose parents were English. Trained as a ballet dancer, and with some practice of choreographing – also during horrendous circumstances in Auschwitz – she was invited to do the choreography for a Smetana opera production in Belfast. It went very well and she was soon teaching and choreographing dance full time in a hall at the YMCA, but:

> it became quite dangerous in the 70s with a group of young children and the bombs flying. I found a nice hall in Lisburn Park, a church, a good part of town. My pupils came from all parts of town. It became clear what a wonderful factor dance is in bringing people together. In the process they became friends and not only for the class, but for life! It never mattered whether they were Catholic or Protestant: they are friends to this day!

In her eighties when I met her, Helen Lewis showed me a black-and-white picture of the last dance production she choreographed, titled *The Dance of Anne Frank*. Together with the late Patricia Mulholland, who had a dance company drawing on traditional Irish dance in Belfast, Helen Lewis is regarded as the founder of dance theatre in Northern Ireland. In the Republic of Ireland, Joan Davies opened the Dublin Contemporary Dance Studio, which offered contemporary dance classes, sometimes taught by professional teachers from abroad. The idea was to establish a full-time school and performing company, and to this end the Dublin Contemporary Dance Theatre was established in 1979 with Joan Davies as director. Davies had learnt Graham technique in London, and was to devote her next ten years to the new company in Dublin.

Even though there is now a lot of crossover between classical ballet on one hand and contemporary dance and dance theatre on the other, there has been a history of ideological and artistic tensions between these two highly specialized dance forms that both require some familiarity in order to be appreciated. They are partly different sensibilities, but unfortunately class backgrounds and the issue of cultural capital often comes into preferences and opportunities in relation to ballet and contemporary dance. Yet if ballet foyers are defined by an upper-middle-class, even upper-class formality and etiquette, which keep many people away from this art form, alternative dance theatre might also make prospective spectators uncomfortable by its special culture of young 'artsy coolness', especially in metropolitan cities. And of course, some alternative dance companies, such as William Forsythe's Ballett Frankfurt,[10] eventually find their way to grand opera houses, thereby transcending, or rather challenging, the boundary between popular culture and 'high' culture (Wulff 1998). In dance scholarship and among dance writers, contemporary dance and dance theatre tend to be regarded as more interesting and important than ballet, not least because this is where choreographic renewal usually occurs. Even though there are many versions of classical ballet productions, shaped by different choreographic styles and schools over time, including famous interpretations of leading roles by dancers from Rudolf Nureyev to

Sylvie Guillem, classical choreography is quite stylized as a form. Yet, ballet keeps impacting on contemporary dance and dance theatre, not only in predictable critique or parody, but also in references to topics of famous ballets, even in entire contemporary versions of classical productions, but more often in moods such as ethereality.

In the Irish dance world, I noticed traces of the tension between ballet and dance theatre, not least ignited by the fact that Ballet Ireland got a big part of the Arts Council dance funding at one point, but then suddenly lost it to dance theatre companies. There was also the notion that ballet was Protestant and middle class, which kept being contradicted by my observations. Susan McCarthy, however, did have an upper-middle-class background. She told me that:

> I begged to go to ballet classes. I started at 4. I had a cousin who did ballet. It was probably the tutus on telly. When I was a child in Leixlep, a village outside Dublin, ballet was a very posh thing to do, a very odd thing to do. It's more normal now than it used to be. Now children from lower income families do ballet.

The reasons for doing ballet have also changed, Susan has noticed when she teaches children ballet. Even though she finds the competitiveness among eight to nine year old girls 'unbelievable', she knows that 'they go for social reasons' (which is the main driving force behind children doing Irish dancing as well, see Chapter 6). Susan also taught thirteen–fourteen year old girls who 'don't want to be there. It's not cool. But in order to be able to do musical theatre and modern dance, they have to do ballet'.

Besides the small Cork City Ballet directed by Alan Foley, who comes out of Joan Denise Moriarty's dance school and Cork Ballet Company, there is now Ballet Ireland based in Dublin. It was set up by Anne Maher and Günther Falusy in 1998. Anne told me about her upbringing in ballet:

> I started dancing at three. My mother took me because all the other girls were dancing. Like so many in Ireland, I started dancing in a church hall. When I was sixteen, I went down to Cork to spend a year with Joan Denise Moriarty. I was able to take class with the company every day. It was wonderful to watch the professional dancers rehearse, but it was terrible when Moriarty was teaching outside Cork and we had to carry very heavy equipment on local buses, old-fashioned big tape-recorders. I used to pretend I was going home.

After teaching for a while at Dublin Ballet, 'until they decided that the company would take a contemporary route', she left for England, where she took classes in London for three months and danced with a small company for a summer. She got a scholarship to Monte Carlo ballet school where she stayed for almost two years. It was after that, in London, that she met Austrian Günther Falusy, whom she later married. They both worked with Vienna Ballet Theatre for ten years. Then in 1998 they went back to Ireland and started Ballet Ireland:

Before that, in summer of 1996, we had registered the company name, started meeting people and the Arts Council. They said they did not know. But we decided to put our money where our mouth was. We wanted to have a shot at it. We hired the Gaiety (Theatre) for a week and put together a series of dates around the country – and we took out a loan. We had auditions here and in London, and hired twelve dancers for a mixed program. The opening night was the last Tuesday in the month of September in 1998. It was absolutely nerve-wracking. But the week went very well. We had some quiet nights in the beginning of the week, the last part was better. And we were absolutely thrilled!

They applied for money from the Arts Council, but it would take a year before they started getting some funding. This continued, but when they saw how dance theatre got 'a considerable amount, more than IR£ 100,000 went to Dance Theatre of Ireland and irish modern dance theatre', they organized a campaign sending out press releases. This triggered a debate in *The Irish Times* about the funding policy of the Arts Council, where especially Michael Seaver (2002) was critical about Ballet Ireland and the amount of money it had been allocated.[11] There was a piece in the breakfast show *Morning Ireland*, on the radio, in support of the company. 'We felt that it had an effect', Anne concluded. They were invited by the Arts Council to apply for multi-year funding and put together a plan for three years, arguing that they would produce a number of the classical ballets on the relatively small scale that was feasible, including *Swan Lake*, and do summer workshops and educational work with primary school pupils. In March 2001, they got IR£ 108,000 from the Arts Council. So they performed *Swan Lake*. On the opening night, the dance officer from the Arts Council complimented them, saying that 'the scale is just perfect'. 'Then in December 2002, we were sent a letter saying that the budget was going to be reduced', Anne sighed, and:

> In January 2003 we received an email saying that our funding had been cut. The reasons were that the scale was too small, the suitability was questioned, as was the nature of the artistic visions. And there was also this thing about opportunity for Irish artists. We did not have all that many dancers from Ireland.

Fundraising *Ballet Gala Extravaganza*

In order to save Ballet Ireland when it had lost almost all its funding, a fundraising *Ballet Gala Extravaganza* was arranged at the National Concert Hall in Dublin in May 2003.[12] On the opening night, there was an air of middle-class confidence in the elegant foyer. Dressed up families, some men in tuxedos and women in evening dresses, couples, and young and older women entered the auditorium; many little girls were jumping around expectantly. Although built for musical concerts, and hence without wings and curtain, there was no live orchestra this night. The accompanying music came from a tape. A big backdrop covered a huge organ. In the first intermission, a private reception was held for national and foreign dignitaries, such as some ambassadors and Irish ministers, with an interest in culture. It was an evening in two acts of a mixed program of seventeen pieces of classical ballet with some folk inspiration, contemporary dance and a few Irish themes. The classical pieces consisted of sections from famous classical ballets put together in new choreographic combinations. The evening ended with *Irish Rhapsody*. The piece started in darkness. As the light came on, it revealed a tight group of seven women and three men standing in the upper left hand side corner of the stage. Looking happy, in modest costume, the women in grey dresses with flowery simple decorations, the men in brown tights and white shirts, started moving in circles with a folk tune in front of a green Celtic knotwork projected on the screen. It brought to mind notions of 'the plain people of Ireland' dancing away at the crossroads. The concert hall was not sold out, but there were enough people in the audience to create a good response: some pieces and solos were very well received with spontaneous clapping. A guest dancer from Vienna State Opera Ballet, Mihail Sosnovschi, brought in to replace an injured dancer, received ovations for his smooth and secure dancing. Lucy Hickey, who danced in three of the pieces, told me later 'at the National Concert Hall – you feel like you are showered in applause!'[13] She also talked about the problems with the funding and commented that of the sixteen dancers: 'two of us are Irish, two half-Irish. That's another reason for the funding cuts: there were more Irish dancers before.' The fundraising gala was successful: Ballet Ireland survived. With some funding it continues to give annual tours and seasons in Dublin and around the country, as well as to some extent in the UK.

Commissioning Irishness

Dance critic Michael Seaver (2003: 232) comments on the development of dance and ballet in Ireland during the twentieth century:

> Establishing the 'Irishness' of dance forms associated with the colonial class became important throughout much of the century. The rich heritage of traditional Irish dance was taken for granted, but it seemed that stamping other dance forms such as ballet with an 'Irishness' – in theme, music or style – helped to make them relevant to the Irish nation. Policy makers were also more comfortable with ballets expressing 'Irishness'.

Referring to Arts Council reports, examplified by the one by Brinson (1985) and the first Arts Plan (1995–97), Michael observes the desire for 'the development of an Irish theatre dance style that interacted with traditional dance forms'. In an interview with me, Michael confirmed that 'dance in Ireland is always going to be linked to traditional dancing ... also socially because of the particular place dancing has in Ireland'. Aware of changing definitions of Irishness, not least in terms of the new multicultural society Ireland is becoming (Finlay 2004b), Seaver anticipates that this will have an impact on dance theatre. During my fieldwork, multiculturality was reflected in the importation of dancers and choreographers from Europe, the United States and Asia, for shorter or longer periods of time. I will return to this issue in Chapter 8.

The policy of the Arts Council to foster Irishness in dance by encouraging connections between modern and traditional dance, which of course makes perfect sense in a national perspective, can however be 'a constant creative pressure', as Michael Seaver (2003: 238) points out: 'There has been a superficial demand for "Irishness", yet the choreographers have asserted their Irishness in more subtle ways. In the words of John Scott: 'Why do we have to add something that has a pronounced Irish reference?''

However, John has choreographed on Irish themes such as *Macalla*, the piece about the conflict in Northern Ireland. And in *Ballads*, David Bolger does a modern investigation into a deeply Irish theme, the cultural consequences of the Great Famine. I would thus argue that there are ways to pursue Irishness in dance in a modern way, within modernity. Michael Seaver (2003: 238) notes how 'cultural ideology in Ireland has in the past polarised into modern versus traditional' and argues that 'it is no wonder that these choreographers have chosen to spurn traditional dance and align to modern international practices'. Yet, it seems to me that choreographers in Ireland are very skilfully avoiding the tradition in its traditional form, by shaping their own tradition in modern versions. According to Michael Seaver (2003: 240) 'the expectation that contemporary dance is only relevant' if it connects with traditional dance is not as pronounced any longer. This focus on traditional dance was enacted both out of 'an expectant Irish psyche and by extension with funding and political bodies'. According to Seaver the situation has turned around: 'it is now traditional Irish dancers who are drawing on contemporary dance to make their work more relevant to twenty-first century Ireland'.

In a transnational context, in the Euro-American dance world, however, in competition with dance companies that are associated with a particular choreographic style, such as that of William Forsythe in Frankfurt-am-Main, or Pina Bausch in Wuppertal, Irish dance theatre companies often launch themselves by way of Irish themes. Then Irishness becomes a trademark, a logo, that is more or less expected from audiences in London, New York or Stockholm. They want to learn about Ireland, but they need familiar signposts in order to find their way. This was what David Bolger did when he decided to revive *Ballads* for his first tour in the United States. The reviews were very positive, even though David and his dancers noted that the critics discussed the Famine as much as the dancing (Wulff 2004). Sometimes, however, critics and audience detect Irishness where none is in fact intended, Liz Roche told me in her capacity of choreographer. One of her early pieces, *Dragons and Tonics*, got a very good recognition, also in Scotland. There was a section, which she did not associate with Irish themes, but everyone else did: because of a lot of footwork and no arms! In 1999 Liz Roche founded Rex Levitates Dance Company, which according to its home page 'focusses on the development of a unique performance language that is relevant to a world audience, while remaining connected to its origins within Irish consciousness.'

A different view of the role of Irishness in dance theatre is voiced in a review of Dance Theatre of Ireland's multi-media piece *Soul Survivor*, about the impact of new technology on human relationships. In the review, which was written by Mike Dixon

(1999) in *Ballett International*, one of the major monthly dance magazines in Europe (published in Germany in German and English), Dixon argues that: 'The Irish themes, which once charaterised the company repertoire, have given way to more accessible and universal subjects, resulting in a more polished and assured-looking ensemble and a company identity that is less insular and more truly European.'

When dance scholar and writer Diana Theodores (1996: 194) worked as a dance critic in Ireland in the 1980s and early 1990s she observed 'the search for a national or a homegrown language of dance – perhaps forged from the traditional dance heritage'. There are three obvious reasons for this: the national project that the establishment of an Irish state continued to entail, the transnational marketing of Irish dance theatre, and the urge to investigate Irishness by Irish choreographers. A fourth reason is that the Arts Council agreed with all this, and has been commissioning Irishness for quite some time from choreographers, companies and repertories they fund. The idea of an Irish dance style, which resonates with Irish culture and traditional movements, fits moreover with the elaborate notions of the five national ballet styles in the transnational ballet world: the French, the Russian, the Danish, the English, and the American styles are believed to reflect '"national personalities" or "nations"' (Wulff 1998: 41), although this is being disputed as dancers learn a number of different national ballet styles, and are able to move between them. Notions of national ballet styles go back to the ballet centres that were set up and developed through ballet schools in France, Russia, Denmark, England and the Unites States (Wulff 1998).[14]

Words, Text and Dance

I had hardly started my fieldwork before I realized that Irish people are as loquacious as they are reputed to be. John Scott was the first choreographer I interviewed in Ireland. We met in Bewley's, a famous café in Grafton Street, a pedestrian shopping street, in central Dublin. John talked enthusiastically for three hours without stopping. I was floored by the amount of data that was flooding in (reflecting to myself that Ireland was of course the country where stream of consciousness was made famous as a literary style.) This would continue three months later at a bar in the gentrified theatre and entertainment Temple Bar area, and with other choreographers, dancers, teachers, writers, producers, arts council officers at innumerable meetings and encounters, planned and unplanned, throughout my fieldwork.

A talent for text and words in dance is of course not uniquely Irish. In the transnational world of dance theatre, it is quite common, with intermittent monologues or dialogues, even conversations, between dancers in performances. Their voices are often used as a type of sound, sometimes uttering unintelligible noises to dance to, or against, rather than uttering words or sentences with a particular meaning. Some choreographers write their own texts, but many include literary sources or other available texts. A forerunner with words in dance, William Forsythe's 'texts are poetic, mathematical combinations, clever plays with words, double entendres, that unexpectedly turn into nonsensical structures and back again' (Wulff 1998: 46). An avid reader, Forsythe also enjoys making intriguing reference to academic discourse.

All this was in Irish dance theatre, as well, although dispersed over different pieces. John Scott, who had travelled to Frankfurt-am-Main to see Forsythe's work live, was the one who was the most directly influenced by Forsythe, especially in the way John related to texts in his dance pieces. In *The Simulacra Stories* by Belgian guest choreographer Joanne Leighton, Dance Theatre of Ireland discussed the process of writing through dancing as a starting point for an investigation of the relationship between dancers and audience. Texts are also projected on screens that can be moving, 'dancing' as it were. On my way through the dance scene in Ireland, I would observe many sections of talk in dance performances. For a while, there seemed to be a trend to have about five dancers (who often constituted the whole cast) moving and talking, sometimes singing, in a soundscape of other voices and noises coming out from a tape, thereby producing a mass scene. In Mary Nunan's piece *Far Flung*, presented at the annual City Dance Festival at the Old Museum in Belfast in 1999, there was a tantalizing tango scene. With fragments of bickering conversation between tangoing partners, five dancers filled up the stage: the spectator 'saw' a mass of moving people on a dance floor. David Bolger created the same amplified effect in *Dish of the Day* the week before at the opening night in Dublin. David used three mirrored walls as a means to suggest a crowded disco scene. As to text and dance, David says that: 'It takes a writer maybe four pages to write down that thing where you can do it in a movement passage that lasts three or four seconds. I'm fascinated with that' (Theodores 2003: 47). About his work with turning Hans Christian Andersen's Danish fairy tale *The Little Mermaid* into choreography, David's experience was that:

> It's nice to take the text and go into the studio and work with some dancers and try and find the themes within the text that suggest movement ... I don't believe that every single story in the world has movement in it, but this story particularly, has a lot of movement. It has lots of problems too in that it is about a mermaid who wants to have legs, who lives under the sea, who wants to marry the prince who lives on land ... I don't want to put drama on movement, I want the drama to be there in the movement ... How do mermaids move? ... Then there's the spirituality of the story, so there are many layers in the way we have been working ... I am really interested in telling stories as a choreographer and I think this way has been quite interesting because we started very much with movement, quite abstract movement, and then started to swing around to storytelling (Theodores 2003: 46,47).

Many choreographers talked about their interest in words and text in dance performances. One of them was Finola Cronin, who had moved back to Ireland after having danced in Pina Bausch's Tanztheater Wuppertal for ten years. Finola was choreographer-in-residence at University College Dublin for three years and later appointed dance specialist with the Arts Council. She made *The Murder Ballads* for the Kilkenny Arts Festival in 2002 about family secrets, corruption and innocence, and has even done some choreographies for traditional storytellers. Finola, who has been a mentor for young choreographers in Dublin, danced with Dublin Contemporary Dance Theatre, the early dance company. Talking about her career as a dancer, she told me: 'I had seen Pina's work and I was interested in the Irish conncection through the spoken word and the drama in her work'. She auditioned with Tanztheater Wuppertal in 1985 and was asked to sign a contract: 'Pina needed somone who could talk! She took me on for my theatrical ability. She needed someone who could speak in English. I did twenty pieces with her'.

With her long red hair, she cut a striking figure on stage. I had seen her, and listened to her clear voice reciting, already in 1996 in Copenhagen (a couple of years before I had even began thinking about doing a study in Ireland) when she came on a tour with Tanztheater Wuppertal. Despite the fact that Pina Bausch had not yet been on tour to Ireland, most Irish choreographers mentioned her influence on their work. Michael Seaver (2003: 237) also acknowledges the prominent position of text in Irish choreography, and how text is involved in dance in a variety of ways.

All this came up in Irish dance theatre. The piece *Made to Measure* opened in March 1999 at the Tivoli Theatre in Dublin. It was choreographed by Portuguese Rui Horta at the invitation of Robert O'Connor and Loretta Yurick, the director couple of Dance Theatre of Ireland, the company that performed the piece. One of the sections consisted of a group of people sitting in a circle on the floor moving their mouths, opening and closing them, as if they were engaged in a heated debate – but no sound was coming out! Strange as it may seem, the fact that the mouths were moving in silence accentuated the talk element of the dance piece.

Words are also prominent in the technological piece *The Secret Project*, by choreographer–writer Jools Gilson-Ellis and digital artist–composer Richard Povall, about secrets of womanhood and girls' friendships. Produced and presented as a live performance at the Institute for Choreography and Dance in Cork, *The Secret Project* is on a website, a CD-ROM and an installation.[15] In this funny and moving multi-media performance, personal and political secrets of womanhood are discussed through the relationship between text (poetry, song, dialogue), exquisite yet powerful movement, and sound. The choreography is partly set, partly improvised. The spoken text, written by Gilson-Ellis, weaves into the soundscape as the dancers speak or sing in English with Irish and English accents, in French and the Irish language. The rather abstract atmosphere of *The Secret Project* is broken in the middle of the piece by a story about a girl who shares her skippingrope with her best friend until she takes it away from the girl and then tries to hit her with it.

Stories of the Soil and Faraway Places

In his elegant little essay on the storyteller, Walter Benjamin (1969a: 84–5, 86) distinguishes between two archaic types of these craftspeople: 'one is embodied in the resident tiller of the soil, and the other in the trading seaman'. Distinguishing between the resident storyteller who 'knows the local tales and traditions', 'the lore of the past' and the traveller 'who has come from afar', bringing 'the lore of faraway places', Benjamin emphasizes that they have a lot in common, and that they do complement each other. Applying this dichotomy of the storyteller to modern Irish writing, Fintan O'Toole (1997a: 83) detects combinations of the two types of storytellers in the oeuvre by James Joyce, but admits that this is rare: in most cases O'Toole sees a contest between the two of them.

An instance when such a contest between stories of Ireland versus stories from faraway places came up during my fieldwork was over funding from the Arts Council in relation to its agenda to commission Irishness both in themes and dancer's national background. As to critical acclaim and audience attendance, I did not notice any difference, or contest, between dance theatre stories on Irish versus foreign themes. And when Michael Keegan Dolan brought back stories from faraway places such as *Giselle*, he adjusted them to an Irish setting, which made them feature both type of stories at once. This duality also applies to Irish choreographers as storytellers: rather than separating them into Benjamin's two types, I see them as 'rooted cosmopolitans', the notion which philosopher Kwame Anthony Appiah (1996: 22) has coined, also in terms of 'the cosmopolitan patriot'. I will develop this discussion on how Irish dance forms contribute to a rooted cosmopolitanism in Ireland more fully in the concluding Chapter 8. For now, I will just say that Irish choreographers have all travelled abroad, and watched dance theatre, some more extensively than others. The interest in dance from faraway places is more important to some than others. Most of them have trained abroad ranging from taking dance and choreographic courses in France and New York lasting a few summer weeks to completing diplomas that entails two to three years study in London. Some have been based abroad as dancers or choreographers. Most of them talked to me about the lack of exposure of dance theatre in Dublin, identifying their area as a new one, a young art form. The biannual International Dance Festival Ireland, which was inaugurated in 2002, is one sign that this perceived isolation is about to change. In the continuum of closeness to the Irish soil at one pole, and closeness to faraway places at the other, Irish choreographers move around occupying different positions through their different stories.

The Danish fairy tale *The Little Mermaid*, which David Bolger made into a dance theatre piece, is a story from a faraway place. Sometimes it was a political engagement which directed choreographers to certain stories from faraway places, such as when Robert O'Connor and Loretta Yurick presented *Freedom's Gait*. Robert told me that this piece is 'like the walk of freedom after having been confined in prison'. The piece deals with identity, relationships, with Irish journalist Brian Keenan who had been held hostage for four and a half years by Islamic Jihad in Lebanon and was released in 1990. Robert and Loretta heard his press conference and were fascinated by the imagery and the poetry he expressed. They contacted Brian Keenan, and asked if they could have a transcript of his statement. They did, but ended up not using it in the piece, only for inspiration. Keenan came to the studio at the end of the rehearsal process, and 'he wept! The man wept!', Robert said. 'We didn't speak for ten minutes'. On the web page of Dance Theatre of Ireland, Keenan has written:

Never could I have imagined that a Dance Company could so eloquently and so movingly capture and articulate so many of the thoughts, feelings and moments of heightened reality that made up the larger part of my four and one-half years captivity...I thank the Dance Theatre of Ireland for translating into movement those inarticulate moments and experiences ... in a sense confirming that we are never alone.

It is possible that Robert and Loretta came up with the idea to do this piece not only because Brian Keenan is Irish (from Belfast), but also because they were born and grew up in the United States, and therefore had been closer to the hostage crisis in 1979–80 when a large number of Americans were held hostage in Teheran.

I saw Michael Keegan Dolan's dance theatre production *The Christmas Show* performed in September 2001 at The Project's Art Centre in Dublin. The production was later co-titled *The Miracle Show*. On his web page, Michael introduces the dance piece as:

Nothing you see here is real. Christmas is the time of The Winter Solstice, Saturnalia, and the celebration of the arrival of a great mystical leader. Most religions have hidden within them the notion that miracles do happen and magical events can occur. This notion goes against a world we have inherited, a world of thought, logic and reason. There is no logic in this show.

This may at first seem like a story without a particular place, at least not Ireland. But it is in fact another dance example of a combination of elements from 'local tales and traditions' in Ireland and 'faraway places' where Christmas also is celebrated as a family ritual more or less steeped in Christianity materialized in the cooking of a turkey and the appearance of Jesus respectively. Specializing in delicate movements, Michael's extensive choreographing for opera companies in England and the United States comes across in colourful sets and expressive steps. In a conversation about his life and career, Michael told me about his interest in theatricality and how, when he was supposed to take part in debating at school, he 'turned them into theatricals!' Carolyn Swift's (2000) review of *The Flowerbed* (see Chapter 4) by Michael, also mentions that it elaborates on a burlesque tone as this Romeo and Juliet parody unfolds:

Wonderfully danced by his Fabulous Beast Dance Theatre, the Montagues and the Capulets become the neighbours from hell, and sword and poison are replaced by garden shears and amphetamines. Mr and Mrs D (Mick Nolan and Bernadette Iglich) are meticulously neat and tidy: he obsessive in his love for his manicured lawn, she obsessed with physical fitness and weight reduction. Neither is much impressed by their mooning teenage son (Jarkko Lehmus). The gross V family moves in next door, constantly eating, chain-smoking and turning up the volume on the telly, and soon Mr D is depositing his son's litter in their garden and they desecrating his lawn with a flowerbed. Mr V's daughter Mary (Rachel Lopez de la Nieta) is sensitive and nature loving. Soon the two young people are in love and open warfare has broken out between their families. The fight scenes are acrobatic and inventive, the love scenes lyrical and moving, while other scenes are side-splittingly funny.

Yet another choreographer who has a background in theatre is Paul Johnson, as a movement director for theatre companies. Now he is making dances for MaNDaNCE, an all male dance theatre company, about male culture from the perspective of an Irish gay man. David Bolger, again, also has a strong theatrical style in his work. He told me in an interview that: 'When I started to choreograph I was interested in how theatre and dance can come together to wake people, make them laugh or cry'.

In *Dish of the Day* from 1999, David was let loose in his cheeky mood. Among other things, he was commenting on the upcoming millennium shift, in particular the threat of the millenium bugs in computers: 'Is the world going to end?' About the many colourful people and props in this piece, he admitted that 'sometimes it's nice to use everything a theatre has to offer!'. *Dish of the Day* was very well received. Like Michael Keegan Dolan's work, it also exemplifed the Irish sense of humour, as testified by Carolyn Swift's (1999) review in *The Irish Times*:

> The audience began laughing almost from the start of the show as the whole cast worked an old music-hall gag from behind the black boards, while white balloons serve as everything from chewing gum to measuring tape, as well as being blown up, burst, used for Isadora Duncan-type lyrical dance and a stunning climax. And of course we get the cooking recipe which gives the piece its name. The audience loved it and so did I.

And so did I, still remembering vividly the breathtaking parody of ballet down on the floor at the Samuel Beckett Centre, described by Carolyn Swift as:

> A frieze of classical dancers is disrupted by James Hosty joining on to the end of the line; Justine Doswell in blonde wig tiptoes on *pointe* through the tulips with a revolving windmill – albeit a toy one – to emphasise the Dutch location, before reclining on a rubber sofa with Eric Lacey as if to re-enact *Dances with Intent*. Instead, the sofa is somehow transformed into the largest *tutu* ever seen as she shows off her fine ballet technique.

What then makes a good story? Benjamin points to the importance of a story being useful either as a 'moral', 'practical advice' or 'proverb maxim'. And a story has to be suggestive, he goes on, explanations and interpretations should not be provided as a part of the storytelling but kept open for the listener to conclude. How the role of the audience for a storyteller's performance shapes the structure of the telling is exemplified in Kirin Narayan's (1989) influential ethnography on folknarrative in Hindu religious teaching. 'A great storyteller will always be rooted in the people', notes Benjamin (1969a: 98, 101, 108) further, and make use of repetition and improvisation in a 'web which all stories together form in the end. One ties on to the next'. When Benjamin talks about how 'soul, eye, and hand are brought into connection' in storytelling, and thus gestures, he could have been thinking of choreographers as storytellers, and how dancers execute these stories through their dance.

Dance critics who have watched a lot of Irish dance theatre over the course of many years do agree that there is Irishness in this dance form, although they see it in different ways. Carolyn Swift (n.d.: 27) identified a collaboration between 'Irish and "foreign" dance' as not traditional yet 'distinctly Irish'. An article with the headline 'Not "Irish" at All' about the International Dance Festival of Ireland in May 2002, does in fact say that 'traditional Irish dancing appears in the dancers' movements' in *Reverse Psychology* presented by Daghdha Dance Company (Musiat 2002: 18–21). Interestingly, the article acknowledges 'the theatrical element and the strong individual performers' without realizing that theatricality and stage personalities are Irish characteristics.

This chapter has discussed the Irish sense of humour and drama articulated through a strong storytelling in dance theatre, and how I, during the course of my fieldwork, discerned a national Irish dance style, not in the choreographic form so much as in theatricality and narrative content. There is a nerve, and a rhythm in the storytelling, which sometimes is hilariously funny, sometimes touches me through delicate moods or portraits of passion. One important part of this dramatic quality, and the reason why it is so effective, is the acting talents of the dancers. They have expressive stage personalities, and they surely know how to tell a story.

Notes

1. Having been an excellent student at University College, Dublin, Brian O'Nolan worked as a civil servant. He also wrote a renowned column for the *Irish Times* signing as Myles na Gopalen.

2. Potatoes were of course the main staple food for most people, as well as for animals, in rural Ireland in the past (see Bourke 2003). This dependency was thus again one reason why potato crop failures caused the Great Famine: there was no alternative food supply (Fitzpatrick 1995).

3. This obviously also applies to other art worlds, especially visual art such as painting.

4. Éilís Ní Dhuibhne (1999b: 53) notes that a talent for writing can be found in all historical ethnic groups on the island: among four Irish authors who have been awarded the Nobel Prize in literature are Shaw, Yeats and Beckett who were Dublin Protestants, and Heaney who is a Northern Irish Catholic. When Ní Dhuibhne rightly singles out Joyce as 'the most well-known and influential of all Irish writers', we are reminded that he was not a Nobel prize winner. Ní Dhuibhne also points at the lack of Irish women in this context. Now there is a new generation of remarkable women writers in Ireland, some of whom contributed to my study, not only through their novels, short stories and poems, but also through my encounters with them in person via network links into the dance world, as well as that of academia.

5. Swedish folklorist Carl Wilhelm von Sydow was pivotal in training collectors and urging the collection of stories in Ireland on the grand scale which was to be later developed by Séamus Ó Duilearga (James Delargy 1969) as documented in *The Gaelic Storyteller*. As

Ó Giolláin (2000: 138) has summarized: 'the continuity of the medieval Gaelic literary tradition in the oral tradition through the vicissitudes of Ireland's history, the interplay between the two, the loss of so much, and the antiquity of that tradition'. Ó Giollain relates how storytelling competitions were organized from 1901 with ten competitors. By 1914 there were two competitions with about a hundred competitors taking part in each.

6.   Irish critics are of course not only local, but also transnational. They review dance from abroad, both in Europe and the United States, for Irish newspapers and magazines, as well as report on the Irish dance scene as correspondents for international dance magazines. Applying Sally Banes' four characteristics of the writing style of dance reviews: description, interpretation, evaluation, and contextualization, all of them tend to be found in the same review by Irish critics, even though the younger critics usually emphasized social and historical contextualization (Banes 1994; Wulff 2004).

7.   See de Valois (1959), MacMahon (1998), Ellis (1999) and O'Toole (2003).

8.   For a similar event in Belfast when the Free Presbyterian Church demonstrated against a dance theatre performance, see Wulff (2003).

9.   In an exposition of Synge and his interest in Irish folklore, Ó Giolláin (2000) mentions the critical debate involving the Gaelic League over 'Synge's unromantic portrayal of the peasantry' in *The Playboy of the Western World*. The dispute took the form of riots at the Abbey Theatre on the opening night.

10.   Ballett Frankfurt was transformed into the private The Forsythe Company in 2005.

11.   See Maher (2002) for a reply.

12.   A legendary world centre for theatre, Dublin of course has a number of grand theatre houses – but no opera house. There are opera houses in Wexford, Cork and Belfast. The opera house in Cork is the home of Cork City Ballet, and it also offers touring ballet and dance companies performance opportunities both from Ireland and abroad, as do the other two opera houses on the island.

13.   Lucy Hickey gave me an interesting piece of information about crossover in the dance world: most of the dancers in Ballet Ireland have also been in *Riverdance*.

14.   An Italian ballet centre in Milan has been connected with an Italian ballet style but not in terms of a national ballet style, which has to do with the fact that Italy is still not quite united as a nation (Wulff 1998).

15.   In a video of the hour long performance in Cork City and in a post-performance discussion with the dancers and the audience, Gilson-Ellis (who is also one of the three dancers, all women) explains how the soundscape of the performance was designed: some sound was made by the dancers as they moved, their movements were videoed by a camera in the back of the auditorium. The video camera was connected to a computer (the BigEye motion capture software) which was processing this information into sound, a pre-recorded piece of music or text. The only technology that was visible for the audience was the tiny microphones the dancers carried close to their mouths.

Chapter 6

Winning the World's

An anthropologist going to Ennis, Co. Clare, in the west of Ireland, is undoubtedly reminded of the urban part of Conrad M. Arensberg and Solon T. Kimball's (1968[1940]) influential community study in the 1930s. It was thus with a feeling of treading classical grounds that I made my way into Ennis in the early spring of 1999. I noticed banners across the streets saying that restaurants and shops were welcoming the World Championship dancers to Ennis. Then I saw a young girl with a multitude of small curlers in her hair, and my reverence for the anthropological inheritance was replaced by a puzzlement by the present. To me, this was a private appearance that was displayed in a public domain. Walking around town as a matter of course with curlers in your hair seemed to be a curious blurring of the private and the public. When I spotted another girl with green plastic curlers sticking out around her head, making it look like a colourful hedgehog, my idle reflection suddenly turned into active ethnographic observation. This girl was also completely comfortable and moreover in the company of two other girls and three women. Amused, I realized that the girls walking around town with curlers in their hair were going to compete in the Dance Championships and were in the process of making their 'bouncing curls', which I knew is a key concept in Irish dance competitions. 'Bouncing curls' are considered to be one of the features of the 'presentation' of a dance, something that is a part of the adorned feminine look of girl and women Irish dancers.

I went into a restaurant in order to have dinner. A girl in her early teens with curlers in her hair entered followed by two men. They sat down at a table next to me. I could hear the waitress wishing the girl 'Good Luck!'. No one seemed to think that it was improper to wear curlers in a restaurant. On the contrary, they were a part of a symbolic capital and special aesthetics saying: 'I'm an Irish dancer! I might win the World's!'

Drawing on week-long, but intense, field stints at Championships in Irish Dancing, this chapter will explore the debate over Irishness and tradition in the contemporary Irish dance competition community in terms of modernity, emotion, play, politics and rivalry. One question in this debate concerns whether one has to be Irish in order to win the World's and the All Ireland's, a sensitive topic in the Irish dancing community, which has to do with the relationship between the Irish from Ireland and the Irish diaspora within the Irish competitive dancing community. The notion of tradition, and its multiple and moving meanings, is central in this community. This is a tradition which found its form in opposition to a colonial power, a circumstance which still defines the debate. On an analytical level, however, the World's was a modern phenomenon when it first came about, as was The Irish Dancing Commission long before that when it started creating modern forms for what was perceived as Irish dance with traditional and modern variants within it. Now, the World's has grown into a format and a scale, with thousands of competitors travelling from far away, which turns out to be a feature of contemporary modernity in a web of European and cosmopolitan modernities. The challenge of *Riverdance* to the World Championships, this Irish dance show which, again, grew out of traditional Irish dancing and the competitions, will also be considered.

In line with nationalist movements across Europe at the end of the nineteenth century, the Gaelic League initiated a nationalist cultural revival in Ireland while the country was still under English occupation. Interestingly, Orvar Löfgren (1993) notes that the ideology behind these nationalist movements was imported from revolutionary national experiments in North and South America. Diarmuid Ó Giolláin (2000) describes how the Gaelic League, *Conradh na Gaeilge*, was inaugurated by politicians and scholars such as Douglas Hyde, who was to become the first president of Ireland. In the beginning the Gaelic League was a rather small association, but in the early 1900s it grew quickly into almost fifty thousand members. By way of travelling teachers, the League provided education and entertainment around the country, and it 'undermined the automatic deference to English culture and helped to give a sense of self-respect and self-confidence in Irish culture to the Catholic young' (Ó Giolláin 2000: 120). The League brought together different strata of Irish society, and as Tom Garvin (1981) points out, it was a breeding ground for government ministers and civil servants during the first five decades of the Irish independece.

Löfgren (1993) also introduces the notion of a toolkit for nation building that each aspiring nation fills with distinct contents. In Ireland, the Gaelic League thus focussed on preserving and promoting the Irish language, but included other cultural forms such as dance in this de-Anglicization effort to create an Irish Ireland. According to Whelan (2005: 144) the initiative to introduce 'a social dimension to the language movement' first came from Fionán MacColuim who worked as a clerk in the India Office in London where he was a member of the Gaelic League London branch. It was MacColium who, inspired by Scottish *céilithe* in London arranged the original Irish céilí[1] at Bloomsbury Hall in London in 1897. It was through MacColium's special interest in Co. Kerry, which also had shaped the canon for the Irish language, that the Munster style of Irish dancing became the dominant Irish dancing style. It was considered important to identify Irish dancing in contrast with dance forms that were regarded as foreign, usually English.[2]

As a part of this agenda, the Gaelic League organized dancing classes and *feisanna* (Irish for festivals), competitions. The latter took place both locally, on parish levels, and nationally, and were to develop into the All Ireland Championships. By the first decades of the twentieth century, feisanna were held in London, Glasgow and in the United States among the Irish diaspora communities.

In 1929, the Gaelic League set up *An Coimisiún le Rincí Gaelacha*, the Irish Dancing Commission, which continues to regulate Irish dancing styles and examines teachers and adjudicators for the competitions. Since 1970, the Irish Dancing Commission has been responsible arranging the annual World Championships in Irish Dancing. The World's is the biggest competition in Irish dancing, and the only one that requires that competitors qualify.

My analytical entrance to the World's is via the concept of spectacle, defined by Frank E. Manning (1992: 291) as: 'a large-scale, extravagant cultural production that is replete with striking visual imagery and dramatic action and that is watched by a mass audience'. Manning exemplifies this definition with sports such as the Olympic Games (MacAloon 1981, 1984; Archetti 1999), World Cup soccer matches, festivals, public entertainment extravaganzas, exhibitions, civic and political ceremonies, and special religious events. Manning also includes Victor Turner's (1982) ideas of spectacle as a modern performance of play and reflexivity. The reflexivity at the World's has to do with meanings of Irishness and forms of modernity phrased in terms of tradition.

For ten days about four thousand Irish dancers convened in Ennis, Co Clare, a town in the west of Ireland. Apart from Ireland, North and South, they came from England and Canada. Many had travelled from the United States, even as far away as from Australia and New Zealand. Most of the competitors were children and teenagers, the youngest were only ten years old, few were over twenty-one years old. They all had to be accompanied by a parent or a dance teacher. This predominantly girls' sport has recently seen a growth of boys' groups, which was attributed to the success of Michael Flatley who was the first male star of *Riverdance*. This show has, again, often been acknowledged as the 'modern' version of traditional Irish dancing. The explosive success of the show led to more than twice as many registrations in Irish dancing schools (Brennan 1999). After more than ten years of global touring, however, *Riverdance* seems to have reached its peak, according to my interviews with *Riverdance* people and observations in connections with performances, while traditional and competitive dancing is alive and well.

There are many ethnographic examples of ethnicity and nationalism being managed and manipulated through dance such as J. Clyde Mitchell's (1956) classic study of the Kalela dance as a 'tribal' marker in Northern Rhodesia. European folk dances have been identified as ethnic dances either in opposition to a dominant nationalism, or by Löfgren (1993) among others, as an element in nation building. With the growing social science interest in nationalism, dance scholars have looked at ethnic and national dance in colonial as well as postcolonial contexts. Stillman (1996) has written about Hawaiian dance, hula, competitions and how creativity in these competitions has transformed this tradition.

'It's like a Fever!': Spectacle of Nationalism and Emotion

In the hotel where the Championships were taking place, I soon found the office, where I observed and was told about the policy to speak Irish in the Irish Dancing Commission. Although the meetings are held in English the minutes are both in

Irish and English, as are the Championships syllabus and all other written information about it. A non-Irish speaker immediately notices that the Irish version comes first. 'It's prerogative to speak Irish', a coordinator informed me without my having asked anything about it, 'We try to promote the Irish language', she went on. Dance teachers in Ireland are expected to pass the Irish exam, but not those who teach Irish dancing abroad.

In the auditorium the competition was in full swing. I was again struck by the blurring of the private and the public, performance and reality, frontstage and backstage. The audience consisted of families of the competitors, mostly mothers but also fathers and grandmothers helping to look after baby siblings on a family outing as it were. There were dance teachers and groups of competitors, boys and girls, many with curlers in different sizes and colours. Here the curlers signified yet another subtle message of distinction: 'I'm going to dance sporting my *own* hair, not a wig!' Some people claimed that natural hair bounces better with the music than wigs, although this actually depends on the quality of the hair. Wigs are a major concern (Brennan 1999: 157, 158) in the Irish dancing world: 'you have to "work" the wig – to make it look and feel natural', meaning 'treat it like real hair'. There has also been a critique against 'mass wigging of dancers', especially of young dancers wearing very big wigs. Still, wigs may be an alternative to curlers for as Orla Griffin, who has taken part in many competitions and danced with *Riverdance*, said to me in an interview: 'Most dancers wear their hair curly. You have to sleep with curlers. If you can't sleep with curlers, you can wear a wig. You have to look the same in the beginning and the end'. Senior women in the Irish dancing world talked about how years ago it took hours and hours to put in the rollers. The wigs save a lot of time. They were also quite expensive at prices between IR£70 and 95. Three years later at the All Ireland Championship in Killarney, Co. Kerry, I saw very few curlers. By then wigs were standard. Almost every competing girl was wearing a wig.

In the auditorium at the World's in Ennis, noone was paying constant attention to the monotonous flow of competitions that had started at 8 a.m. and went on until 10 p.m. Instead, mothers and friends tended to the hair of girls, while fathers talked to fathers, and young children ran around. 'We're here to win the World's!' I overheard mothers and teachers inciting each other and 'Imagine being the best in the world in your age group!'. This made me think of a comment that one of the dancer in *Riverdance* made backstage in Stockholm about 'pushy mothers' in the competitions who 'nearly have heart attacks'.

There were four types of dance in the Championships: single, with two dancers peforming different solo step-dancing combinations to the same music, céilí, with eight dancers, figure dancing, with eight to sixteen dancers, and dance drama,[3] with eight to twenty people on stage. Dance drama or figure dancing, (see Chapter 2) is like a pageant featuring stories. This year they included 'Night to remember', with passengers on The Titanic dancing on the deck, 'The Umbrella', about a priest who has a new umbrella, 'The Fair of Spancill Hill', dealing with homesick immigrants in America who dream about Ireland, 'The Spirit of the Celts', focussing on the arrival of Christianity to Ireland and 'The Vikings of Tara', describing the invasion of Vikings, which utlimately won. Before every drama, the member of the Irish Dancing Commission who was in charge of the competition read a poem, often written by the teacher, on historical or Celtic themes such as the Famine, emigration and homesickness among the Irish diaspora.

The solo step-dancing was separated into soft shoe dance (slip jig or reel) and hard shoe dance (hornpipe or double jig). The two types of dance are danced with so-called 'softies', shoes looking like laced ballet shoes for what is called 'light dancing', and 'hardies' with big heels that are used to make the characterstic clicks in Irish step dancing. Hard shoe dance is preferably performed on wooden stages in order to make the clicks louder. Sometimes the music was turned down so the adjudicators were able to '*listen* the dancing'. Musicians, on the other hand, who had to sit close to the dancers, complained that the level of noise from the hard shoe dancing was a brutalizing experience for them. The dances had names like 'Trip to the cottage', 'The Hunt' and 'St Patrick's Day'.

Some competitors were warming up in the back of the auditorium. Others were half dressed in bra or T-shirts and shorts as well as wigs, tiaras and stage make up as they were waiting for their turn to dance. And afterwards they were so warm that they unzipped their costumes in the middle of the auditorium. In the Programme for the 30th Irish World Dance Championships (1999: 50) I found a list of rules of order, or 'Notices'. The last one said:

AN COIMISIUN AND WEST COUNTY HOTEL WILL NOT ALLOW DANCERS TO WALK AROUND THE HALL IN THEIR UNDERWEAR. AT ALL TIMES DANCERS MUST BE PROPERLY ATTIRED.

In the ladies' room close to the auditorium was a big mirror and on a wall a sign warned:

> In the interest of safety,
> Dance Practice
> is **not** permitted
> in the Toilets.

However, no one seemed to care. There was more often than not a small crowd of girls trying out steps in front of the mirror. These two rules, and the panache with which they were broken, contributed to the atmosphere of school pranks which defined the Championship at times.

One of the corners of the auditorium, which was used as a dressing room, was littered with clothes, costumes and other belongings. The three adjudicators were sitting in front of the stage, each at a separate table. The number of adjudicators varies depending on the type of dance. There is thus a panel of three adjudicators for the solos, a panel of five for the céilí dances, and seven for the figure dancing. To the right of the stage was the score board. On stage was a piano, harmonica and a fiddle. There was electronic music equipment including a tape recorder and big speakers on the side of the stage. Unlike other theatre performances, but not sports competitions, there was no proper back stage where transformations into stage personas, or in this case Irish competitive dancers, could take place. The competitors were, in other words, exposed to the audience and the adjudicators before and after their performance, and not only during those three minutes when they were doing their routine on stage.

Celtic Costumes

At first the seemingly endless parade of Irish dancers was alienating to me. The girls came on stage looking like marionette dolls wearing their colourful costumes with Celtic embroidery and appliqué, different styles representing different dancing schools. The costumes were traditionally bright green with some orange, although many were black, red or navy among other colours. Although there is a second-hand market for dancing costumes, many parents paid hundreds of IR£ for their daughters' hand-made costumes ranging from IR£400 to 1000.

At the All Ireland's in 2002, Michelle Lawrence, a pretty sixteen-year-old girl from Co. Tipperary won the solo step dancing for senior girls (aged 16–17). Her father used to be a milkman, now her parents run a B&B together. For quite some time, they had been paying substantial amounts of money for their daughter's dancing: classes, entrance fees to the competitions, and travels, but above all for her costume. It was in the bar at the hotel that I first heard the sum mentioned that Michelle's parents had paid for her costume. The following days I checked this piece of information, outside the light-hearted bar context, with her dance teacher, her mother and an Irish costume maker, and then I had to believe that Michelle's costume had cost IR£2000. This hand-made velvet and silk dress displayed the Rock of Cashel, a famous landmark in her home town Cashel, on the front, and on her shawl, going down her back, there was a map of the world where a rhinestone indicated the location of Ireland. The prize for Michelle's victory this year was a big cup, which her father pointed out to me with pride, was from 1946. In line with the tradition, Michelle wore medals from earlier victories with her costume: on a ribbon around her neck was a medal from the World's, on the right of her costume was pinned a Munster medal (from a Regional competition) and on the left side her All Ireland medal was displayed.

Women dancers at the World's mentioned that these heavy and stiff costumes are not very complimentary for the figure. I did notice, however, that when they were dancing on stage the skirts that were supposed not to be shorter than four inches above the knee, did swing up and reveal not only thighs, but also underwear that was carefully matched with the lining of the skirts. The dancers were, in other words, well aware of the fact that this might be a way to attract attention after all.

At the World's in 1999, Séamus O'Shea, the Chairperson of the Irish Dancing Commission, was embarrassed by the neon colours that had been used lately, saying to me: 'It's sort of an illusion they have. If you make the colours bright enough they will get noticed! It brings scam! People mock it! I want people to admire them!'

But at the All Ireland's in 2002, shiny costumes were more common than not. Talking to a seamstress who makes and sells Irish dancing costumes, she also told me that this style was a way to be noticed by the adjudicators, 'if you are not very good or very pretty. If they're good enough dancers, they don't need that'. There was no reference to Euro-American fashion outside the dancing community, where this type of glittering clothing was quite widespread at the time. The metallic shiny dancing costumes were made of raw silk mixed with other fabrics such as polyester and very bright gabardine. These costumes were thinner and softer, and thus more comfortable, than the old style, more delicate and much more shiny. On stage, the spotlights caught the sparkling glitter also from head-dresses and tiaras.

A whole team of people would be involved in the making of a costume: a cutter, a designer, an embroiderer, and a seamstress who usually put it together in four to five days, five costumes in a week. The seamstress talked about how the top dancers change costume every year, and then get half price for them when they sell them second hand, unless they are out of fashion.

From the beginning, Irish dancers wore the clothes of that time, their everyday or Sunday best dress. As John Cullinane (1996: 27) points out: 'the English occupation of Ireland throughout the 19th century resulted in there being no typical Irish or national dress'. But as if this was not enough, Robb (1998) refers to the longstanding English ambition to get the Irish to wear clothes in line with English fashion. 'The wearing of the green' was banned (Cronin and Adair 2002: xiii).[4] However, in the early twentieth century the Gaelic League introduced a national costume as one way to promote Irishness: kilts for men and long dresses with shawls for women. The preferred colour was indeed green, the national colour, while red should be avoided as it was connected with the English. This national dress would develop into dancing costumes.[5] Some of the boys still wore kilts at the World's in 1999, although this was clearly a disappearing practice since it was considered 'sissy'. Most male Irish dancers performed dressed in black trousers and a white or black shirt. However, as one of the senior dancing teachers told me 'I miss the kilts to be honest, the black trousers hide a lot!'

Where is the Dance? The Posture Puzzle

With my background in ballet (Wulff 1998), where the movements of arms and legs are coordinated in every detail, I found the stiff upper body and straight arms strange, but was impressed with the extremely fast and elaborate footwork. Belfast choreographer Helen Lewis specified that 'it wasn't only the arms, it was the posture - shoulders, arms, bodies, heads in Irish dancing, they would not use!' She showed me how they turn without turning the head, and went on: 'They would not turn their back towards the audience. Expression is taboo, totally taboo, it's all in the steps!' The dramatic contrast between the straight upper body and the elaborate footwork is sometimes described as 'God in the upper body and the Devil in the feet'. Hall (1995, 1996) talks about the *posture puzzle* as a combination of physical education, the requirements of competitions, and the policy of nationalism. When I asked Irish dancing people about the origins of the erect posture and the straight arms, I usually got the answer: 'the tradition'. Some senior people talked about the idea that it was 'to develop a dance form which would reflect well on the Irish character'. This seems to have been a response to English stereotypes about the Irish as 'unruly' during colonialism. It follows Foucault's (1979) celebrated statement about how the impact of discipline forms docile, political bodies that learn to be more capable, but in fact are subordinated.

Jokes abound about the source of the straight arms such as 'when they were dancing at the crossroads, it was windy, so the girls had to hold their skirts down', or 'it was a way to hide the dancing when the English landlords were looking in through the windows and they only saw the upper body'. The fear of priests in the past surfaces in the suggestion that 'it was a way to hide the dancing from the priests who were walking outside the hedge and only saw the upper body'. A more elaborate story goes like this:

> Once upon a time, the Irish used to dance with their hands in the air and the smiles on their faces. But the English kidnapped some dancers and took them to dance for the Queen. In protest they danced with deadpan faces and their hands at their sides.[6]

Senior people in the Irish dancing world pointed out to me that in the past the arms had been relaxed, but with the regulation of the championships by the Irish Dancing Commission the dancing was to be concentrated to the feet. From a movement technical point of view, the lack of arm activity could be explained by the fact that all energy is needed for the forceful footwork. Another suggestion is that the erect posture and straight arms ironically might have been brought to Ireland by the English through the *Galliard*, a Renaissance dance with Italian roots, which was developed in France and taken up by the English. The *Galliard* is supposed to have influenced some European folk dances (see Sutton 1998). Interestingly, the success of *Riverdance* is claimed by *Riverdance* people, including Michael Flatley himself whose idea it was, to have come about to a great extent because the dancers do use their arms, although an outsider to Irish dancing would perhaps not think so.

It did not take very long before I was drawn into the excitement of the competitions at the World's, and even found it difficult to leave the auditorium for a short break. Like the others, I was mesmerized and soon engaged by victories and disappointments of individual competitors, their mothers, teachers and schools. And there was an appealing incident when the frames of the spectacle were threatened, revealing the passion of the dancers: eight girls wearing orange costumes were dancing the Ladies' Céilí. Suddenly the electricity went off. It became completely dark in the auditorium. The musicians stopped playing but the girls went on dancing! When the lights came back on, and the music started again, it was out of tune with the steps, so then the girls finally gave up and walked off stage. John Cullinane, the member of the Irish Dancing Commission who was in charge of the competition invited the girls to 'redance' after the next team. 'They were electrifying us!' he joked and 'Now the next team will dance with the lights on!' After which the first team came back, and did very well, perhaps spurred on by the mishap. They were not placed, but they were rewarded with loud applause.

'It's like a fever!' both dancers and mothers kept saying, and I fully agreed. A woman teacher talked about competing as 'a poison' and added that 'when they win, it's still not enough!' A male teacher, who now takes dance students to competitions and once did win the World's, reminisced about this triumphant moment in terms of every superlative he could think of: 'It was the highpoint of my life! An extraordinary event! Mind blowing! Euphoric!'

An eighteen-year-old American woman of Irish origin who had been competing in the United States and Ireland for many years told me that since she was a little girl, her main goal had been to win the World's, although she only knew of two American girls who had won. But she was aiming at winning the World's before she hopefully would go on to *Riverdance* or *Lord of the Dance*. She described the experience of euphoria and the excitement of competing:

> I love competing! There is no other feeling like competing with performing. I just love it! The hairy thing with competing is when you get up on stage and everyone just gets silent and stares at me. At the All Ireland's this guy was staring at me and when I finshed he was just in shock! I nailed him down! It was an amazing feeling! I know I don't want to compete for the rest of my life. It's very stressful. I'll probably quit competing if I win the World's. It's so nerve-racking, I was so nervous, I almost got sick on stage!

Hall (1999) has analysed stories told by dance teachers about the stress at the World Championships in the early 1990s. The stories are about competitors who vomited and a woman teacher who was so badly taken when one of her students did not get a 'recall' (i.e., a chance to dance in the final round), that a doctor had to be called.

During the first days of the Championships the youngest dancers competed. Many of them reminded me of the fact that Irish dancing is still mainly a hobby: here was one dancer after the other, and one team after the other, who did not show any particular talent for dancing, they were not really coordinated in their own movements nor did they seem to move with the music. To them, the Championships were mostly a social occasion where 'you meet an awful lot of friends'.[7] To compete in Irish dancing is still a common feature of growing up in Ireland and a means to embody the history in the process. Parents and teachers are aware that the Championships are the rationale of Irish dancing, which simultaneously provides a good education in Irishness. This is in line with Hall's (1995) identification of Irish dancing as a physical education steeped in a romantic national expression. The level of dancing rose and became more even, and finally excellent with the older dancers, some of whom were professional Irish dancers working in the dance shows.

But if the attention was somewhat unfocussed in the auditorium during the flow of competitions, everyone suddenly became completely attentive once the results appeared on the score board. As the excitement mounted, people moved towards the stage and stood up on chairs in order to see the score board properly. The air was thick with apprehension. Accompanied by Irish music the winners were announced: the name of the dancers, their school and home city (but not country). They went on stage to collect cups. Those who had had a recall (but consequently not been ranked) received medals, which, in line with the long tradition, some dancers, such as Michelle at the All Ireland's, pin on their costume at the next competition. All dancers who take part in the Championships get a certificate and a key ring with the emblem of the Irish Dancing Commission. A member of the Irish Dancing Commission calls: 'Hip, hip!' into the microphone and the audience responds: 'Hurrah!' clapping their hands in appreciation. This is the moment when years of work, intense practice five to six days a week, may or may not pay off. Euphoria is mixed with disappointment. And there are half victories, such as the American woman who came second in the Junior Ladies group (age 17–19). While the Irish woman who won for the second time disappeared from the hotel immediately afterwards, the American woman was treated as a winner by her school and friends taking turns drinking champagne from her cup in the bar. Still, it was obvious that she was not pleased, but was looking forward to the next World Championships which was going to be held in Belfast in April 2000, when she very much wanted to win. I did not get to see her dance in Belfast, but I learnt that she was placed third, and the Irish woman, the 'holder', won again.

Politics and Rivalry

According to Meyer (1995: 35) it is crucial that adjudicators 'demonstrate a knowledge of dance politics' in addition to that of dance aesthetics. All Irish dancers, mothers and teachers I have talked to have emphasized spontaneously that there is a lot of politics in competitions. Or that the top five to ten dancers are equally good, so it is in fact impossible to rank them. A woman dancer found it irritating that mothers were talking to adjudicators before their daughters were going to compete. And a dance teacher commented on the American woman coming second by saying that it might have been to her advantage that there were many North American adjudicators on the panel. The teacher anticipated that the American woman might win in 2000, even if she was not the best then, or as good as now. She also referred to the importance of having a reputation, which the American woman knew about, telling me on another occasion that it is good that the adjudicators know who you are. Still, the title holder is in a better position, and should preferably be Irish. Although there was a certain hesitancy about admitting this, I did find that the idea that the Irish are the better solo dancers dominated at the Championships, while the Australians or the Americans were regarded as 'less strong'. Or at least they were treated as such, since I was repeatedly told by dancers, both champions and others, that 'it's down to the preference of the adjudicator', often in terms of style, school or region, which was sometimes phrased as 'different traditions'. Then there was the English woman of Irish origin, who won the All Ireland's in 2002, who accordingly said: 'It used to be the case, the Irish were better than the English and the Americans. Now it's an open competition'.

It is likely that my status as a visitor at the World's made not only dancers, teachers and mothers, but also adjudicators, more open and ready to confide in me about politics, especially the idea that winners should come from Ireland. This was also discussed by dancers with *Riverdance* backstage in Stockholm.

Despite the numerous written rules, of order and of the competitions (about age, steps, music, costumes, etc.) there were no formal rules for adjudicating, although I got a sense of conventions inolving posture, timing and good footwork. Incidentally, the dancers seemed to agree on them. A woman adjudicator confessed a bit reluctantly: 'When many are good you're splitting hairs to decide who's gonna win. I guess it's a subjective thing: you look for what you like. My favourite competitions are the ones where I don't know anybody. Generally most panels tend to agree.' There are about 1500 registered teachers in Irish dancing. Those who have passed the adjudicator exam can apply to serve as adjudicators at the World's if they have two years experience of a major feis, such as the All Ireland's. There is a raffle to select adjudicators every day of the Championships, and the results are posted on a notice board so the adjudicators know the day before if they can judge. And the dancers and their mothers know who the adjudicators will be.

Mothers of dance students and sports students, who take a special interest in their children's activities, are a familiar phenomenon in dance and sports communities.[8] This is, as should be clear by now, certainly the case in the community of Irish competitive dancing as well. Mothers of Irish dancers are said to monitor their children's dancing either because they never got to do Irish dancing themselves, or because they did and now they want their children to have the same experience themselves. From my participant observation at the World's in Ennis, I understood, however, that Irish dancing mothers were not only supporting their children in this endeavour for their children's own sake, but the mothers got their own pleasure and excitement out of this absorbing hobby. Mothers of children who go to the same dance school form friendship cliques and clusters, and may even be sisters. To them the competitions might also be an opportunity for travel and partying. Yet there was no doubt about the force of the mothers' involvement in their children's dancing. I noted that mothers talked about their children's dancing in terms of we, such as 'we use wigs'. And there were no limits to the pride of a mother whose daughter got a recall, which was celebrated with a small bottle of champagne shared among her friends and their mothers (and me) back at the B&B where we all were staying. Then there was another mother, who actually came from Ennis, and whose daughter had been placed very low. The mother was disappointed, and as we were having lunch at the hotel she burst out: 'The adjudicators know some of the dancers!' and went on about how expensive it was to take part in competitions. 'Write the truth!' she urged me: 'What it's really like!'[9]

Older dancers told me how rivalry could make younger dancers try to destroy each other's dancing by bumping into each other on stage, 'by accident' as it were, during the solo step dancing when two rival dancers perform at the same time. They also talked about the problem of being on stage with someone who was really slow, or not very good, and who did not know where he or she was going, since that might entail not only a risk of injury if they collided, but such uncertainty might also adversely affect the performance of the dancer who was more confident. Time on stage is short, and the adjudicators will not look at you only. If a dancer falls on stage, he or she is allowed to redance unless they have hurt themselves. Then, of course, it happens that dancers who feel that they are not doing as well as they could, fall on purpose in order to get a second chance to do better.

Dance Competitions and Irishness

As Paul Spencer (1985b) notes, dance competitions are used as a means of boundary display, something he exemplifies with the Azande beer dance and the Tikopia night dances described by Evans-Pritchard and Firth. This is dance as confrontation, a warning that if we do not get our way there will be a violent encounter. This is different from the ambiguous atmosphere of framed play which characterizes the championships in Irish dance, although there is the risk of disappointment and emotional drama not only for competitors but, again, also for mothers and teachers. This risk is in fact the essence of play in dance championships. But then there is always another championship, another chance to win, and also to win again and again, for that is the nature of the dance championships. This chance quality, as well as an urge to confirm victories, are important for keeping the excitement and the whole endeavour of the Championships going. Here is, to paraphrase Victor Turner (1982), an example of 'the human seriousness of play'. Turner contrasted the notion of play in the light and free sense, with that of work in the heavy and obligatory sense, which showed that play might well be an aspect of work. Yet Turner argues that industrialization, urbanization and professionalization, which once created a division of leisure and work, also produced specialized performative genres such as folk drama and major sports events which combine play and work.

The theme of dance competitions, as well as music, sports and storytelling competitions, recurs frequently in Irish society, both historically and in present times. As Helen Brennan told me: 'This country is obsessed with competitions, winning medals! It's always been the same way. It's about locality and a sense of place'.

There have long been informal competitions. People might initiate dance competitions in the middle of the flow of everyday life in the kitchen or in the back yard. Informal or semi-informal competitions tended to start spontaneously and might develop into endurance tests. This was usually friendly rivalry, but there was also professional and other rivalry that might provoke local dance competitions, having to do with religious rituals and pre–Christian practices in earlier times. Competitiveness, rivalry and challenge are often mentioned in accounts of dance in Ireland, according to Brennan (1999).

Dance competitions are included as short sections in Irish dance shows such as *Feet of Flames*, which was choreographed by Michael Flatley after he left *Riverdance*. In *Feet of Flames*, Flatley dances the 'good guy' who competes with the 'bad guy' over a belt, which Flatley wins. Belts are still sometimes used as trophies in formal dance competitions, both for men and women, and have the names of the winners engraved on them. *Riverdance* also includes a dance competition: it is in a tap section where African–American male dancers show off, outshining each other. And in *Straight with Curves*, a dance theatre production choreographed by David Bolger, which caused a scandal at the Belfast Festival in 1996 because of a short nude section (see Wulff 2003), two male dancers engage in a competition of physical appearance (displaying their muscles), and a woman joins in.

If it may be an advantage to be Irish in order to win the World's, what exactly does this Irishness consist of? This becomes especially relevant because of the increasing attendance of the Irish diaspora and non-Irish people from abroad. Irish descent in the United States is clearly not enough. The overwhelming number of foreigners who claim to be 'a little Irish' through a grandparent or a great aunt rarely seem to impress the Irish living in Ireland. This is also the case in the Irish dancing community in Ireland where the Irish diaspora dancers tend to be conceptualized as one element in the tension between the Irish in Ireland and the Irish diaspora in general. The latter were, however, also said by some Irish from Ireland to be very good at keeping up the tradition in music and dance, much better than they themselves. The Irish diaspora, on the other hand, were eager to keep up with the tradition by going to the World's, like a Canadian woman dance teacher and adjudicator who commented:

> The World's is a great place to see the best Irish dancers, apart from the shows. This is what all the show people had to do before the shows. All these kids had to do a lot of work before they came here, you see the tradition, the roots, as opposed to the shows. You have to come and see so you know what you have to do.

She added that 'you don't want to leave the history'. Thus tradition appears to be elusive in this instance, always somewhere else: some Irish in Ireland thought it was hiding abroad, while some Irish diaspora people were looking for it in Ireland.

Alice Reddon, winner of women's competition in the age group 19–21 at the All Ireland's in 2002, was English, but of Irish origin. While I was interviewing her, an older man came up asking her 'How did it go?' As this was one of the central competitions, he must have known that she had won, and was in fact checking if she was Irish, and if so how much. '*Both* parents', Alice confirmed. 'Both your parents!' The man seemed pleased with that. Irish families and frequent annual visits in Ireland mattered even for those coming from England, Canada, the United States and Australia. It made them more Irish. As Alice phrased it: 'When you're brought up in an Irish family, and go to Ireland to visit every year, they never sit down and talk to you about it. I always like to know that that my Mum and Dad were Irish. I count myself as half/half. My Mum is quite traditional Irish, but yeah, I'm English.'

Irish dancing competitions are an important way to socialize children and teenagers in Irishness, even though they may not be aware of this while it is happening. Yet the 'social thing' the dancers, especially the younger ones, appreciate with competitions has much to do with growing up in Ireland and learning something about the history in the process. This will sooner or later reveal for them that Irishness is diversified, seemingly contradictory and often contextual, even in Ireland. And that it has been under threat. An Anglo-Irish identity in Ireland may produce feelings of exclusion in Irish contexts, and vice versa. There is also a distinction between those who grew up speaking Irish at home and at school on one hand, and those who speak English with an Irish accent on the other. Irishness is, in other words, a shifting contrastive quality.

Perhaps predictably, I found the World's quite a cosmopolitan event. I had expected the somewhat smaller All Ireland's to be more thoroughly Irish, but it turned out to be a cosmopolitan competition as well, with Irish dancers from as far away as Australia and North America, also from the United Kingdom. One of the senior dance teachers from Limerick who was approaching seventy told me about his life in Irish dancing:

> In the beginning of the 1970s we would have two to three Americans. They came to Limerick from Brussels and elsewhere. We did it in Spain, Ireland, Belgium. We did it in the 60s, 70s, 80s, 90s, at small festivals. We loved it, and then, all of a sudden, you have this *Riverdance!* Then everyone wanted to do it! We've been doing it all the time! Now the Kerry group has asked us to go to Taiwan. I don't know where it is, to be honest, Far East, we'd love to go, if we are allowed to by the mothers, then we go!

This teacher had started dancing late, at nine, but did 'win a couple of medals and a few cups here and there' before moving on to become a dance teacher. He described the necessity of having 'light and shape' in Irish dancing. As a teacher, he said, 'It is very important that you get their confidence and that you get their feet!' And even though he enjoyed teaching young children and seeing them 'shaping', he did talk about how difficult this particular dance form is to learn for most children, and that a child's success as an Irish dancer depends on parents who can pay for costume, travel and entrance fees.

Helen Brennan is concerned about the tradition. At one of our meetings, which had the form of an interview, she told me that she took a special interest in solo-dancing in Co. Clare because she saw it as being 'in danger of extinction'. In *The Story of Irish Dance*, Brennan (1999) makes a distinction between competitive dancing, as a modification of the old Munster style step-dancing, which is being taught at the modern dance schools (established in the 1920s and 1930s), and traditional dancing, which has grown out of social regional dance such as sean-nós and some forms of set-dancing. The latter were taught by dancing masters and teachers in the old days. Brennan is not really in favour of the dance schools and the formal competitions. She is worried that the competitions will change what she regards as the traditional and regional styles. There is, for example, the custom to slow down the tempo at the competitions in order to 'put in all the embellishment', or as one of the dancers formulated it, 'pack in as many steps as possible'.

It is not only Helen Brennan who is worried about competitions, so is Mary Fox, a renowned set-dancing teacher in Northern Ireland. Mary travels widely in Europe giving workshops in set-dancing often in connection with Irish festivals. When I talked to her during a traditional music session at the *Kitchen Bar* in Belfast, she told me that she finds competitions artificial, not least because of the make-up and the costumes. And she, too, thinks that the competitions change Irish dancing negatively. A musician who plays the fiddle at competitions and works as a traditional arts officer at the Arts Council of Northern Ireland, and thus has a certain influence on funding for dance, told me that there were debates at the Arts Council about whether or not dance competitions really were healthy for the children.

Compared to the music competitions, dance competitions are often regarded as 'crazy' by people who do not dance themselves.

Dance Drama and the Irish Diaspora

Breandán Breathnach (1983), has said that the dance drama is the most popular of the competitions at the World's. And it certainly attracted a lot of attention and audience at the Championships in Ennis. In the historical context of Irish dancing and championships, dance drama is a relatively new phenomenon. This competition, which includes decor and dress, and echoes the pantomime dances of the eighteenth century (Meyer 1995), was first introduced in the early 1970s (Breathnach 1983), telling stories about myth, history, customs, daily life and politics in Ireland. Dance drama also resembles occupational mime dances originating in the sixteenth and seventeenth century which were 'based on the rhythmic movements used while planting potatoes with a special stick' (de Barra 1998: 111). This was incidentally also the type of movements that were performed with the occupational songs on farms in the past and that inspired Father Pat Ahern to start making dance theatre pieces in the early 1970s for his Siamsa Tíre company.

The dance drama at the World's can be seen as one link to the land, but so is, on a larger scale, the massive Irish dancing diaspora. People acquire some Irishness by dancing Irish dance far away, creating a symbolic ethnicity (cf. Gans 1979) of nostalgic loyalty to Ireland, the homeland of their parents or grandparents, as a point of orientation. Diaspora Irish dancers travel in growing numbers to Ireland and take part in the World's, but as we have seen, no matter how skilled they are as Irish dancers, they may not be considered Irish enough to beat someone who was born and grew up in Ireland, preferably in the South. Yet both Irish dancers in Ireland and in the diaspora express national emotions for Ireland as they construct Ireland as a place through their dancing.

Although there has been Irish dancing in the diaspora since it came about, and feisanna in many places in the diaspora for almost a century, the Irish Dancing Commission was largely an Irish organization up until the 1960s. Now John Cullinane (1994: 195), identifies it as an international organization with 'many more Irish dancers and teachers resident outside Ireland than within Ireland', especially in America. This has led American teachers to demand an input into the Commission, but this is not approved by Irish members from Ireland who argue that it may reduce the Irishness of Irish dancing.

Tradition as Modernity

This chapter has moved towards a discussion of Irishness and tradition in terms of modernity at the World's and All Ireland Championships in Irish Dancing. The notion of tradition is prominent in the Irish competitive dancing community, although it is divided by generations, nations, regions and schools. Dance forms which have once been identified as traditional Irish dancing will keep that label, but other forms which were once considered modern will be added to the traditional category. In a larger perspective, however, the World's was modern from the beginning, and so was the Irish Dancing Commission long before that, when it started promoting Irishness in line with the nationalist cultural revival. I have argued that the World's is still modern although in different changing ways. Today the size, the elaborate venues in hotels including a selling area (where competitors can buy costumes, shoes, video tapes of Irish dancing, photographs of themselves on stage, etc.), and the growing number of competitors from abroad, all make the World's and the All Ireland's modern, even cosmopolitan, phenomena.

I would like to return to Victor Turner's (1982) suggestion that a spectacle, or a dance competition in this case, can be seen as a modern performance of play and reflexivity. This brings back Paul Connerton's (1989) idea that the past is kept in a bodily memory through ritual performances. When it comes to Irish dancing this memory is also passed on between generations, from one Irish body to another one. Meyer (1995: 35) describes Irish dancing schools and competitions as liminal spaces for expressions of Irish identity cultivating the 'memory of the old ways'. In the Irish competitive dancing community, the past, the tradition, is cultivated by the dance drama and rules of regulation and conduct as well as conventions about the dancing. This is the structural nostalgia (Herzfeld 1997) of the multifaceted and often elusive tradition of Irish dancing. As Herzfeld (1997: 109) has said, 'the static image of an unspoilt and irrecoverable past often plays an important part in present actions'. It is in this light that we should see the 'strictness' of the regulations of Irish dancing, including the erect posture, the stiff and heavy costumes, and the emphasis on Irishness from Ireland at the World's. Even though it also matters that, as choreographer David Bolger noted about the posture in Irish dancing: 'Because the footwork is so tricky, it makes it easier to move if the posture is straight!' Yet protecting the strictness and the Irishness may be a way to celebrate the memory of balanced social relations, a social harmony, from the past. For even though the past in Ireland was far from entirely harmonious, there were aspects of a certain small-scale sense of community which *were* harmonious, and that are now forever gone. Irish dancing at the World's is an embodied tradition, which, like many other national performances of sports and dance, thrives on strong emotions towards the land. The competitive Irish dancing community is not positioned on one side in the rural–urban divide, however, which is often referred to in discussions on Irish society. The World's can, again, be traced back to the land through the dance drama and the diaspora thereby connecting the rural with the urban through the dance schools and competitions that take place in semi-rural or urban settings. The World's is in between the rural and the urban, it has a bit of both, and via Irish dancing diaspora and *Riverdance*, it also has global ties.

The different forms of Irish dancing did change before *Riverdance* created a new genre of its own, but as we will see in the next chapter, not as much. The success of *Riverdance* provoked much debate about tradition in the competitive Irish dancing community. The World's felt challenged by *Riverdance*, but even though it did so in the name of 'tradition', it did so as one modern variant of traditional Irish dance facing competition from another. This is why the tradition of Irish dancing at the World's emerges as a form of modernity.

Notes

1. A céilí also means 'an evening visit, a friendly call' according to Brennan (1999: 30). There are now many céilís arranged all over Ireland, North and South, often as a part of the recent set-dancing revival. People get together at céilís and dance set-dancing for hours on end. See Cullinane (1998) and Brennan (1999) for the history and debates such as questions of authenticity of steps in connection with céilí dancing. céilí is also a type of dance in Irish dancing.

2. Among the dances that were discarded were set dances, so called sets, because of links to the French *cotillion*, documented already in the eighteenth century in France, a *contredanse* which probably evolved from a type of English country dance. The *cotillion* developed into the *quadrille* and seems to have been brought to Ireland in the early 1800s with military people. These 'sets of quadrilles' were different from set dances in solo dancing (Hall 1995; Friel 2004; Murphy 2000). See O'Connor's (1997b) article 'Safe Sets' on modern set-dancing as a liberating communitas for women in Dublin.

3. The dance drama has been analysed as an oral poetic form expressing Gaelic culture through a kinetic syntax in an article by Meyer (1995).

4. On St Patrick's Day in Dublin in 2002, my dance critic friend Seona MacReamoinn invited me to a family dinner that night. Seona was looking for a particular scarf, telling me, 'I'm going to wear something green'. A few days later, I asked choreographer Cathy O'Kennedy if she had celebrated St Pat's. 'No', she replied, 'I didn't do anything. Just bought a green dress for my granddaughter'.

5. In Scotland and Brittany traditional dress is also linked to traditional dancing, Malcolm Chapman (1995: 26–27) notes. Originating from the late eighteenth century in Scotland and from the late nineteenth century in Brittany, these dresses are a 'repeated statement about the modern condition.' According to Chapman, traditional dress is 'frozen in its frame' for romantic and political reasons.

6. I owe this story to fellow anthropologist Thomas Taafe whose Irish mother told it to him.

7. When I interviewed Joanne Doyle, who was one of the women dancers who had replaced Jean Butler as the female lead in *Riverdance*, she told me enthusiastically about Irish dancing and that 'everyone does it'. I should add that not exactly every child in Ireland does it, but, again, many do. Not everyone enjoys it, however. There are those who are uncomfortable with the discipline, some just do not like dancing at all and/or find Irish dancing awkward even '*backward*' (italics in original, Foley 2001: 38).

8. See Wulff (1998) on ballet mothers. In his account of preadolescent boys in Little League baseball in the United States, Fine (1987) describes parents as typically over involved in the games, especially when it comes to letting offspring forget a defeat.

9. This turned out to be a frequent reaction among many parents of Irish dancers I was to meet later on.

Chapter 7

The *Riverdance* Moment

On 30 April 1994, Europe stopped for seven minutes. *Riverdance*, which was first created as an interval entertainment in the Eurovision Song Contest, mesmerized millions of television viewers.[1] Many people have reported on reactions such as 'my jaw hit the floor!' to watching this event. No one was expecting that it would happen, even though looking back, the dancer Cormac O'Shea recollects how they had been wondering at the dress rehearsal: 'Why are people clapping so much? Then at the opening night! It was just hysterical! The dress rehearsal kind of prepared us, but it was just very shocking! It went very well. There was an extra spark when the pressure was on!'

It seems as if something extraordinary occurred during the live broadcast that night from Dublin. The leading team, Irish–Americans Jean Butler and Michael Flatley, and the troupe of Irish dancers, rose to the level beyond the rehearsal process, where new artistry emerges. Watching a video clip of this breakthrough, I have been scrutinizing a moment in the middle when Butler and Flatley together go into flow (cf. Csikszentmihalyi and Csikszentmihalyi 1988; Wulff 2006) and how they, at the end, drenched in a deafening applause, look at each other completely overwhelmed by the peak dancing.

This seven minute slot on European television was a unifying moment in Ireland. As Terry Moylan, renowned set-dancer and writer, expressed it: 'You gasped and you could feel the whole country gasping with you' (Wulff 2004: 293). This ties into my argument from Chapter 3 about the unifying quality of ritual performances, especially as an expression of collective memory. *Riverdance* was a part of a new phase in Ireland's history and economic climate, and would, in its full-length version, shoot to global success, attracting new attention to Ireland, its history, culture and place in the modern world. But this commercial show also stirred an engaged public Irish debate, not only in the dancing community which I reported on in Chapter 6, but quite extensively among academics, journalists and music people.[2] In his accessible book on *Riverdance* as a business enterprise, Ó Cinnéide (2002; see also 1999) devotes a chapter to the culture versus showbusiness debate. This debate was still going on when I set out on my study in 1998. *Riverdance* evoked strong emotions for or against it. Everyone seemed to have an opinion about the show. I observed a curious combination of pride and embarrassment in Ireland over the nature of the show and its commercial success. An Irish anthropologist explained to me that it was not quite 'done' among the 'chattering classes' to appreciate this light-hearted entertainment. *Riverdance* clearly raised critical questions about who among the Irish should have the right to represent Ireland abroad, and what this representation should look like.

Like all dance forms, Irish dancing has, again, not been static. It kept being modified even before *Riverdance* established a new genre, the Irish dance show. This was, however, a more sudden and larger break with the past than previous change in Irish dancing. To begin with 'the nationalist theme in *Riverdance* is constructed differently than its Gaelic League forebear', as Frank Hall (1997: 140) says. Instead of 'exclusion and opposition to dominant cultural forms', this is a confident nationalism which positions itself 'as a member of something larger', of Europe. John Cullinane says he had seen the changes that *Riverdance* brought emerging over a number of years 'occurring behind closed doors, almost all the innovations in *Riverdance* had been introduced in traditional Irish dancing since twenty years'. The composer Bill Whelan, who wrote the music for *Riverdance*, had worked for Siamsa Tíre and contributed the music to their *The Seville Suite* in 1992, and in 1993 he composed the music to *The Spirit of Mayo*, a dance production which also can be said to prefigure *Riverdance*. But *Riverdance* was the moment when all this came together.

Riverdance is an excellent example of a phenomenon which constitutes the rupture of modernity, which Appadurai (1996: 3) suggests has occurred during the recent past as 'media transform the field of mass mediation because they offer new resources and new disciplines for the construction of imagined selves and imagined worlds'. This is taking place, Appadurai continues, 'through the immediacy of their absorption into public discourse, and through their tendency to be associated with glamour, cosmopolitanism, and the new electronic media' featuring for example 'spectacular entertainment'. These instances all apply to *Riverdance*: the show itself, some of the life around it (including the fact that the stars became world media personalities), and the reception of the show.

A rupture of modernity is the contextual point of departure for this chapter, which, with many dance and music people in the traditional as well as the dance theatre community in Ireland, positions *Riverdance* as an instance of high kitsch in the global marketplace. I am also going to consider *Riverdance* in terms of Irish crossover and technology. Cultural analyses of crossover or hybridity combinations tend to acknowledge one major, dominant part in a web of different components. In this case, there is no political domination of one major part over the others, however. On the contrary, *Riverdance* is often seen as an instance of Ireland's cultural and political independence. This Irish crossover of music and dance is conveyed through advanced new technology with lights and sounds such as live electronic music, sections of pre-recorded step sound on tape and small microphones on some of the dancers' shoes. Other technology and media such as television and video have been central in the widespread marketing of the show.

David Lloyd (1999: 90, 93–100) has identified an 'apparent inevitability of the devolution of "authentic national culture" into kitsch'. In the essay 'The Recovery of

Kitsch', Lloyd dwells on how 'the commodification of certain styles and the mechanical reproduction of standardised forms of affect that have traditionally been the hallmarks of kitsch have their close counterparts in cultural nationalism'. Connecting to the topic of social and collective memory, Lloyd goes on to argue for kitsch as repertoire for national resistance by exemplifying with politicized murals in West Belfast, a Ninja turtle harp[3] and a black-and-white image of an emigrant ship, one of the 'coffin ships' where many people died of exhaustion before they reached the United States. This image of such tragedy is placed above the bar of the Irish Cultural Center in San Francisco.

The Show: Irish Crossover

Although there is now a certain *Riverdance* fatigue, the breakthrough in the Eurovision Song Contest was remarkable and spurred the producer Moya Doherty and John McColgan to expand the seven minutes that had been broadcast into a two-hour full-length stage show. It took some time to get the finances together, however, 'because noone really believed in the project!' as set designer Robert Ballagh commented, and Doherty and McColgan did take a big personal financial risk (Smyth 1996). Little did they know that soon they would not have to worry at all about money.

The show features scenes of Irish dancing and music alternating with crossover of flamenco, Russian folk ballet, African–American tap dance mixed with gospel and an Irish choir, Anúna. As I talked about *Riverdance* with writer and musician Fintan Vallely, he pointed out to me that 'the music sounds more Irish than it is. There are Islamic and Eastern motifs'. This East European style with Balkan rhythms opened up new choreographic opportunities, which were crucial for the originality of the show. The crossover was thus there already in the first seven minute version. The full-length show presents crossover of different forms of Irish dance from sean-nós steps and set-dancing to tap-dancing and the stylized form of Irish dancing.[4]

Beginning by recalling the origin of humanity, the show proceeds by praising Ireland, its land and legend, moves on to depicting the distress of emigration and the excitement of urban life in the New World. This is mixed with a crossover journey around the globe. Between the dance sections poetry is read by a male voice. The historical flashbacks and the poetry connect to what we all remember about Ireland from school and perhaps have seen during a holiday week since then. But also the music, with its distinct Irish fiddle sound coming through Balkan rhythms in an electronic shape, is familiar to a general public. It is played by eleven musicians on stage. The show ends with a happy homecoming to Ireland.

In February 1995 *Riverdance – The Show* opened at the Point Theatre in Dublin. It finished with a standing ovation which lasted for almost thirty minutes. A British agent who saw the show the next night arranged for ten performances at the Labatt's Apollo Theatre in London. It became one hundred and fifty-one! (Smyth 1996). That was the beginning of worldwide touring which still is going on. One early milestone for the company was when *Riverdance* came to Radio City Music Hall in New York for St Patrick's week in 1996. The big size of this venue and the grand reception marked the real step out in the world both for the management, the dancers and other people working with the show. This was the beginning of the huge scale of the show. In an interview with set-designer Robert Ballagh he recalled this event:

> The first time I realized that *Riverdance* was bigger than Ireland was when we were at Radio City Music Hall in New York. There are so many Irish people in America, the audience at the general [rehearsal], there was staff and families, nearly two thousand tickets. We had to pay for extra staff while the ordinary staff was watching the general. There were blacks and Asians in the audience, not only Irish. They went wild! We seem to have touched some common nerve in humanity!

There were soon three troupes named after Irish rivers: the Liffey and Lee, and the Lagan was added. They toured in different parts of the world: the Liffey company toured in Europe and the Lagan in the United States. Later the Shannon was formed for the Broadway run (www.riverdance.com). The companies became the Avoca, the Boyne and the Foyle. The latter company came about for the *Riverdance* return to Dublin in 2004. The new companies were set up specifically to be more mobile. They are not first, second and third casts, but all are supposed to be equally good. Dance coordinators see to it that they are keeping up the standard, as well as the uniformity of the execution. Although there are many different styles, not least regional, in Irish dancing, *Riverdance* is supposed to look the same. In order to accomplish this, the dance coordinators do a lot of travelling between the troupes. *Riverdance* has toured in England, Scotland, the United States, Canada, Australia, Japan, Scandinavia and Central and Southern Europe. In the summers of 2000 and 2004 *Riverdance* came back to Ireland for jubilee performances, otherwise the touring has on the whole been abroad. Dancers from The Flying Squad, the 'understudy' company, used to perform in Ireland at charity events, parties and weddings.

In the long run, television has been the primary marketing media for *Riverdance*: television trailers, often documentaries, but always featuring the long line of Irish step dancers beating the floor, have kept announcing that the live show is on its way to your country, or coming back for the second, third or even fourth or fifth time. As late as in 2004 *Riverdance* was said to have 'played to 18 million people and grossed over US$ 1 billion' (Lavery 2004). To a certain extent, the vertiginous figure of 18 million covers the same fans watching the show over and over again. There is also a large number of people who have caught a glimpse of a television trailer – yet long enough to have registered the phenomenon of *Riverdance*. Because of the national and global media exposure of the touring, the television trailers and programmes, videos, CDs etc., *Riverdance* gets the attention of an audience that is not present on their tours, or perhaps have only seen the show live once or twice, but keep track of it. This imagined *Riverdance* community of fan followings, agents, marketing people, and show biz people continue to have an impact on the success of the show.

In his account of *Riverdance*, journalist Sam Smyth (1996) recalls that Michael Flatley left the show just before the London opening night, and Colin Dunne, another Irish dancer and winner of world dancing titles, took his place. And *Riverdance* survived, even flourished, while Michael Flatley went on to collect new victories with *Lord of the Dance* and *Feet of Flames*. There had been a controversy over the choreographic rights, which was complicated by the fact that the choreography is not notated. Who contributed what choreographic sections and who did most of the choreography were questions that became increasingly disputed as the success grew. There was for instance the powerful long Chorus line of thirty-two Irish dancers pounding out their steps in rhythmical unison. The effect of this long line was clearly crucial for the success of the show, and the fact that it could be packaged into easily recognizable sound and sight bites and played time after time on television, radio, in restaurant, pubs, shops and at airports. There had been long lines in Irish dancing before, but not this long. The *Riverdance* line rather recalls Broadway shows. Although the choreographers[5] are formally acknowledged in the programme, it is noteworthy that in advertisements and posters for this dance show no choreographer is credited, only the composer, the producer and the director. The reason may be that there were as many as nine choreographers, and this list (which people would not have time to read as they pass it in the street or skim through the newspaper), would also take a lot of space on the posters.

The Sound of Dance

Riverdance has attracted people from many different countries and cultures, men as well as women, in all ages and classes. This seems to happen in large part because of the catching percussion beat that speeds up the pulse. But what really struck me as a dance scholar the first time I saw the show, was, again, the complete coordination of the troupe. This kind of 'togetherness', to get that many dancers in a line to do the same steps in total unison, is very difficult. In *Riverdance*, there is a lot of beating the floor: the legs go like drumsticks. Later when I started talking to the dancers, they told me that the visual impression of perfect coordination was in fact partly technologically created by a sound manipulation: sections of prerecorded step sound 'even out' irregularities in the dancers' execution. If one of the dancers in the long Chorus line misses a step, or makes a mistake, this is not likely to show. The dancers were grateful for this 'support sound', saying that it made them feel safer.

The 'support sound' is very helpful, according to composer Bill Whelan, when it comes to reaching out in the huge arenas and theatre houses where *Riverdance* is performed. The small microphones on the shoes of some of the dancers also contribute to this.

This emphasis on step sound in *Riverdance* should be related to the importance of the sound of dance, the clicks, in traditional and competitive Irish dancing. The acoustic apparatus in traditional Irish dancing has even been identified as the 'primary signifying function' in a hierarchy of different forms of Irish dance (Meyer 1995: 36). In order to produce the clicks people used to take down a door and dance on in earlier times, both at competitions and at home in the back yard (Brennan 1999), although this custom is sometimes said to have come about because the floors in the cottages were made of earth. To dance on 'the timber of emigrant ships' (Brennan 1999: 14) on the way to America or Australia also produced good clicks. As historian William H. McNeill (1995) argues, coordinated rhythmic movement, the muscular bonding of drill, exemplifying with dance, callisthenics and military academies, creates a sense of community. This concerns all different forms of Irish step dance, but is especially interesting when there is an audience present such as at championships and when *Riverdance* is performed. For then this togetherness that is produced includes the audience, indeed it is an important part of the explanation of the success of *Riverdance*.

In line with Feld's (1996: 97) acoustemological perspective 'sound is central to making sense' especially of memories and experiences of place (see Chapter 4).[6] Analysing the parades in Northern Ireland in terms of ritual events, Jarman (1997: 10) brings up the fact that the absorbing effect of 'rhythmic repetition of sounds, whether liturgy, singing, chanting or music helps to create a sense of collective identity where before there was only a collection of individuals'. An obvious example of this is the prominence of the percussive step beat in *Riverdance*, which makes the pulse go faster. The crescendos of the signature section with the long line of Irish dancers is built with step sounds alternating with instrumental sections. As the speed and the volume increase, the clever use of false stops adds to the tantalizing experience. When the climax suddenly comes – you want more!

Even though *Riverdance* has performed with fourteen dancers in small theatres such as the Samuel Beckett Theatre at Trinity College Dublin, it has also played to six thousand people, and with similar effect, composer Bill Whelan told me. Yet the huge scale of the live show is significant for the concept,[7] the audience experience and not least the quality of the sound: the set is enormous and the technological equipment, with twinkling red, white and green lights, computers and mixing tables back stage, is impressive and there in order to create blazing rock show lighting on stage. The lighting is very important for the live experience of the show: as it is synchronized with the rhythm, it accentuates the impact of the beat.

So technology has been central for *Riverdance*, not only in the show, but also for the marketing. As *Riverdance* grew from an interval filling to a full-length show that started touring abroad, the marketing became more targeted. *Riverdance* is thus often performed in connection with local Irish festivals. Yet *Riverdance* broke through on television, and the real clue to the mega fame of *Riverdance* is the television programmes and trailers of and about the show. The television background of the producer Moya Doherty and director John McColgan clearly mattered for this use of television. Many people working with *Riverdance* backstage in the production team also come out of RTÉ public broadcasting in Ireland. The television trailers have reached and made an impression on even a larger amount of people than have seen the live performances: allegedly more than one billion people are supposed to have watched it on television. Before *Riverdance* comes on tour to a new country, at least one program is broadcast as a trailer to the live performance. The four videos have also been important for the success. Between 1994 and 1998 more than six million videos were sold. The first video recording *Riverdance – The Show*, is said to be the best-selling video in the world (Media Information Pack 1998: 4–5). The composer Bill Whelan won a Grammy Award for the music CD in 1997.

The Irish Response

While raising his back, choreographer David Bolger was pleased to talk about how he watched *Riverdance* breaking through: 'The Eurovision was fantastic! I nearly cried! So powerful and emotional! I was so proud!'

With all the attention and the different forms of the show appearing everywhere in Ireland, he admitted a few year later, however, that 'we are getting tired of *Riverdance*'. So was Lucy Dundon, one of the dancers who moved between different dance theatre productions in Dublin. 'You can only beat a horse so many times!' she said but recalled that: 'When I first saw it, the very first time: I was on the edge of my seat! I was like wow! That really blew my head away. And then when the whole show came I was really disappointed.'

The seven-minute breakthrough of *Riverdance* 'dramatically altered the Irish perception of Irish step dance and the people's perception of themselves', Irish dance scholar and dancer Catherine Foley (2001: 38) argues. There was a new sense of empowerment, especially in a global context. Yet, Foley points out, there were still Irish people who saw Irish step dance as 'backward in its nationalistic, rigid aesthetic and *not* cultured in line with Western art aesthetics'. Again, as with the concept of tradition which does not always stay put in an 'indigenous' or an 'analytical' category in Ireland, but often appear in both, intellectuals and writers who engaged in the debate over *Riverdance* might also appear as dancers or musicians in my field. Catherine Foley was one of them, and dance critic and musician Michael Seaver was another one. Even though there are both rural and urban scenes in *Riverdance*, Michael pointed out that in the rural–urban divide in Ireland, Siamsa Tíre can be thought of as representing the rural tradition and *Riverdance* the urban. And that:

> *Riverdance* has really had an interesting effect, a poisonous chalice, making people more aware of dance, I was very interested at the time, we used to play at all the Eurovisions. People in the orchestra told me they got a standing ovation, I saw it and thought: 'Was that it?', but the shine and the gloss that was put on it was fantastic, a break from the past: this was traditional dance, it was still Irish enough, indicative of the economic climate. Irish culture is now for want of a better word: celebrated. The success of the culture is more celebrated than the culture. The ways people enjoyed its success, this Irish thing, you enjoy Ireland being successful. Thirty dancers coming, the unison, there was a kind of narrative which Irish people love!

As Fintan O'Toole (1997b: 144, 152) notes 'the razzle-dazzle and the spectacle, the sexiness and the celebration, are inextricable from a narrative of emigration, displacement and loss'. It probably matters, too, for the Irish appreciation of the show, that it concludes with a happy homecoming to Ireland. Yet, O'Toole finds the 'dramatic coherence' weak and says that this is where the show fails to make the 'narrative point that Irish culture has taken its place in the international melting pot' as substantially as it could have. It may be O'Toole's experience as a theatre critic in Dublin which has formed his view on what a dramatic narrative should be like. A dance and music show is a different genre with different conventions than theatre plays. Bill Whelan told me how the narrative of *Riverdance* came about: 'I saw the whole show as being a series of images to dance music, elemental things. The first half of the show, little tableaux that can be performed on their own.'

One Irish response to *Riverdance* has been irony and humour. Stand-up comedian Dennis Leary did a take-off of the show, and there was a tea-bag advertisement on television with a glimpse of the signature section. Choreographer Mary Nunan talked about this advertisement. She had not seen the show live, only one of the videos and this tea-bag advertisment. When she overheard people around her asking each other if they had seen *Riverdance*, a common reply was: 'I've seen the tea-bag ad! That's enough!' And with a mischievous smile, Seona MacReamoinn, dance critic of *The Sunday Tribune*, showed me how, sitting down: 'People bang their knees and tap their feet – then everyone knows what it is!' Seona did think that *Riverdance* was 'brilliant', but that the importance of the show has been exaggerated, that many people in Ireland overreacted after the Eurovision Song Contest: 'The claims it was making! I don't think it was as radical and revolutionary as many people claimed in the beginning. People just went hysterical! I kept thinking: Have these people ever watched television?' She pointed out that *Riverdance* has not improved the conditions for modern dance theatre in Ireland. Except for some recent funding for 'theatre–dance initiatives in Ireland' by the production company Abhann Productions (Seaver 2003: 235), this dance form did not get very much more money or audience out of the *Riverdance* fame. When Seona MacReamoinn, at an early point before the global success was a fact, wrote a critical article about the show, she got a stream of negative responses: 'It was as if I had been disloyal to Ireland!'

One type of internal Irish critique of *Riverdance* was the early worry that the show was instance of appropriation of a local cultural form by the global marketplace. Irish sociologist Barbara O'Connor (1997a: 60) saw how this might risk 'closing down possibilities for Irish dance', i.e., those features that do not fit into the global frame. This capitalist commodity scenario has also been suggested by sociologist Joyce Sherlock (1999: 205, 209, 213). Admitting to having been captured by 'the vivacious precision, dignity, discipline and power of the group dances and the resonance of the music' as being 'astonishingly moving' and evoking 'somatic remembering', Sherlock maintains that the euphoria of *Riverdance* might hide the 'the real struggles in consumer capitalism and dance of all kinds'.

The show was thus regarded as posing a threat to the authenticity of traditional Irish dancing. Some of the intricacies of traditional dancing had indeed been removed from the show. There could be three reasons for this: firstly, it was a way to make it easier for the long line of Irish dancers to be in unison, secondly, to present a version of Irish dancing which would be accessible to newcomers to this dance form, and thirdly, to accommodate to the format of a big show on a large stage with thousands of spectators in the audience. The intricacies of Irish dancing were, however, still intact in the traditional and competitive dancing community. As dancer Cormac O'Shea saw this:

> *Riverdance* is a coordination, a spectacle when it really comes together. There are a lot of intricate things we can do that we don't do in the show. The things we do in the show are good for the audience, nothing distracts from the dancing. There are better things you can dance, more difficult things you can dance. In a sense *Riverdance* is quite simple.

By now we know that these extinction scenarios did not happen. Traditional and competitive Irish dancing is alive and well. The fact that dancers and musicians in *Riverdance* have been able to buy houses from the money they earned when they worked with the show is a lasting consequence of this profit making. This aspect of commercialism should be related to the importance of owning property for Irish people, which often was explained to me in terms of the legacy of colonialism (see Chapter 4).

In this spirit and inspired by the megalithic tombs at Newgrange in Ireland, Robert Ballagh designed the sets for *Riverdance*. To Ballagh, who has a background in mass art and also designed Irish stamps and bank notes, the commodity critique of the show does not make democratic sense. In line with Walter Benjamin's (1969b) idea about the revolutionary power of reproduction of art, Ballagh has an ideological interest in making art that can be reproduced on a mass market.

A common reaction among dance critics, scholars and dance people in Ireland to *Riverdance* has been that the show has 'made Irish dancing sexy'. This audience reaction needs to be contextualized by the notion of the restrictiveness of traditional Irish dancing both when it comes to steps and costumes. And contrary to traditional Irish dancing, *Riverdance* communicates with its audience. The *Riverdance* costumes, soft short skirts and black tights for the women, and open skirts and black leather trousers for the men, are often cited as a part of the sexiness of the show. Yet traditional Irish dancers like to talk about 'how sexy Irish dancing was before *Riverdance*'. This then refers to doing dance which O'Connor (1997b) has written about in terms of 'Safe Sets'. O'Connor shows how set-dancing classes can provide a space for flirtation and fun. This is a dance occasion when everyone gets to dance, and when it is over, single women do not run the risk of unwanted company but can safely make their way home on their own. Brennan (1999: 155) says about *Riverdance* that 'this was Irish dance as it had never been seen before: an unashamedly spectacular display which, for once, accepted the sexual undertones of the dance and revelled in its power'.

The Irishness of *Riverdance* is another topic of debate, especially the dancing. The belief that 'Irish descent' matters in Irish dancing, has turned into a promotion ploy for *Riverdance*. On one level it is recognized that one does not have to be Irish to dance *Riverdance*, and that anyone who starts early enough can learn Irish dancing, but there is a tendency to cling to the nationalist idea that 'it helps if there is Irish in the blood', as producer Julian Erskine told me, 'Irish descent is the key'. This reflects the notion of national ballet styles in the Western transnational classical ballet world. As 'national personality' is said to guide how people dance, dancers from the English school are for instance identified as dancing 'magnificently, but slightly reserved' (Wulff 1998: 41).

One contradiction of this is that there are only a few national ballet styles and many nations, another one is that good dancers can learn to switch between different styles. Yet national ballet styles are still used as a way to launch ballet dancers and companies transnationally, which can be seen as similar to *Riverdance.*

Most of the dancers in the *Riverdance* troupes were born and raised in Ireland, North and South, but there were also dancers who grew up in England, the United States, Canada or Australia. They have all learnt Irish dancing since they were children. Many of the dancers went to the same dancing school in Dublin, The O'Shea Dancing School. This means that they have taken part in competitions and won championships in traditional Irish dancing both in Ireland and abroad, and also competed against each other, even their friends, many times.

Backstage

As so much has been said and written about *Riverdance*, the debate has certainly run high, let us go backstage, and listen to the voices and views of the people who produced and performed the show. I saw three performances of *Riverdance* in Stockholm, two from the auditorium and one from backstage. I met and interviewed dancers, producers, a dance coordinator, the composer and the set-designer backstage at the Globen arena in Stockholm, elsewhere in Ireland at championships, in studios and at the *Riverdance* office in Dublin.

In studios and offices of people working with *Riverdance* I have seen world maps posted entitled '*Riverdance* – The Global Schedule 1998' stating tour dates and places for each of the three companies. Not only the management but also the designer Ballagh gets show-report faxes from the performances. Ballagh is informed when something has happend with the sets. Such problems can be potentially dangerous for the dancers (and other people who work backstage) and need to be taken care of. Occasionally the dancers have threatened not to go on stage if something has broken, such as once in Australia when there was a water leak on stage. The show did start, but not until the leak was fixed. Such immediate feedback of what is going on with the show far away in other countries contributes to the interlocking of the global structure of *Riverdance.*

The dancers in *Riverdance* never thought they were going to be professional dancers. Unlike in other dance worlds, the concept 'Irish dancer' refers to a student who is taking classes and is competing in Irish dancing, doing it as a hobby. *Riverdance* has entailed a sudden professionalization of this dance form, not least when it comes to daily training. It has also given the young students in Irish dancing a goal to work for, apart from becoming dance teachers. Orla Griffin in the *Riverdance* troupe talked about the expense of costumes, wigs, dance lessons and travel to competitions (cf. Chapter 6): '*Riverdance*', she said, 'was the first time to get something back for Irish dancing 'now Irish dancers are getting paid to dance[8] instead of paying to dance'. There has been a certain turnover of the dancers. Some have stopped and returned to college or started teaching Irish dancing.

Before joining *Riverdance*, the dancers certainly spent a lot of time practising. The life story of Joanne Doyle, the woman lead, was thus structured by dancing. She started ballet classes at age three, but changed to Irish dancing when she was four years old: 'I was very energetic as a child', she told me, 'with Irish dancing I got out of my mother's hair twice a week'. In fact, she went on:

> I can never remember not dancing. I was dancing in front of the mirror. I was not playing, I was dancing! Every child when you go to school, you do it. It's like learning the national anthem. It's great craic, a social thing. It's better fun if people don't know the steps! You are at the same level for four or five years and then the rhythm clicks in your head!

She had been in dancing schools until she was twelve years old. When she was seven her dancing teacher had called her mother and suggested she moved to another school where she could get classes three times a week. Like everyone else, she took part in many competitions, but noted with relief that her mother had never forced her to compete or expected her to win in the way other mothers of Irish dances often did. Rather: 'I did love the social elements of competitions. During the summers we went on tours with the school, even abroad. It was like going on holiday with your friends! I was doing what I liked the best!'

Talking about the success of *Riverdance*, Joanne Doyle noted:

> The entertainment industry, television and film are so big now. People have forgotten live performances. The world has been waiting for something like this. Irish dancing was like an untapped resource. The costumes, the staging, the music, it just exploded on stage. A lot of people, they haven't seen Irish dancing before. They can't explain it, it's very fresh. We needed to go back and find the 'rooty' thing. It was the right time. We had Andrew Lloyd Webber musicals, then this came. It reminded people that everything began with the theatre. *Riverdance* is an adrenalin wash! If you wish to you can scream and dance up and down the aisle, like at rock concerts. Here you can take part in the experience!

About daily life with the show, she told me that she practices every day:

> I come in at five o'clock, wash my hair and put my hair up in a bun, do my make-up, put on my costume, stretch, rehearse, get a massage as close to the show as possible, stretch again, then I stop for twenty minutes. Go back stage, do jumps in the wings. I'm nearly sweating before I go on stage.

And on stage 'it's like being in a dream or being under water. You don't really see the faces, you don't really hear the applause'. The most memorable moment was on her first tour to London when her grandmother was in the audience without having been told that her granddaughter was doing the lead: 'I saw her – and started crying!' Then there was the exceptional performance before the show split with a hundred dancers on stage forming two lines: 'that was unbelievable!'

To daily life backstage belongs being coached by dance coordinators. During my fieldwork Carol Leavy Joyce was one of them. When I met her in Dublin, she talked about how they have to consider at auditions that some dancers cope better than others on the road, and what they would look like in a line. Elaborating on Irish dancing she said: 'Irish dance in itself is a fantastic art! We grew up with it and the competitions. Then came *Riverdance* which offers dancers an opportunity to come along and express themselves: it's not restricting! It's the right combination for a dancer, and everybody is a star!' She was pleased to note that 'the level of Irish dance in this company has increased' and that *Riverdance* had brought a 'complete revival', with Irish dance appearing everywhere from charity events to a video by U2. Like many others in the Irish dancing community she referred to the impact of the Famine: 'Anybody can do Irish dance. Where there has been an Irish culture, places the Irish emigrated at the time of the Famine, they brought music and dance'.

In her coaching, Carol starts with the signature section and breaks it down into steps, first, second movement. In morning class, dancers wear dance shoes, in the afternoon they change into runners or soft shoes. They are told to concentrate on the movements, to dance through the music. At competitions, it is common that dancers dance off beat, while in *Riverdance* they are expected to dance through the flow, with the music. Carol says that she often has to urge the dancers to relax and remind them that 'you're not competing!' The idea behind the *Riverdance* choreography is to follow the music and go with the music. Just to make sure, she spends a lot of time looking at every dancer one to one checking the execution of the actual footwork.

The making of the full-length show for the opening night at the Point Theatre in Dublin in 1995 was a hectic time for everyone involved. The global scale was already emerging. Bill Whelan recalls how he worked for fourteen hours a day writing the music in relation to the choreography as it was being created by Jean Butler and Michael Flatley in the studio. Sometimes he connected intimately with the choreography, sometimes not at all. He would complete the picture first in sketch form and then go back into the studio. When it came to the Russian dance, he sent the tape to Moscow. And with the Spanish dance, the choreographer Maria Pagés would ask for one or two changes. Robert Ballagh told a similar story about intense work with the sets the weeks before the opening night of the full-length show:

> The scenery would be projections rather. All the images for the back projector were made in London. I designed the whole thing, we pulled all this together very fast, all the images, little oil paintings. A courier would come here with the tape of the music. We did it all in a month. It was very frenetic, a lot of guessing. I've had so many opportunities to correct my mistakes, still, it kind of breaks all the rules all over the place. Out of naivety we accidentally were going into this huge phenomenon. The scenery was being made in New York, in London. It's difficult to control everything, you can't go everywhere all the time. You'd be on planes the whole time, phone conversations are poor substitute, but when things get this big you have no choice. Only a few companies in the world build sets this big such as *The Lion King, Phantom of the Opera* and *Rolling Stones*.

All through this process, Ballagh had been given three guidelines by the management: to respect the tradition, to present the tradition in a modern way and that the set had to be Irish.

When I met with one of the producers, Julian Erskine, in Dublin in 1998, he was beaming with enthusiasm over the show: 'There is a thing about the show. It takes you over! You love the show, everyone of us who works with the show loves it. We put the show on sale in Dublin. It decided to go big on itself! We're being pulled by he show!' They also seemed to be pulled by the promotors, English, American, and Australian, who knew how to deal with global marketing, not least in London and New York. Erskine was full of record-breaking stories about *Riverdance* such as after a performance in Oberhausen with 'a non-English speaking audience, they were still clapping in the auditorium when the cast was getting on the bus!' He also told me that the intention was to keep going as long as they could, not only were they 'looking at South Africa and Asia', but they were aiming for 'the whole of the Pacific rim!'

Reverberations of *Riverdance*

In this chapter I have analysed the *Riverdance* moment in terms of a rupture of modernity which the breakthrough of *Riverdance* illustrates. This and the following global success of the live show came about through technology and Irish crossover supported by the new confidence that the economic boom had produced in Ireland. The crossover in music and dance of *Riverdance* offers something for everyone to recognize or at least relate to.

Riverdance permeated Ireland for many years in different forms, from sound bites in pubs and sight bites of dancing in a tea-bag advertisement on television, to debate in culture pages in the newspapers. The show was all over the island, yet interestingly very little in the form of the live performance, since virtually all of those shows took place on foreign tours. But everyone seemed to have a strong opinion about the quality, authenticity and political and cultural significance of the show. *Riverdance* raised an extensive debate in Ireland. The scale of the live show was huge, as was its geographical reach between London and Tokyo, New York and Stockholm. The show also appeared in small versions at charity events and parties in Ireland. Many people I met during my fieldwork outside the *Riverdance* context had a relative or a friend working with the show.

In his chapter titled 'Speed Limits: Ireland, Globalisation and the War against Time', Michael Cronin (2002: 64) mentions that a performance of *Riverdance* marked 'the opening of the European Central Bank in Frankfurt in 1998'. The show was supposed to symbolize 'the flow of capital through the European union' and 'profitable velocity'. In 1998, Moya Doherty and John McColgan, the producers, used some of their profit to launch a *Riverdance* Fulbright Scholarship, for two places for dance at the Irish Studies Programme of Boston College in Massachusetts. And *Riverdance* has contributed to funding the World and All Ireland Championships in Irish dancing.

The academic critique of *Riverdance* as an instance of commodification in the global marketplace suggested that the global format of the show would distort and dilute local dance traditions. This has not happened. Instead this larger exposure of

Irish dancing has made Irish dancing more accessible and known. There has been a new demand for classes in Irish dancing. *Riverdance* has moreover entailed a professionalization of Irish dancing when it comes to training practice (including schemes for preventing injuries) and lead to a job market for Irish dancers not only as dance teachers but also in other dance shows. Whatever views we might have of the show, the fact remains that it works as a performance.

There were dance shows before and after *Riverdance*, especially in the United States, but not with such a pronounced national Irish theme as in *Riverdance*. The show created a new genre, the Irish dance show. When *Riverdance* was followed by one Irish dance show after another, however, it turned out that none of them would come close to the success of the original show. The concept was already taken by *Riverdance*. There was only room for one Irish dance show in the competitive global marketplace. The follow-up shows featured very specific Irish legends and Gaelic references that most people outside of Ireland did not know about.

The *Riverdance* costumes, soft short skirts and black tights, were imitated for a while at the Worlds Championships in Irish dancing. One significant effect of *Riverdance* on the championships, this predominantly girls' sport, on the other hand, has been that the boys' competition group has grown because of Michael Flatley. The tendency among boys to replace the kilt with black trousers is also attributed to Flatley's influence. A cultural form can thus also generate an alternative force, even nourish local form (cf. Giddens 1991; Appadurai 1996).

It is significant that new social units such as *Riverdance* create new collective representations. In fact, *Riverdance* has created a number of representations and re-representations of different collectivities of Irish nationalism. *Riverdance* provoked a debate over representations of Irishness. The Irish are not a homogeneous collectivity. Still, there is no doubt that *Riverdance* does represent a major force of modernity in Ireland. We just have to accept that representations are always partial and negotiated processes, even those representations that reveal a major new force in a society.

Dance is usually analysed from the visual point of view, but in this chapter I have shown the impact of the sound of Irish dance, and the interplay between sight and sound especially in relation to the support sound in the show. In conclusion, the themes of displacement and longing in the narrative of *Riverdance* have clearly struck a general human note touching masses of people who have no Irish descent or connections at all. The sound of Irish step dance invites us all not only to an imagined Ireland, a homeland of the past (Brabazon and Stock 1999), but also to a contemporary generic Celtic cosmopolitanism.[9]

Notes

1. According to the Media Information Pack (1998: 5), the *Riverdance* management estimated that 300 million viewers were watching this event.
2. See Courtney (1994), Swift (1995), O'Connor (1997a), O'Toole (1997b), Vallely (1995) among many others.
3. The harp is the national emblem of the Republic of Ireland appearing on 'government stationary, Garda caps and coin currency' (Vallely 1999: 169). It is significant that the harp was on one side of the old Irish pound and is kept on Irish Euro coins. The harp is also the symbol of Guinness brewery.
4. For discussions on crossover and hybridity in *Riverdance*, see O'Connor (1997a), Ó Laoire (2005), Foley (2001), Sherlock (1999) among others.
5. The choreographers that are mentioned in the *Riverdance – The Show* programme (undated) for having contributed sections of 'original choreography' to the show are Michael Flately, Jean Butler, Maria Pagés, Colin Dunne, Mavis Ascott, Paula Nic Cionnath, Tarik Winston and Tara Little, as well as the Moscow Folk Ballet Company.
6. See also Feld (2000: 183–184) on acoustemology.
7. O'Connor (1997a: 55) talks about the 'big scale of production' and the 'wide stage', which differ from traditional dancing in kitchens and competitive dancing on smaller stages. Foley (2001: 40) mentions the 'big stage' of *Riverdance* and the 'Western theatrical manner' of the show.
8. I conducted this interview in 1999 when the Irish currency was still in Irish pounds. The dancers in the *Riverdance* troupe were paid IR£400–800 per week.
9. It was Martin Stokes who first observed that *Riverdance* could be thought of in terms of a contemporary generic cosmopolitanism (personal communication).

Chapter 8

Rooted Cosmopolitanism

Originating from Zimbabwe, now based in Belfast Tura Arutura danced a solo titled Artfrique in October 2002 in Derry, Northern Ireland.[1] The solo opened a conference on community dance for an all-white audience of dance practitioners: we saw Tura emerging from the backdrop wearing a black mask covering his face and a feather head dress, which he took off and put on the stage floor. He executed a series of crossover steps from contemporary stage dance and hip hop accompanied by drums on a tape and the rhythmical rattling sound of small bells on bands around his ankles.

A black mask covering an African man's face sparkles all kinds of associations from making a point of 'blackness' to hiding it, or hiding something else, perhaps protecting some part of a 'blackness'. An occasion like this is inevitably framed by Western appreciation of African art and performance. Some would think of this in terms of (unintentional) 'othering', 'exoticizing', while I see an African performer who tries to accommodate his or her tradition to a new setting, for an uninitiated audience. As this short powerful performance took place in a (Northern) Irish context, and was composed of these generic American and African visual and aural elements, this was not only a multicultural, but a cosmopolitan event. And it was a big success.[2]

To the discussion about Irish Ireland versus global Ireland, the idea of Cosmopolitan Ireland is added. If cosmopolitanism in its earlier meaning of an elite form of life and travel, without any particular engagement in place, does not apply to a young nation which relatively recently became independent and thus understandably has a special commitment to its national culture and land, it is important to clarify to what definition of cosmopolitanism my data on dance in Ireland takes us: and it is to a definition which includes and connects local dance in Ireland with global forms of Irish dance that travel far away.

Philosopher Kwame Anthony Appiah (1996: 22), of Ghanaian background, identifies 'the cosmopolitan patriot' as someone who:

> can entertain the possibility of a world in which everyone is a rooted
> cosmopolitan, attached to a home of his or her own, with its own cultural

particularities, but taking pleasure from the presence of other, different places that are home to other different, people.

I have considered Irish choreographers and dancers as cosmopolitan storytellers because of their Benjaminesque manner of combining stories from the soil with faraway places, also by transforming the latter to Irish contexts. Irish dance theatre is moreover cosmopolitan through crossover of steps and stories, and to some extent through global touring. This concluding chapter will pull together the main lines of my argument that emerge from the different chapters in the book. It will suggest that in an overall perspective where different dance forms are intertwined, the link to the land is always nearby. It is more in focus in certain contexts than others, but sooner or later, it reappears. By now it should be clear how close the link to the Irish land is, how short as it were, to a national and global level, and that this land is an anchor for a rooted cosmopolitanism.

Contemporary Cosmopolitanism and History

In the recent revival in social theory of cosmopolitanism discussed by authors such as Vertovec and Cohen (2002), but also Timothy Brennan (1997, 2001), there is a duality of cosmopolitanism which makes account of culture as well as politics.[3] Hannerz (2004b, 2005) writes about this in terms of 'the two faces of cosmopolitanism', where the aesthetic and intellectual strand is one face while concern with far-reaching political problems makes up the other one. As examples of ethnographies of contemporary cosmopolitans, Hannerz (2004b) mentions Werbner (1999) on a Pakistani *haji* who thus had been on the pilgrimage to Mecca, Wardle (2000) on Jamaican proletarian city dwellers with transnational kinship networks that have contributed to a cosmopolitan philosophy, and Ferguson (1999) on Copperbelt street sophisticates aiming to break with tradition.

In the analysis of dance in Ireland, we need both these faces of cosmopolitanism. Some of James Clifford's (1997a) passing point about 'discrepant cosmopolitans' emanating from displacement forced by violent conflicts over economy, politics and culture also helps to explain Ireland through dance, especially those instances when Irish people had to leave Ireland during the Famine or during different historical periods because of unemployment. Colonialism certainly produced violence, not least during the Easter Rising in 1916, and the Troubles has made people leave their homes in the North. Yet, as Hannerz (2004b) maintains, travel and mobility do not necessarily entail cosmopolitanism, but circumstances around large numbers of people en route are likely to produce cosmopolitanism, even reluctant cosmopolitanism. Travelling, also in the form of emigration, may train a habit to handle new situations, while staying at home with a cosmopolitan approach could, for instance, mean a readiness to accept new settlers. And again, cosmopolitanism is not an elite privilege, but an approach which can be the result of an exposure to difference. This informs Hannerz' (1991: 239) ideas about cultural cosmopolitanism as 'a willingness to engage with the Other. It is an intellectual and aesthetic stance of openness toward divergent cultural experiences, a search for contrasts rather than uniformity.'

Such 'divergent cultural experiences' are to be found in the crossover dance and music in *Riverdance*, but also in life around the show, not least through the extensive international touring and media attention that is still going on. If there is less crossover in the actual steps and stories of competitive Irish dancing, the culture of the championships is clearly cosmopolitan. Just like *Riverdance* performances, especially opening nights, the championships in Irish dancing are regarded as cultural events, which means that dignitaries such as politicians and famous Irish artists are invited to highpoints of the annual weeks of these competitions. The glamour that travel and big hotels bring for the young Irish dancers, who are mostly of working-class or lower-middle-class backgrounds, often compensates for losses in the championships, as well as the hard work that many of them put into practicing Irish dance over a number of years. The girls dress up in colourful costumes, with Celtic embroidery, wigs and plastic tiaras, embodying a stylized creature from an Irish legend. This could even be the case for boys who still wear kilts, rather than those who wear black trousers and a white or black shirt. The championships also provide opportunities to meet old and new friends (even occasionally relatives), not only from Ireland, North and South, but also from the United States, Canada, Australia, England and Scotland.

Interestingly, all this contemporary dance cosmopolitanism in Ireland is taking place against a backdrop of more than hundred years of cultural and national diversity through urban and national influences in the Gaeltachts in the west of Ireland. Éilís Ní Dhuibhne conveyed a piece of cosmopolitan ethnography from there to me in a long email, suggesting that this cosmopolitanism has lead to some more protection of the local culture and way of life. At the same time, there is a tolerance, even an appreciation, of alternatives:

> For more than a hundred years the Gaeltachts, much more than any other regions in rural Ireland, have been visited by, studied and explored by outsiders from the cities and other countries. This means that the people of the Gaeltachts have been exposed to urban and international influences for a long time; for instance, in the Gaeltacht we visit in Dunquin, Co Kerry, local people have enjoyed friendships and contacts with Swedes, Norwegians, English and Americans, for at least a hundred years. They have been aware of other worlds outside Ireland to a greater extent, I think, than people in the rural English speaking parts of the country.
>
> For many years, about thirty I suppose, the Gaeltachts have also been settled by outsiders – people from Germany, America, England and Wales, for instance, have lived more or less permanently in the Dingle Gaeltacht since the 1970s. In addition there is the huge influx of summer visitors, long term ones who own houses in the regions and live there for two or three months, as well as all the short term tourists.
>
> For a long time, the Gaeltachts have been more cosmopolitan in the sense of having cultural and national diversity, than any other part of Ireland. This exposure to outside influences, and absorption of outside influences, means that Gaeltacht people to some extent have become more protective of

their own culture and way of life. But I think in general the external influences have been beneficial: they have heightened local awareness of the value of their culture and way of life, endorsed their uniqueness, while at the same time leavening it with new values. For instance, to give a practical example, a town like Dingle, in the Kerry Gaeltacht, had health food shops, vegetarian restaurants, that sort of thing, long before they were common anywhere else in Ireland. It was, simply, more modern, than anywhere with the possible exception of Dublin.

This is ironic, given that it is also one of the only towns in Ireland where the old language is still spoken. It is true that a lot of the modernity, the cosmopolitanism, of a town like Dingle expresses itself in symbols of alternative' ways of life – so health food, acupuncture, yoga, vegetarianism, are the sort of expressions of modernism that are most typical. Also art, pottery, weaving. People from outside have brought, say, artistic skills to the place, settled in themselves, and then after a while a lot of local people become artists. Also writers. The Gaeltachts, especially the Kerry one, perhaps the most 'go ahead' Gaeltacht, has been a hive of creativity for almost a century. The people there are, I think, sophisticated citizens of the world, by contrast with the citizens of many, most, English speaking places in rural Ireland. This does not mean that they won't have conservative religious and political views, but they have a tolerance of alternatives that perhaps is a hallmark of true internationalism or cosmopolitanism.

Cosmopolitan Ireland is often discussed in contrast with the nation, such as by Declan Kiberd (1996: 156, 198) in his milestone *Inventing Ireland: The Literature of a Modern Nation*. Kiberd goes back to the literary revival around the time of the Gaelic League and the cultural nationalism beginning in the 1890s. 'The real debate', says Kiberd, 'of the revivalist generation was about whether the literature it created should be national or cosmopolitan in tone'. Yeats advocated nationalism, John Eglinton cosmopolitanism while George Russell tried to combine the two sides. Writing about Ireland in light of the challenge of cosmopolitanism in the early twenty-first century, Delanty (2004: 184) emphasizes that 'the nation has become pluralised and open to new imaginaries about belonging, community and identity'. This, Delanty goes on, is especially obvious through reactions to 'multiple cultural identities and cosmopolitan self-understanding'. With his focus on citizenship and national culture, Delanty sees these as separated from states, which is a sign of a cosmopolitanism as 'a civic conception of the nation'. If Delanty's perspective is striving ahead, Gibbons' (1996: 3) identification of Ireland as 'a First World country, but with a Third World memory' includes the past as a prominent part of present Irish national identity. While suggesting that the Irish past provides a readiness for 'international solidarity and an embrace of cultural diversity in a modern social policy', Gibbons (2002: 102, 104, 105) refers to this in terms of 'rooted cosmopolitanism'. This is indeed not a romantic ideal, but has had 'its formative role in Irish foreign policy, particularly during the brief phase of the Cold War in which, as a non-aligned nation, exerted an influence at the United Nations out of all proportion to its size', which took place during decolonization in the late 1950s and early 1960s. This 'uneven development' makes for a complex Irish cosmopolitanism, as Gibbons says: going from 'chronic unemployment and emigration to being a host-culture for immigration in the 1990s is accordingly welcomed as a sign of growing multiculturalism'. Gibbons repeats that in order to form a 'genuine engagement with cultural difference', the hardships of the past in Ireland must not be forgotten. He thereby refutes the notion, which has been voiced in the debate about Ireland and 'openness towards the other' (Gibbons 1994: 29; see also Finlay 2004a), that such an engagement would require an abandonment of Irish identity.

Cosmopolitan Connections: Dance Festivals

As I began attending dance festivals in Ireland, I noted that some were locally oriented altough presenting one or two international acts, while other festivals were aiming for an international tone and scale throughout. It made analytical sense to think of them in terms of cosmopolitan connections, also because they were reviewed by European, and sometimes American, dance critics in daily newspapers and dance magazines in Europe and the United States. The local festivals, as well as some dance galas, included Irish artists who had acquired an international fame, such as Gillian Revie. Born in Bangor, Northern Ireland, she had become a first soloist with the Royal Ballet in London. In October 2000 Gillian Revie was the first recipient of the Award for Outstanding Achievement in Dance Performance on the occasion of the annual black-tie Gala Night Celebration of Dance Northern Ireland held at the Lyric Theatre in Belfast. It was obvious that Gillian Revie was delighted to get the prize. The Gala was opened by the Lord Mayor of Belfast, and a man and a woman team, from Ulster television and BBC Northern Ireland respectively, were hosting the fifteen dance acts that ranged from young girls doing ballet steps to Latin American and African dance, Irish dancing and a duet from a production by Dance Theatre of Ireland. A group of small boys from a Loyalist area danced very well with a lot of joy. They got a loud and long applause. Practically all the performers were Northern Irish. The fact that Tura Arutura danced a piece of African dance does not make this whole Gala into a cosmopolitan event, however: it was a local dance event with cosmopolitan features.

Over the years of my fieldwork, I attended a number of dance festivals, especially in the North where different organizations were very active in setting up new festivals and recreating annual celebrations. The longstanding success of the Belfast Festival at Queen's University, a high quality festival for culture and the arts (which also included some dance events) which had been a very popular autumn event for decades, was probably an inspiration for this upsurge in festivals in Belfast, concurrently with a general trend to organize new festivals in the 1990s especially in Europe and the United States. The Belfast Festival was an arena where local and global artists and audience met. Many people travelled from Dublin to attend performances, some of which were recurring highlights, and certain performers were (Northern) Irish who came home for this. This was one instance of collaboration between the North and the South – but also of competition. Should artists from the North be prioritized over artists from the South? In many ways this Festival took place in front of an international audience with critics from major European newspapers and art magazines, who did not know all that much about Irish identity politics. Yet it was a critic from a Belfast newspaper, choreographer John Scott told me, a bit disappointed, who had called his Dublin company Dance Theatre of Ireland 'the home Irish company' and the dancers 'our dancers'. During the weeks of the Belfast Festival, the whole city was brimming with it in venues all over town. Everyone was talking about it, evaluating it, comparing this year's attractions with those of previous years. Still a major event, there seems to have been a certain scaling down of the Belfast Festival recently. Yet as Jane Coyle (2002) commented on the Fortieth Belfast Festival in *The Irish Times*, it 'was full of controversy and wonders'. The controversy was over an Israeli dance company, Yossi Yungman Dance Company, and their one performance, which was funded by the Israeli government. Twelve art practitioners voiced their concern in an open letter to the media about the Festival being associated with this government. The wonders were plays, music, poetry readings, circus and art exhibitions. But the headline of the review, 'Belfast, where culture is contested', hints at the news that came through during the opening week of the Festival: Belfast had lost its bid for the European Capital of Culture 2008. Coyle reports on 'a combination of disappointment among the organisers and relief among some members of the arts community, who had expressed grave misgivings about the bid'. The failure of the bid is explained by Fiona Magowan (2005) in an analysis based on John Blacking's vision of healing the Northern Irish conflict through music, which happened to coincide with the aim of the bid thirty years later. The bid was not even shortlisted because of a lack of shared culture to be summoned, or created, in Northern Ireland, at least for the time being.

My first dance festival in Ireland was the City Dance Festival Belfast in June 1999. It was an annual outdoor festival held on the lawn (or in a tent when it was raining) outside the Cresecent Arts Centre, and in this year was a part of a national dance week with England, Scotland and Wales. The Festival had started a few years earlier as a show case for dance classes such as salsa, ballet, contemporary dance, street dance and set-dancing that are run at the Crescent Arts Centre. Many of the performers were children or teenagers such as the group of mentally retarded young boys who did a happy hip hop section choreographed by Anthea McWilliams. Not particularly fit, the boys still went into the rhythms with great gusto and skill, creating rapport with the audience. There was also a section of Irish dancing danced by a girl in a green costume with 'Saints and Scholars' embroidered on a sleeve and a map of Ireland on the front of the shawl.[4] Two years later, Irish dancing was almost absent at the Belfast City Council Week of Dance, organized by Dance Northern Ireland and the Belfast City Council at the invitation of the World Health Organisation for active living in European cities. This was a major Festival, which took place all over Belfast with dance performances in market places, a shopping mall and a hospital. There was an array of workshops on different popular dance styles, and a disco dance competition for children and young teenagers attended by a large number of competitors and their parents.

In Ulster Hall, a concert hall, a tea dance was arranged for senior citizens. About a hundred elderly women and a couple of men had been bussed there from community centres and were now seated at tables around a big dance floor having tea and cut sandwiches. I was at a table with four ladies while we were each handed a certificate with our names for having taken part in 'a physical activity – tea dance' since the Festival was promoting dance as a healthy activity. With some puzzlement the elderly ladies were reading the headline 'Get a life, get active' on the top of the certificate. A couple dressed in ballroom costume, the woman blond in a long mint-green dress with glittering tinsel and the man in black tails and shining shoes, began waltzing to music from an accordion, a fiddle and a tape-recorder. I asked the lady next to me why there were so few men at this tea dance. 'The men are in the bar!' she joked, her friendly pretty face smiling. She was not going to dance herself, she explained, as she had a bad leg, she displayed her bandage to me. But many of the other women in the hall went up, and danced couple dances – with each other. I talked to a big lady sitting opposite me, thinking that she was an unlikely dancer too because of her bulky body. But I sure was wrong: when the music started up a quick-step tune, the big lady rose and danced – and danced like noone else in the whole hall, and few dancers I have ever seen! Her legs and feet were flowing in complete unison with the rhythm, making it her own. Light as a feather was her big body as she swung it across the floor with complete pleasure and perfection. No mistakes, no hesitations there: she had dance in her body, I observed spellbound from the table. Like the other ladies at the table, the big lady used to do Irish dancing. It turned out that they were indeed Catholics, although eager to stress that there were people from 'both sides of the community' at the tea dance. One of the ladies asked me what I thought of 'that, this peace wall and that'. I replied that I did not understand it, and she concluded the topic with 'Well, we're too old for that now!' And she did not seem to mind. Instead we returned our attention to the dance floor looking out over this moving mass of elderly ladies uninhibited in this moment of true excitement.

The Belfast City Council Week of Dance also included workshops on line dancing, an American style of dancing in a line facing the audience dressed in cowboy hats and boots. This dance form had caused Reverend Ian Paisley, who was campaigning for the imminent election, to issue a statement where he was condemning line dancing for 'being as sinful as any other type of dancing with its sexual gesture and touching'. This brings back memories of the Public Dance Hall Act from 1935 and the ban on crossroads dancing and house dances. The line dancing statement first came a month before the Festival, but Paisley repeated it during the Festival thereby steering the media towards his campaign for a few days (Wulff 2003: 183). The Festival led up to a grand finale with a reception and fundraising gala held in Whitla Hall at Queen's University of Belfast. The patron of Dance Northern Ireland, English dancer Wayne Sleep, had flown in for the gala night as a special attraction. Together with a woman partner, he did a song and dance section from *Cabaret*, the musical.

In 2002, two major international dance festivals were launched in Ireland, one in the North, the annual EarthQuake Festival of International Dance in Belfast, and the other one in the South, the biannual International Dance Festival Ireland in Dublin. I went to the second EarthQuake Festival in Belfast, in March 2003. The theme was 'bringing dance to the people'.

The main venue was the Waterfront Hall, a stylish light building for concerts and other performances, also exhibitions. With its beautiful location by the river Lagan, the white circular Waterfront Hall is an eye catcher in the Belfast city landscape of old red-brick terraced houses and newer business, hotel and shopping areas. This Festival had cosmopolitan connections and ambitions that were expressed in invitations to leading dance companies such as the multicultural Phoenix Dance Theatre from Leeds in England, and two senior student companies, Paris Conservatoire and American Ballet Theatre Studio Company from New York. 'Phoenix rises in Belfast' was the title of Seona MacReamoinn's (2003) enthusiastic review of the company's performance. She came up to Belfast for this performance in order to review it for *The Sunday Tribune* in the South, and raved: 'Physical, exuberant dance movement, beautifully executed, marked the mixed bill of works presented by Phoenix Dance Theatre from Britain, who were making their Irish debut as part of the Earthquake festival of Dance in Belfast last week.' The review ended: 'All in all, a class act'. There were also a great many workshops both in schools and community centres, and at the Waterfront Hall, as well as masterclasses in ballet and dance taught by well-known teachers, and a 'dance and disability' seminar. The workshops displayed quite a variety, from baby dance and disco, jazz, tap and line dancing, to salsa and tea dance. Following the historical development of ballet and dance theatre, it was appropriate to start the Festival with classical ballet, the award-winning film *Backstage at the Kirov* by Derek Hart, an ex-dancer and film director, which is about a dancer's career, especially her rehearsals and performances of *Swan Lake*, and then move on to dance theatre.

Even though Dublin, with its focus on culture, literature and the arts, hosts many festivals, especially the theatre festival in the autumn (which sometimes features dance theatre), the fact that this is a bigger city than Belfast means that a dance festival, even an international one, is less noticeable in the city as a whole, than an international dance festival is in Belfast. But obviously certain flagship events, such as Merce Cunningham Dance Company performing in the Abbey Theatre at the International Dance Festival Ireland in May 2002, got a lot of media coverage. Cunningham presented both early classical work such as *Summerspace* from 1958, which still engages audiences, and recent completely cutting-edge pieces. Dance critic Christine Madden (2002: 10, 18) wrote about Cunningham:

> One of the great creators and guiding lights of dance in the 20th century, he continues to work choreographically through his close rapport with the dancers in his company and his ingenious use of computer technology in the form of 'motion capture'. Hooking up various parts of dancers' bodies with sensors, phrases danced out were fed into and recorded into a database, which then replicated their movement on screen – and could of course be altered and manipulated. Biped … exploited this technique to riveting effect.

Summarizing the Festival, Madden noted that: 'Judging roughly by the plain counting-bums-on-seats method, the International Dance festival was a great success: the acts drew in their audiences and filled the various venues, fuelling a buzz as the weeks passed.'

Irish Culture: One, Two, Multi

The concept of culture has recurred in different discussions in this book, sometimes on an analytical level, sometimes on an indigenous. What then is Irish culture? From an anthropological point of view, on an analytical level, Irish culture is an excellent example of diversity of ideas and expressions that are connected, and contested, even politically, in a social organization of meaning. Culture is socially organized, and much sharing is contextual and partial, yet held together in a structure (Hannerz 1992). There is the divisional nature of Irish culture including the North and the South, Catholics and Protestants, Irish and Anglo-Irish, the rural and the urban that importantly all are linked criss-cross in various ways. Paedar Kirby, Luke Gibbons and Michael Cronin (2002: 16) argue that 'no society could exist without some common values, beliefs and meanings to hold it together'. Yet according to Máiréad Nic Craith (2004: 208) 'culture is a concept that encapsulates the notion of difference'.

The idea of Ireland, North and South, as a multicultural society has been gaining force, even though this is mostly happening in the cities. And like any form of multiculturalism, whether one of policy, market interests, or analytical and indigenous, there are creative connections between some groups, as well as hierarchy, power struggles, even racism in other instances, as Tovey and Share (2000) testify. Writing about nationalism and multiculturalism in Ireland, Finlay (2004a, b) goes back to cultural pluralism, aiming to incorporate Catholic and Protestant communities, which developed into a multicultural agenda with immigrant groups moving in.

St Patrick's Parade: A Multicultural Event in a Cosmopolitan Context

One of the most famous Irish annual national rituals, St Patrick's Day, with festivals and parades, is advertised as a multicultural event, and the designation emerges in anthropological analyses, as well. In Basegmez' (2005: 254, 255) vivid ethnography of the Irish music scene, she had an opportunity to follow musicians preparing and playing in parades on 'Paddy's Day' both in Dublin and Galway that were featured in terms of multiculturalism. Aware that all ethnic groups were not included in this, Basegmez yet saw most young musicians embracing quite a variety of groups, especially in Galway where Travellers, unemployed people and community groups were given space in the parade.[5] In Dublin, Basegmez watched drummers rehearsing and playing in African and Cuban sections in the parade, and reports on traditional Irish music, rock and pop, and the Afro-Cuban drumming in the parade, that all seemed to be a display of world music rather than of anything particularly Irish. But Basegmez points out that:

> the celebrations in Dublin in 1997 were immense, perhaps even exaggerated. This Day was marketed all over Europe in order to attract tourists. There were, for instance, announcements on MTV and NBC, saying that Dublin was the right place to be in Europe on St Patrick's Day. 120 acts involving around 1500 performers appeared in the parade and in street performances.

Observing that 'the celebration of Irishness by non-Irish people is, however, more like a masquerade, or perhaps a "cool thing to do"', she admits being drawn into feeling Irish for a while herself.

I went to the St Patrick's Festival on 17 March 2002 in Dublin. It started two nights before with the 'Glimmering': a mass of school children paraded carrying lanterns accompanied by suggestive drumming in the wet foggy darkness down to the river Liffey. On the river, a flotilla of small wooden boats of fire came on, and soon a spectacular revolving wheel of fire began turning, lighting up the quays where crowds of families, old couples and teenagers had flocked. The day of the big parade, my friend, Seona MacReamoinn, had bought real shamrock for me, which she fastened with a pin on my lapel (cf. the significance of 'the wearing of the green' in Chapter 6). Through the many facets and levels of national celebration, commercial enterprise, artistic representations and scholarly analysis, I was touched by this inclusive gesture. It did make me feel 'a little Irish' as the saying goes, on this day when 'the axiom proclaims, "everyone is Irish"', as Wilson and Donnan (2006: 108) point out. Their analysis of St Patrick's Day parades reveals these as 'prime occasion not just for the expression of ethnicity and national belonging but for its contestation and potential fragmentation'. Such contestation, even exclusivity, is exemplified with different interests among groups in the North, and problems for gays participating in the parades in New York City and Boston.[6]

Applying a historical perspective, Seán Mac Réamoinn (1987: 165, 166) says that 'the Industrial Parade of today is the glossier successor of those held in early years of this century, part of the movement towards national self-reliance'. The very first St Patrick's parade probably took place in the United States, according to Cronin and Adair (2002), which makes sense in light of the large Irish diaspora for whom it was important to confirm their Irishness together with other Irish people, new settlers in a country with an elaborate tradition of parades. Yet, with an American presence in the Dublin parades, and the eventual boost by the Celtic Tiger, these parades have grown and become more elaborate than they used to be. Spending a great night, the night before 17 March with Seona MacReamoinn and her circle of friends in their favourite pub, and at a dinner afterwards, I got to hear many jokes and comments about the parades in the past. In the middle of a giggling fit, one woman described, and this was not a joke: 'It was very short, only two floats, and then some tractors and – Arnott's delivery truck!'[7] The utter boredom of this day in the past was conveyed by Seán Mac Réamoinn , when he told me that: 'Three days of the year, the pubs used to be closed: Christmas Day, Good Friday and St Pat's! It used to be so boring. As children in the 1930s we hated St Pat's because there was nothing to do – not even mass! We were not allowed to do anything!' This contrasts sharply with the joyous popular family feast of St Patrick in Dublin nowadays, even though it has its critics too for being driven by commerce and commodified, both the parades and the parties, as well as the green beer, shamrocks as face paint, and other Irish tourist paraphernalia, such as leprechaun green hats and plastic shamrock tiaras, worn by members of the huge crowd which is attracted to the city centre of Dublin on this day.[8]

In 2002, the theme of the parade was 'Join the Dream Theme', which had spurred a number of groups to present stories about dreaming. As I was standing in the rain, alternating with sunny spells, in the middle of the colourful crowd, watching the parade go by to marching music, Latin and jazz rhythms, and other catching beats, I saw groups ranging from Ireland's reserve forces and Garda (the Irish police) equestrian team to the Lord Mayor in his golden State Coach originating from 1791, drawn by horses. St Patrick himself came walking down the street, bearded, dressed in his green cape and sandals carrying his long stick. There were marching bands from California and England, the Chinese Dragon dancers, a vintage-car rally, youth bands from Dublin and Co. Down in the North, and a samba school. Just as I had began thinking that the parade seemed all white after all, a banner appeared saying 'Know Racism, The National Anti Racism Awareness Programme'. It got the first applause. Guinness had sponsored one of the stories about dreaming titled 'Inspired: Dreamtime Awakening' with motifs from Australian Aboriginal myth. When the NYPD (New York Police Department) came out, a shiver went through the crowd. This was only six months after 11 September where there had been many Irish losses. Not only is the Irish contingent considerable in the NYPD, but some of them had been taking part in rescue activities during the 911 event. The troupe was greeted with loud applause and cheers. There was a huge Chinese dragon crawling down the street, pom-pom girls from Co. Tipperary, a Norwegian brass band, a Scottish bagpipe band and a Japanese group, the latter sponsored by Toyota. Children marched by, waving flags from different countries, mostly Irish green-white-orange tricolours. Apart from a carnival group from Co. Donegal performing the Irish myth about Balor, and good versus evil, inspired by Caribbean costume and West African and Japanese musical styles, and a pipe band from Co. Down, I noted an absence of Irish music and dancing in this year's St Patrick's parade. At the end of the parade, St Patrick came back as an old man, with white hair and beard.[9]

If the parade was a family event, then a so called 'monster céilí', a huge dance gathering which was arranged after the parade by St Stephen's Green park, was mostly a youth event, for groups of teenagers and young people. I observed a big happy crowd doing an 'Irish samba', and one person after another who did not seem to know each other beforehand, hooking up to form a long 'snake' in the pouring rain to traditional music on stage. They had a great time, bouncing up and down, perhaps to keep warm, perhaps because this was how this event had been advertised and performed previously. It is also a common dance style at rock concerts. The actual céilí dancing, including set-dancing instructions, never took off, however. The whole event was regretfully commented on in a critical letter by Terry Moylan (2002) to *The Irish Times*. A prominent set-dancing teacher, Terry Moylan had been in charge of the set-dancing at previous 'monster céilithe', but found the 'bouncing around' insincere, and withdrew his assistance.

Conclusions: Dance and Rooted Cosmopolitanism

Moving towards a conclusion of this chapter, and this book, my first reflection is that the grounds for social life are shifting, and consequently the methods of anthropologists. This book is supported by my multi-local yo-yo fieldwork (see Afterword). By going to Ireland over the course of a number of years doing participant observation and interviews at competitions, festivals, and performances I gradually became immersed in my field. I have seen the economic boom and the beginning of its decline. Multi-local fieldwork is often assumed to be deterritorialized, but that has not at all been the case in my fieldwork in Ireland. It is a part of the well-established interest in Ireland as a region in anthropology, sociology, European ethnology, folklore and interdisciplinary Irish Studies.

Throughout my fieldwork I observed and was told about a duality of the culture in Ireland. Writer Éilís Ní Dhuibhne phrased it as 'there is always a difference between the official representation and what is going on in reality', and choreographer John Scott said that 'we're a two-faced people. Since the occupation there is an outer and an inner identity. We switch between resilience and then it all comes out in eruptions!' In dance, such eruptions take the form of creative wit or dark drama. But there are also delicate moods in dance that discuss circumstances that can be difficult to talk about in everyday life, and that suggest an alternative interpretation. The voices and views in this anthropology of dance study have brought out stories about Irish culture both in the past during the occupation, as well as in the contemporary cosmopolitan world. Some of the duality of Irish culture can be conceptualized in terms of cultural intimacy, a notion coined by Michael Herzfeld (1997: 94; see also Shryock 2004) meaning 'the sharing of known and recognizable traits that not only define insiderhood but are also felt to be disapproved by powerful outsiders. The term's hints of domesticity are especially apposite in the context of nationalism'.

This ethnography of different, but connected, dance forms in Ireland adds a crucial piece to the understanding of dance more generally in relation to geopolitics: abstract dance and movements also communicate stories about their societies. In Irish dance, these stories often take the form of memories of displacement, longing, and resistance. These memories are presented in cutting-edge dance theatre performances, in *Riverdance* showbiz that thrives on touring, and by thousands of Irish dancers who embody the history and travel vast distances to championships. In Riverdance, the long Chorus line of thirty-two Irish step dancers at first recalls Broadway shows (although there are also long lines in Irish set-dancing), but then moves on to tell an Irish tale about a new sense of independence and political confidence, and of commercial success. For whether one is a fan or a foe of *Riverdance*, the fact remains: this is a successful performance.

Basegmez (2005: 246) identified a global orientation among musicians in Ireland in the late 1990s, and how this in many ways had replaced the opposition to the English. This appreciation of global connections in the music scene, co-existed with an anxiety among some local, traditional musicians that traditional music would lose its authenticity and turn into a global commodity. Other musicians were open to musical influences from different traditions outside Ireland, seeing these rather as ways to develop Irish music, and revitalize Irishness. As Basegmez says: 'These musicans wanted to combine a cosmopolitan identity with a sense of national belonging'. I saw cosmopolitan ambitions in the dance world that were not always realized, dance people who felt left out of this context, others who rejected the idea, finding it unappealing, yet some of whom I would identify as cosmopolitan in lifestyle and outlook without identifying themselves as such. It is entirely possible to be more or less cosmopolitan and to different degrees. This unevenness, coupled with inequality in relation to dance cosmopolitanism, are all included in cosmopolitanism as a modern process.

And finally, like much in Irish culture, the social memory of Ireland as a dancing place, both from a national and a transnational perspective, evolves around notions of displacement, longing and resistance. Despite critique and contestation, even ridicule, crossroads dancing is also remembered as an idyllic practice. The dance theatre piece about the Famine suggests displacement in the form of emigration which would produce longing for Ireland, and for those who left. Emigration and homesickness are also included in the narrative of *Riverdance*, although the show does present a happy ending with a homecoming to Ireland. When it comes to competitive dancing, a prominent element is the diaspora dancing themselves Irish far away, creating a nostalgic loyalty to Ireland, the homeland of their parents or grandparents. On an analytical level, this homeland (cf Brabazon and Stock 1999), as well as many other constructions of Ireland as a homeland featured in different forms of dance, is located in the past. It is an imagined Ireland to which one cannot go back.

This book on dance in Ireland began with the establishment of Irish dancing classes and competitions as one element in the national cultural revival movement in the 1890s and moved on to the Public Dance Hall Act from 1935, which banned – but did not stop – dancing at the crossroads, and other popular dance forms such as house and barn dances. Irish dance theatre which sometimes features traditional Irish steps and music, has developed into a major dance form with an international reputation. It can be traced back to dance plays at the Abbey Theatre in Dublin that Yeates and Ninette de Valois staged already in the 1920s and 1930s. *Riverdance*, the Irish dance show which came out of Irish competitive dancing, had a seven-minute breakthrough in the Eurovision in 1994, and as a full length show, skyrocketed to global success. It is crucial that Irish dance has been cosmopolitan long before *Riverdance* came along, as have sections of Irish society: competitive dancing has been practiced and taught in many places across the globe among members of the Irish diaspora and other people, yet coordinated through the Irish Dancing Commission in Ireland. Like many contemporary cosmopolitans, Irish dancers and choreographers enjoy opportunities to travel and get access to 'divergent cultural experiences' (Hannerz 1991: 231). As Delanty (2004: 201) hints, young people are major agents in 'shaping a potential cosmopolitanism'. In Ireland, this is a rooted cosmopolitanism at the crossroads of Irish tradition and European modernity, nurtured by strong links back to the Irish land.

Notes

1. This city is referred to as 'Derry' in Northern Irish Catholic parlance, and 'Londonderry' by Northern Irish Protestants. The latter was the most common designation when international and British media reported on violence in connection with the Troubles in this city. Here I use the designation 'Derry' as this was the one preferred by the organizers, Dance Northern Ireland, of this conference 'Dance in the Community'. It was an opportunity for community

dance practitioners and specialists in Ireland, North and South, as well as the United Kingdom, to meet and discuss development, collaboration and funding of community dance.

2. Tura Arutura has lived in Northern Ireland since the early 1990s with his wife (of Northern Irish background) and two children. He teaches 'African and Street Dances' and also works as a broadcaster hosting a multicultural programme on a local radio station.

3. There is for example *Cosmopolitanism* by Breckenridge, Pollock, Bhabha and Chakrabarty (2002), which stresses non-Western, i.e., Asian and West African cosmopolitanisms.

4. Island of 'saints and scholars' is a traditional designation of Ireland, scholars in this case usually referring to students, learned people who study (rather than doing scholarly research).

5. Travellers are an indigenous minority group in Ireland.

6. For St Patrick's Day celebrations and a diversity of meanings attributed to it ranging from commemoration of a slave uprising, displaying Irish connections, or an opportunity to party on the Caribbean island of Montserrat, see Skinner (2004, forthcoming).

7. Arnott's is a department store in Dublin.

8. The little leprechaun with his characteristic big green hat is a male figure from Irish mythology.

9. This could also be interpreted as a reference to the idea that there might have been two St Patricks, as discussed by Seán Mac Réamoinn (1987). See also Persson (2002) on old and new meanings of climbing Croagh Patrick, the holy mountain of Ireland.

Afterword

Yo-yo Fieldwork

As yo-yo fieldwork is a new term, yet, I would argue, an increasingly common strategy to do fieldwork, I am going to discuss this methodological practice. Fieldwork tends to be hailed as the distinguishing feature of the discipline of anthropology, despite the fact that it is actually the theoretical insights that are generated through fieldwork (and that could not have been generated in any other way) that, in combination with a comparative perspective, is our major contribution to academic knowledge.

How then is fieldwork defined within anthropology? And no less importantly: how do we *de facto* conduct fieldwork today? For at the same time as there is an anxious debate in the discipline about emerging methods such as mobile and multi-local fieldwork, there is an obvious shift towards more flexible forms and methodological pluralism, polymorphous engagements, as Hugh Gusterson (1997) has phrased it. In order to keep up with the mobility and speed of contemporary social life, anthropology requires a new set of methods such as the expanding practice of mobile and multi-local fieldwork. Traditional fieldwork with one year of more or less uninterrupted participant observation in a village or an urban neighbourhood as a unit, does not always do anymore, it does not necessarily answer the research questions that come out of modern social life where so much is in motion.

Multi-local and mobile fieldwork have been discussed and documented by Marcus (1998 [1995]), Clifford (1997a,b), Hannerz (1998, 2003a,b), and in *Anthropological Journal on European Cultures (AJEC)* special issue on 'Shifting Grounds: Experiments in Doing Ethnography' (2002). My fieldwork in Ireland accentuated questions of time and place. At stake were two movements: firstly, the yo-yo movement between Stockholm and Dublin by air, secondly, my moving around all over the island both in the Republic of Ireland and Northern Ireland by bus, train and to some extent by domestic flights and car. This is a generic multi-local fieldwork in line with Hannerz' (2003b: 21) definition that 'several local fields … are also linked to each other in some kind of cohesive structure'. This is '*one* field, which consists of a network of localities – "several fields in one"'. What is going on in one locality has an impact on the next locality, deliberately or not. And consequently, a multi-local field is also translocal: an understanding of the localities includes relationships between them, as well.

Built around culture theory, globalization, the media and occupational cultures, Stockholm anthropology early provided training in multi-local fieldwork since the communities we researched operated multi-locally, although in different ways. Ulf Björklund (2001) has written about his journey, which altogether lasted for almost one year, through the Armenian diaspora in Paris, California, Boston and New York, followed by Jerusalem, Nicosia and Istanbul. By moving around in these often interconnected circles, Björklund learnt about the beliefs, views, activities, sensibilities and relationships of this diaspora. Aware that he met Armenians in their capacity of Armenians in the centres of the diaspora, where issues of ethnicity and nationalism are emphasized, but that he has not really seen the variety of Armenianness in the peripheries, Björklund argues that his multi-local movements have yet been in accord with the social scope of this old diaspora population. To move around multi-locally was also the best way for Christina Garsten (1994) to study the organizational culture of the transnational computer company Apple. Garsten did fieldwork in three localities: the Swedish office in Stockholm, the international headquarters in Silicon Valley in California and the European headquarters in Paris, thereby covering both centres and one periphery as well as the links between them in this transnational organization. Another occupational culture, multi-local by definition, is the emerging profession of interculturalists whose job it is to teach businesspeople to handle cultural differences. This is the topic of Tommy Dahlén's (1997) study, which was conducted with participant observation and interviews mainly at conferences and courses in intercultural communication, varying from one-day workshops with consultants and big annual international conferences organized by SIETAR (Society for Intercultural Education, Training and Research) to term-long courses at Lesley College in the United States. This is a typical network field where localities are less important. One significant aspect of this fieldwork was that part of the field was temporary, emerging for a short period of time: even though some of the conferences and courses took place with regular intervals, they were not there continuously. Such temporary fields that are connected to more permanent structures are now necessary to deal with for anthropologists, in our aim to make account of contemporary life. So is the occurrence of fields that are temporarily on the move in multi-local fieldwork, that is when a field is moving away for a while and then coming back, as it were. It can be people going on holiday, business trips or other kinds of travel such as when the ballet dancers I was studying in Stockholm (Wulff 1998, 2000) went on tour to Japan, or their colleagues in New York all went to Washington, D.C., to perform. If I had not been able to go with the dancers to Japan and Washington, D.C., I would have been the only one left behind: a fieldworker without a field.

'Looking for a Field' is the subtitle of a chapter by Hasse Huss (2001) about his multi-local fieldwork on the making of reggae music, which was planned as a one local study of toasting (Jamaican rap music) in Kingston, Jamaica, but was to extend to London, Tokyo and Osaka. It was obvious for Huss that he would go to Jamaica, this small Third world nation which against all odds has produced a global music industry. It did not take long before he realized, however, that most people he was going to meet during his fieldwork were part of small or big transnational networks of family and friends. This was especially the case with the music makers. Huss was also struck by the unlikely presence of the Japanese in Kingston: music producers, toasters and fans, all there because of the great interest in reggae in Japan. And a translocal network took shape with a set of 'deterritorialised common values ... about music and music making' (Huss 2001: 273) reducing the importance of particular places after all. A set of deterritorialized common values were also central in Galina Lindquist's (1997) study of urban shamans and new age performed at courses, parties, and ceremonies based in Sweden but taking her to Denmark, England and France. At the same time, these urban shamans appropriated their own holy places in the Swedish forest for their ceremonies. This is yet another aspect of the meaning of place.

Hannerz (2003b: 18) writes about his multi-local fieldwork among foreign correspondents in Jerusalem, Cape Town, Hong Kong and Tokyo:

> A little like the foreign correspondents themselves, I have moved in and out of various places, trying to get an idea of who they are and what happens before their reports about the state of the world reach us viewers, listeners and readers. But besides meeting the correspondents in various places, I have also tried to follow their reporting, read their memoirs and report books, and meet some of the international news editors at their home news stations.

Hannerz (2003b: 18) continues by recalling how different his first fieldwork was, in an African–American neighbourhood in Washington, D.C., in the 1960s (Hannerz 2004 [1969]). That field was characterized by 'face-to-face-relationships' that were managed 'within walking distance'.

This does not mean that there is an inherent lack of face-to-face relationships in multi-local fieldwork. When I went to Ireland I connected to a lively dense network of people in and around the dance world. It is useful and true that many Irish people are convivial and great storytellers, but the small scale of Irish society also matters. I kept running into informants in various contexts that I was not expecting to meet in that place or during that visit. As I was around for so long, my informants included me in their world. They took for granted that I came to major dance events such as local competitions in the countryside, premieres and international dance festivals in Dublin and Belfast. And even though I did not take part in the most mundane everyday life of the dance world, I have shared a little of that too. It did not provide any particularly useful data, however – for that I had to be around at performances, competitions and festivals.

Time and Immersion

It is clear that time is a crucial issue in multi-local fieldwork. A common misunderstanding about this type of fieldwork is that it by definition entails shorter time in the field, at least in each field site. For this study I spent thirty-three weeks in the field, or in all more than eight months. My study of the transnational ballet world (Wulff 1998) included four field sites: one year with the Royal Swedish Ballet in Stockholm, and three months each with the Royal Ballet in London, the American Ballet Theatre in New York and Ballett Frankfurt in Frankfurt-am-Main, altogether almost two years in the field. Importantly, the duration of my fieldwork in Ireland thus corresponds on the whole with a traditional period of time in the field. But taken together my study lasted over a longer period of time, which is something that Hannerz (2003b) has noted tends to be the case in multi-local fieldwork.

My methodological strategy, to move around the island, to go to different places where dance events occur, was motivated by the fact that dance events relate to each other. An analysis of *Riverdance* required, again, a familiarity with competitive dancing, for example. Importantly, Irish dance people also move around the island taking part in different dance events. By going to Ireland many times over a number of years, I gradually became immersed in my field along a time axis, and can therefore take part in theoretical discussions of the relationship between mobility, time and place. This is an instance of how a field is demarcated by place as well as by the mobility of people and events.

A yo-yo fieldwork moreover allows for time to write conference and seminar papers and articles for publication between field stints, which is useful not least as a way to relate to the academic world in the field. Academic contacts and conferences in the field region add significant dimensions to the understanding of an ongoing study.

A special twist on my academic involvement with Ireland happened when I sent an early article on my yo-yo fieldwork to Anthea, my choreographer friend in Belfast. In the article I talk about how my field was dispersed all over the island, which had me doing fieldwork along the lines of George Marcus' (1998[1995]) six strategies for multi-local fieldwork, or multi-sited ethnography: follow the people, follow the thing, the metaphor, follow the plot, story or allegory, the life or biography, or follow the conflict. These strategies turn out to overlap (cf. Hannerz 2004a): for instance, when I went to Carraroe in the west of Ireland for the dance competition in sean-nós step dancing, I followed dancers and audience, the dance and the competition, as well as the idea of the west of Ireland as a place that still is associated with 'authentic' Irish life. In the article I write about this stint. The next time Anthea was back on the road with her boyfriend, they sent me this enthusiastic (meta)message identifying themselves as my 'field co-informants':

> Hi Helena,
> Greetings from Gary and I in Clifden/Lennane/Cong/Westport ... between sunshine & showers. We have your article with us and read it every day, although we won't make it to Carraroe unfortunately. We will however walk in your footsteps elsewhere as your field co-informants as this is after all the area where the film 'The Field' was filmed ... how appropriate (have you ever seen it?).[1] We will follow the field, the yellow brick road, the sun rising to meet us (hopefully) and the people, the food, the drink and of course the dancing. We have a short but simple tale of our first night in Westport and the dancing magic (created by ourselves). We will be in touch again at the next Connemara internet cafe.
> Regards,
> Anthea & Gary

Another important aspect of time in my multi-local yo-yo fieldwork in Ireland is that I made use of the time during my field weeks differently than I have done in my previous field studies. When I was in the field in Ireland I had to use my time even more efficiently than I, if I am completely honest, always did in my traditional field studies. In Ireland I had to push myself forward if I was going to get anything done, which I did. My field weeks were filled with activities, meetings, interviews. Most of them were arranged via email or phone before I went to Ireland, but I tried to leave some space for improvisation, to be able to seize sudden opportunities, which is an aspect of all fieldwork.

A spin-off effect of a multi-local yo-yo fieldwork, where one is not in the field continuously, and which also has to do with the usage of time, is that one gets information about what is happening when one is off-field, so to speak. Such in-between periods of fieldwork, off-fieldwork, are clearly of a different nature than the after-fieldwork state, after having exited the field (cf. Wulff 2000). During off-fieldwork the fieldworker is temporarily physically away from the field, but not mentally. The fieldwork was still going on through my polymorphous engagements such as reading contemporary Irish fiction and watching new Irish film because they portray aspects of modern Irish society that related to my study. Another reason to keep up with the latest novels and films was that my informants did, and then brought them up in conversations with me. My fieldwork was also going on through information and communication technologies when I was at home in Stockholm. This is definitely a new widespread aspect of fieldwork. I received emails and postal mail, both formal information from organizations and also informal letters from key informants about what was going on. I kept up with web pages of Irish newspapers and dance companies, and spent a lot of time watching dance videos that my informants gave me or sent me, or that I bought in Ireland. Watching dance videos is a time-consuming activity, but it was a vital part of my fieldwork, since video is vital in the dance world as in so many other contemporary social worlds (although increasingly replaced by DVD). For me, watching dance video was a way to prepare for meetings with informants who had choreographed the dance pieces on the video or danced in them, to keep up with what my informants were doing while I was away from the field, and to learn about previous work that they did not perform live anymore. I did not make videos myself, however, I only took still pictures.[2] I was thus documenting a process rather than a slice of time, which used to be the case in traditional fieldwork.

The importance of being there is emphasized in Watson's (1999) volume about modern fieldwork, and this quality is of course central also in long-term multi-local fieldwork. Communication via email, web pages, and video was essential for my fieldwork on dance in Ireland, but it would not have been enough, it was rather a way to keep in touch with the field and to complement face-to-face contacts during participant observation in the field. In my yo-yo type of fieldwork, my repeated returns served to strengthen (cf. Hannerz 2003b) my bonds to the field.

One of the chapters in *Foreign News* by Ulf Hannerz (2004a) is titled 'Writing Time'. It deals with how foreign correspondents write, also in relation to time. Since they are fond of the idea that they write 'the first draft of history' Hannerz goes back to *Annales* historian Fernand Braudel's (1980: 25ff) concepts of three types of history writing with three different time spans: history of events, medium-term history which covers a couple of decades and *la longue durée*, the time spans which might last for centuries. While journalists typically focus on events, anthropologists have traditionally conceived of an 'ethnographic present' as timeless. Hannerz (2004: 230) discusses long-term fieldwork with continuous involvement and recurring visits in the same field. Even though the actual length of the stay or the number of return visits are in fact not what matters but rather 'a cultivated sensibility towards the passage of time: the medium-term history of the present as a state of mind'.

Going back and forth to Ireland in my yo-yo manner over a number of years enabled me to create such 'a cultivated sensibility towards the passage of time' especially in relation to events in Irish history but also to the economic boom, the so called Celtic Tiger, which I observed almost at its height, and then starting to go downhill.

Just like traditional anthropology, my multi-local study thus has a region. There are similarities with another form of more established type of long-term fieldwork, which meant that the anthropologist kept in touch with the field more or less sporadically for several decades. It was common to spend some longer periods there, and go back now and then to visit. During the course of a yo-yo fieldwork, the field is always present, at least in the back of one's mind. I kept thinking about theoretical questions, planning methodological manoeuvers for my next field trip, reading popular and academic literature and writing about my study. The prerequisite for a yo-yo fieldwork is obviously that it is relatively easy and cheap to get to the field, and above all that the fieldworker is able to arrange life and work at home in a way that makes it possible to go away now and then, almost in a commuting manner.

There is a sense of a divisional nature of Irish society which tends to be traced back to colonialism (see Swan 2005 among others). I did notice social distance and divisions even between people and places that are rather close geographically such as the Republic of Ireland and Northern Ireland, Catholics and Protestants, Irish and Anglo-Irish, the rural and the urban, yet kept finding ties between them. They were linked criss-cross in various ways on different levels. This can be related to the idea of the village as a unit for fieldwork, or at least the village as a metaphor, to the idea of Ireland as a village where everyone knows everyone. This idea comes out of the fact that the networks are dense and comprise the whole island, and that Irish society is relatively small scale. In a conversation with fellow anthropologists, Frank Hall who, again, has extended experience of research on competitive Irish dancing (1995, 1996, 1997, 1999), he identified the tightly knit and intertwined networks of dance people, musicians, writers, politicians and academics in Irish society as being 'like Celtic knotwork'. I often noticed, with surprise, that people I met in different contexts turned out to know each other, or at least were connected via only a few network links, just like the intricate but inclusive pattern of a Celtic knotwork.

Notes

1. The film titled *The Field* is about an old man in Ireland who loves the field he has worked his whole life, and when it risks being sold by public auction to an American, the Irishman puts up a fierce fight protecting not only his livelihood but also a dark secret.
2. See Banks (2001) on visual methods in ethnographic research, such as video filming.

Bibliography

Ajayi, Omófolábó S. (1998). *Yoruba Dance: The Semiotics of Movement and Body Attitude in a Nigerian Culture*. Trenton, NJ: Africa World Press.

AJEC (Anthropological Journal on European Cultures) (2002). *Shifting Grounds: Experiments in Doing Ethnography*, special issue.

Almqvist, Bo (1991). 'Irish Migratory Legends on the Supernatural: Sources, Studies and Problems', *Béaloideas*, 59: 1–43.

Appadurai, Arjun (1996). *Modernity at Large: Cultural Dimensions of Globalization*. Minneapolis: University of Minnesota Press.

Appiah, Kwame Anthony (1996). 'Cosmopolitan Patriots', in Joshua Cohen (ed.), *For Love of Country*. Boston, Mass.: Beacon Press.

Archetti, Eduardo (1999). 'The Spectacle of Heroic Masculinity: Vegard Ulvang and Alberto Tomba in the Olympic Winter Games of Albertville', in A.M. Klausen (ed.), *Olympic Games as Performance and Public* Event. New York: Berghahn.

Arensberg, Conrad. (1959[1937]). *The Irish Countryman*. Gloucester, Mass.: Peter Smith.

Arensberg, Conrad M. and Solon T. Kimball (1968[1940]). *Family and Community in Ireland*. Cambridge, Mass.: Harvard University Press.

Aretxaga, Begoña (1997). *Shattering Silence: Women, Nationalism and Political Subjectivity in Northern Ireland*. Princeton, NJ: Princeton University Press.

Argenti, Nicolas (In preparation). *The Intestines of the State: Youth and the Political Transformation in the Cameroon Grassfields*. Chicago: University of Chicago Press.

Armagh and Down Parliamentary papers (1836). Irish Folklore Collections, University College Dublin, XXXII, 63–4.

Arts Plan (1995–7). Report for the Arts Council. Unpublished brochure.

Balanchine, George and Francis Mason (1989). *101 Stories of the Great Ballets: The Scene-by-Scene Stories of the Most Popular Ballets, Old and New*. New York: Anchor Books.

Banes, Sally (1994). 'On Your Fingertips: Writing Dance Criticism', in *Writing Dancing in the Age of Postmodernism*. Hanover, NH: Wesleyan University Press.

———. (1998). *Dancing Women: Female Bodies on Stage*. London: Routledge.

Banks, Marcus (2001). *Visual Methods in Social Research*. London: Sage Publications.

Barra, Séamus de (1998). 'Aloys Fleischmann's Ballet Music', in R. Fleischmann (ed.), *Joan Denise Moriarty*. Dublin: Mercier Press.

Basegmez, Virva (2005). *Irish Scene and Sound: Identity, Authenticity and Transnationality among Young Musicians*. Stockholm Studies in Social Anthropology, 57. Stockholm: Almqvist & Wiksell International.

Bauman, Richard (2001). 'Tradition, Anthropology of', in N.J. Smelser and P.B. Baltes (eds), *International Encyclopedia of the Social and Behavioral Sciences*. Oxford: Pergamon/Elsevier Science, pp. 15819–24.

Bender, Barbara (ed.) (1993). *Landscape: Politics and Perspectives*. Oxford: Berg.

Benjamin, Walter (1969a). 'The Storyteller: Reflections on the Works of Nikolai Leskov', in *Illuminations*. New York: Schocken Books.

———. (1969b). 'The Work of Art in the Age of Mechanical Reproduction', in *Illuminations*. New York: Schocken Books.

Björklund, Ulf (2001). 'Att studera en diaspora: den armeniska förskingringen som fält', in U. Hannerz (ed.), *Flera fält i ett*. Stockholm: Carlssons.

Bourdieu, Pierre (1977). *Outline of a Theory of Practice*, Cambridge: Cambridge University Press.

Bourke, Angela (1999). *The Burning of Bridget Cleary: A True Story*. London: Pimlico.

———. (2003). 'The Virtual Reality of Irish Fairy Legend', in C. Connolly (ed.), *Theorizing Ireland*. Basingstoke: Palgrave Macmillan.

Brabazon, Tara and Paul Stock (1999). '"We Love You Ireland": Riverdance and Stepping through Antipodean Memory', *Irish Studies Review* 7(3): 301–311.

Braudel, Fernand (1980). *On History*. Chicago: Chicago University Press.

Breathnach, Breandán (1983). *Dancing in Ireland*. Milton-Malbay, Co. Clare: DalgCais Publications.

———. (1996[1971]). *Folk Music and Dances of Ireland*. Cork: Ossian Publications

Breckenridge, Carol, Sheldon Pollock, Homi K. Bhabha and Dipesh Chakrabarty (2002). *Cosmopolitanism*. Durham, NC: Duke University Press.

Brennan, Helen (1994a). 'Dancing on a Plate: The Sean-Nós Dance Tradition of Conamara', MA thesis, Belfast: Queen's University of Belfast, Department of Social Anthropology.

———. (1994b). 'Reinventing Tradition: The Boundaries of Irish Dance', *History Ireland*, Summer: 22–4.

———. (1999). *The Story of Irish Dance*. Dingle, Co. Kerry: Brandon.

Brennan, Timothy (1997). *At Home in the World: Cosmopolitanism Now*. Cambridge, Mass.: Harvard University Press.

———. (2001). 'Cosmopolitanism and Internationalism', *New Left Review* 7 (January-February): 75–84.

Brinson, Peter (1985). *The Dancer and the Dance: Developing Theatre Dance in Ireland*. Dublin: Report for the Arts Council.

Brody, Hugh (1986[1973]). *Inishkillane: Change and Decline in the West of Ireland*. London: Faber and Faber.

Browning, Barbara (1995). *Samba: Resistance in Motion*. Bloomington: Indiana University Press.

Bruner, Edward M. (2004). *Culture on Tour: Ethnographies of Travel*. Chicago: University of Chicago Press.

Bryan, Dominic (2000). *Orange Parades: The Politics of Ritual, Tradition and Control*. London: Pluto Press.

Buckland, Theresa J. (ed.) (1999). *Dance in the Field: Theory, Methods and Issues in Dance Ethnography*. London: Macmillan.

Buckley, Anthony D. (ed.) (1998). *Symbols in Northern Ireland*. Belfast: Institute of Irish Studies, Queen's University of Belfast.

Buizléir, Seán de (1936). Ms 172: 35–38, Irish Folklore Collections. Department of Irish Folklore. Dublin: University College Dublin.

Burt, Ramsay (1995). *The Male Dancer: Bodies, Spectacle, Sexualities*. London: Routledge.

Cass, Joan (1993). *Dancing through History*. Englewood Cliffs, NJ: Prentice Halls.

Castells, Manuel (1996). *The Rise of the Network Society*. Oxford: Blackwell.

Chapman, Malcolm (1995). '"Freezing the Frame": Dress and Etnicity in Brittany and Gaelic Scotland', in J. Eicher (ed.), *Dress and Ethnicity*. Oxford: Berg.

Clifford, James (1997a). 'Traveling Cultures', in *Routes*. Cambridge, Mass: Harvard University Press.

———. (1997b). *Routes*. Cambridge, Mass.: Harvard University Press.

Connerton, Paul (1989). *How Societies Remember*. Cambridge: Cambridge University Press.

Connolly, Claire (2003). 'Introduction: Ireland in Theory', in C. Connolly, (ed.), *Theorizing Ireland*. Basingstoke: Palgrave Macmillan.

Cooper Albright, Ann (1997). *Choreographing Difference: The Body and Identity in Contemporary Dance*. Hanover, NH: Wesleyan University Press.

Corcoran, Sean (1991). 'What is Traditional Music?', in P. McNamee (ed.), *Traditional Music: Whose Music? Proceedings of a Co-operation North Conference*. Belfast: Institute of Irish Studies, Queen's University of Belfast.

Courtney, Kevin (1994). 'Go Jump in the Lake, Riverdance', *The Irish Times*, 12 December.

Cowan, Jane (1990). *Dance and the Body Politic in Northern Greece*. Princeton, NJ: Princeton University Press.

Coyle, Jane (2002). 'Belfast, Where Culture is Contested', *The Irish Times*, 12 November.

Cronin, Michael (2002). 'Speed Limits: Ireland, Globalisation and the War against Time', in P. Kirby, L. Gibbons and M. Cronin (eds), *Reinventing Ireland*. London: Pluto Press.

Cronin, Mike and Daryl Adair (2002). *The Wearing of the Green: A History of St Patrick's Day*. London: Routledge.

Csikszentmihalyi, Mihalyi and Selega Csikszentmihalyi (eds.) (1988). *Optimal Experience: Psychological Studies of Flow in Consciousness*. Cambridge: Cambridge University Press.

Cullinane, John. (1990) *Further Aspects of the History of Irish Dancing*. Cork City: Ballineaspig Publications.

———. (1994). 'Irish Dance World-Wide: Irish Migrants and the Shaping of Traditional Irish Dance', in P. O'Sullivan (ed.), *The Creative Migrant*, Volume 3. Leicester: Leicester University Press.

———. (1996). *Irish Dancing Costumes: Their Origins and Evolutions*. Cork City: Cullinane.

———. (1998). *Aspects of the History of Irish Céilí Dancing 1897–1997*. Cork City: Cullinane.

———. (1999[1987]). *Aspects of the History of Irish Dancing in Ireland, England, New Zealand, North America and Australia*. Cork City: Cullinane.

———. (2003). *An Coimisiún le Rincí Gaelacha (Irish Dancing Commission): Its Origins and Evolution*. Cork City: Cullinane.

Curtin, Chris, Hastings Donnan and Thomas M. Wilson (1993). 'Anthropology and Irish Urban Settings', in C. Curtin, H. Donnan and T.M. Wilson (eds), *Irish Urban Cultures*, Belfast: Institute of Irish Studies, Queen's University of Belfast.

Daedalus (2000). *Multiple Modernities*. Winter, 129(1).

Dahlén, Tommy (1997). *Among the Interculturalists*. Stockholm Studies in Social Anthropology, 38. Stockholm: Almqvist & Wiksell International.

Daniel, Yvonne (1995). *Dance and Social Change in Contemporary Cuba*. Bloomington: Indiana University Press.

Delanty, Gerard (2004). 'From Nationality to Citizenship: Cultural Identity and Cosmopolitan Challenges in Ireland', in A. Finlay (ed.), *Nationalism and Multiculturalism*. Münster: LIT Verlag.

Delargy, James H. (1969). *The Gaelic Story-teller*. Chicago: Chicago University Press.

Dixon, Mike (1999). 'Electronic Image, Human Form: The Dance Theatre of Ireland Performs "Soul Survivor"', *Ballett International* 12: 52.

Donnan, Hastings (2005). 'Material Identities: Fixing Ethnicity in the Irish Borderlands', *Identities* 12: 69–105.

Donnan, Hastings and Graham McFarlane (1986). 'Social Anthropology and the Sectarian Divide in Norhern Ireland', in *The Sectarian Divide in Northern Ireland Today*. RAI Occasional Paper No. 41. London: Royal Anthropological Institute,

Donnan, Hastings and Thomas M. Wilson (1999). *Borders: Frontiers of Identity, Nation and State*. Oxford: Berg.

Ellis, Syliva C. (1999). *The Plays of W.B. Yeats: Yeats and the Dancer*. London: Macmillan Press.

Eyerman, Ron (1999). 'Moving Culture', in M. Featherstone and S. Lash (eds), *Spaces of Culture*. London: Sage.

Falk, Signe and Victoria Wulff (2003). 'The Troubles'. Unpublished Paper for The Music High School of Kungsholmen, Stockholm.

Farnell, Brenda M. (1994). 'Ethno-graphics and the Moving Body', *Man* 29: 929–74.

———. (1995). *Do You See What I Mean?* Austin: University of Texas Press

Feld, Steven (1996). 'Waterfalls of Song: An Acoustemology of Place Resounding in Bosavi, Papua New Guinea', in S. Feld and K.H. Basso (eds), *Senses of Place*. Santa Fe, N.Mex.: School of American Research Press.

———. (2000). 'Sound Worlds', in P. Kruth and H. Stobart (eds), *Sound*. Cambridge: Cambridge University Press.

Feld, Steven and Keith H. Basso (1996). 'Introduction', in S. Feld and K.H. Basso (eds), *Senses of Place*. Santa Fe, N.Mex: School of American Research Press.

Feldman, Alan (1991). *Formations of Violence: The Narrative of the Body and Political Terror in Northern Ireland*. Chicago: University of Chicago Press.

Ferguson, James (1999). *Expectations of Modernity: Myths and Meanings of Urban Life on the Zambian Copperbelt*. Berkeley: University of California Press.

Fine, Gary Alan (1987). *With the Boys: Little League Baseball and Preadolescent Culture*. Chicago: University of Chicago Press.

Finlay, Andrew (2004a). 'Introduction', in A. Finlay (ed.), *Nationalism and Multiculturalism*. Münster: LIT Verlag.

———. (ed.) (2004b). *Nationalism and Multiculturalism: Irish Identity, Citizenship and the Peace Process*. Münster: LIT Verlag.

Fitzpatrick, David (1989). 'Ireland Since 1870', in R.F. Foster (ed.), *The Oxford History of Ireland*. Oxford: Oxford University Press

———. (1995). 'Flight from Famine', in C. Póirtéir (ed.), *The Great Irish Famine*. Dublin: Mercier Press.

Fleischman, Ruth (ed.) (1998). *Joan Denise Moriarty: Founder of Irish National Ballet*. Dublin: Mercier Press.

Flynn, Arthur (1998). *Irish Dance*. Belfast: Appletree Press.

Foley, Catherine (1988a). 'Irish Traditional Step Dance in North Kerry: A Contextual and Structural Analysis'. Ph.D. thesis. London: The Laban Centre for Movement and Dance.

———. (1988b). 'Irish Traditional Step-Dance in Cork', *Traditional Dance* 5–6: 159–174.

———. (2001). 'Perceptions of Irish Step Dance: National, Global and Local,' *Dance Research Journal* 33(1): 32–45.

FORTE (1996). *Access all Areas: Irish Music and International Industry*. Report to the Minstry for Arts, Culture, and Gaeltacht. Dublin: The Stationary Office.

Foster, Roy F. (2002). *The Irish Story: Telling Tales and Making it up in Ireland*. London: Penguin.

Foster, Susan L. (1986). *Reading Dancing: Bodies and Subjects in Contemporary American Dance*. Berkeley: University of California Press.

———. (1995), 'An Introduction to Moving Bodies', in S.L. Foster (ed.), *Choreographing Histoy*, Bloomington: Indiana University Press.

————. (ed.) (1996). *Corporealities: Dancing Knowledge, Culture and Power.* London: Routledge.

Foucault, Michel (1979). *Discipline and Punish.* New York: Vintage.

Franko, Mark (1995). *Dancing Modernism/Performing Politics.* Bloomington: Indiana University Press.

Fredengren, Christina (2002). *Crannogs: A Study of People's Interactions with Lakes, with Particular Reference to Lough Gara in the North-West of Ireland.* Bray, Co. Wicklow: Worldwell Ltd.

Friel, Mary (2004). *Dancing as a Social Pastime in the South-East of Ireland, 1800–1897.* Dublin: Four Courts Press.

Gans, Herbert J. (1979). 'Symbolic Ethnicity: The Future of Ethnic Groups and Cultures in America', *Ethnic and Racial Studies* 2:1–19.

Garsten, Christina (1994). *Apple World: Core and Periphery in a Transnational Organizational Culture.* Stockholm Studies in Social Anthropology, 33. Stockholm: Almqvist & Wiksell International.

Garsten, Christina and Helena Wulff (eds) 2003. *New Technologies at Work: People, Screens and Social Virtuality.* Oxford: Berg.

Garvin, Tom (1981). *The Evolution of Irish Nationalist Politics.* Dublin: Gill & Macmillan.

Gibbons, Luke (1994). 'Dialogue Without the Other? A Reply to Francis Mulhern', *Radical Philosophy* 67: 28–31.

Gibbons, Luke (1996). 'Identity Without a Centre: Allegory, History and Irish Nationalism', in *Transformations in Irish Culture.* Cork: Cork University Press in Association with Field Day Essays.

————. (2002). 'The Global Cure?: History, Therapy and the Celtic Tiger', in P. Kirby, L. Gibbons and M. Cronin (eds), *Reinventing Ireland.* London: Pluto Press.

Giddens, Anthony (1991). *The Consequences of Modernity.* Cambridge: Polity Press.

Gillis, John R. (2001). 'Places Remoter and Islanded', *Michigan Quarterly Review* 40(1): 39–58.

Glassie, Henry (1982). *Passing the Time in Ballymenone.* Dublin: The O'Brien Press.

Gmelch, George (1985 [1977]). *The Irish Tinkers: The Urbanization of an Itinerant People.* Propspect Heights, Il: Waveland.

Graham, Brian (ed.) (1997). *In Search of Ireland: A Cultural Geography.* London: Routledge.

Grau, Andrée (1993). 'John Blacking and the development of Dance Anthropology in the UK', *Dance Research*, 25(2): 21–31.

Guilbault, S. (1983). *How New York Stole the Idea of Modern Art.* Chicago: University of Chicago Press.

Gupta, Akhil and James Ferguson (1992). 'Beyond "Culture": Space, Identity, and the Poltitics of Difference', *Cultural Anthropology* 7(1): 6-23.

Gusterson, Hugh (1997). 'Studying up revisited', *Political and Legal Anthropology Review* 20(1): 114–19.

Halbwachs, Maurice (1980). *The Collective Memory.* New York: Harper & Row.

Hall, Frank A. (1995). 'Irish Dancing: Discipline as Art, Sport, and Duty', Ph.D. thesis, Bloomington: Indiana University.

————. (1996). 'Posture in Irish Dancing', *Visual Anthropology* 8: 251–66.

————. (1997). 'Our Mr. Joyce is a Fine Man, But Have You Seen *Riverdance*?', *New Hibernia Review* 1(3): 134–42.

————. (1999). 'Madness and Recall: Storied Data on Irish Dancing', in T.J. Buckland (ed.), *Dance in the Field.* London: Macmillan.

Handler, Richard (1986). 'Authenticity', *Anthropology Today* 2(1): 2–4.

Hanna, Judith Lynne (1987[1979]). *To Dance is Human: A Theory of Nonverbal Communication.* Chicago: University of Chicago Press.

———. (1988). *Dance, Sex and Gender: Signs of Identity, Dominance, Defiance, and Desire.* Chicago: University of Chicago Press.

Hannerz, Ulf (2004[1969]). *Soulside: Inquiries into Ghetto Culture and Community.* Chicago University Press.

———. (1991). 'Cosmopolitans and Locals in World Culture', in M. Featherstone (ed.), *Global Culture.* London: Sage.

———. (1992). *Cultural Complexity: Studies in the Social Organization of Meaning.* New York: Columbia University Press.

———. (1996). *Transnational Connections: Culture, People, Places.* London: Routledge.

———. (1998). 'Transnational Research', in H.R. Bernard (ed.), *Handbook of Methods in Cultural Anthropology.* Walnut Creek, CA: Altamira.

———. (2003a). 'Being there ... and there ... and there! Reflections on Multi-site Ethnography', *Ethnography* 4: 229–44.

———. (2003b). 'Several Sites in One', in T. Hylland Eriksen (ed.), *Globalisation,* London: Pluto.

———. (2004a). *Foreign News: Exploring the World of Foreign Correspondents.* Chicago: University of Chicago Press.

———. (2004b). 'Cosmopolitanism', in J. Vincent and D. Nugent (eds.), *Companion to the Anthropology of Politics.* Oxford: Blackwell.

———. (2005). 'Two faces of Cosmopolitanism: Culture and Politics', *Statsvetenskaplig Tidskrift,* special issue on Cosmopolitanism, 107: 199–213.

Harris, Rosemary (1972). *Prejudice and Tolerance in Ulster: A Study of Neighbours and 'Strangers' in a Border Community.* Manchester: Manchester University Press.

Herzfeld, Michael (1997). *Cultural Intimacy: Social Poetics in the Nation-State.* New York: Routledge.

Hirsch, Eric (1995). 'Introduction. Landscape: Between Place and Space', in E. Hirsch and M. O'Hanlon (eds), *The Anthropology of Landscape.* Oxford: Clarendon.

Hirsch, Eric and Michael O'Hanlon (eds) (1995). *The Anthropology of Landscape: Perspectives on Place and Space.* Oxford: Clarendon.

Hobsbawm, Eric (1983). 'Introduction: Inventing Traditions', in E. Hobsbawm and T. Ranger (eds), *The Invention of Tradition.* Cambridge: Cambridge University Press.

Holmes, Douglas R. and George E. Marcus (2005). 'Cultures of Expertise and the Management of Globalization: Toward the Re-Functioning of Ethnography', in A. Ong and S.J. Collier (eds), *Global Assemblages.* Oxford: Blackwell Publishing.

Huss, Hasse (2001). 'I reggaens kvarter: på jakt efter ett fält'. In U. Hannerz (ed.), *Flera fält i ett.* Stockholm: Carlssons.

Irish Ecclesiastical Record (1926). January–June vol. XXVII.

Jarman, Neil (1997). *Material Conflicts: Parades and Visual Displays in Northern Ireland.* Oxford: Berg.

Jenkins, Richard (1983). *Lads, Citizens and Ordinary Kids: Working-class Youth Life-Styles in Belfast.* London: Routledge & Kegan Paul.

Kaeppler, Adrienne L. (1978). 'Dance in Anthropological Perspective', *Annual Review of Anthropology* 7: 31–49.

———. (1985). 'Structured Movement Systems in Tonga', in P. Spencer (ed.), *Society and the Dance.* Cambridge: Cambridge University Press.

Kelleher Jr, William F. (2003). *The Troubles in Ballybogoin: Memory and Identity in Northern Ireland.* Ann Arbor: The University of Michigan Press.

Kiberd, Declan (1996). *Inventing Ireland: The Literature of the Modern Nation.* London: Vintage.

Kirby, Paedar, Luke Gibbons and Michael Cronin (2002). 'Introduction: The Reinvention of Ireland: A Critical Perspective', in P. Kirby, L. Gibbons and M. Cronin (eds), *Reinventing Ireland.* London: Pluto Press.

Kockel, Ullrich (1993). *The Gentle Subversion: Informal Economy and Regional Development in the West of Ireland.* Bremen: ESIS.

———. (Forthcoming). 'Reflexive Tradition and Heritage Production', in U. Kockel and M. Nic Craith, *Cultural Heritages as Reflexive Traditions.* Basingstoke: Palgrave.

Lanclos, Donna M. (2003). *At Play in Belfast: Children's Folklore and Identities in Northern Ireland.* New Brunswick, NJ: Rutgers University Press.

Lavery, Brian (2004). '"Riverdance" aims to tap into the future', *International Herald Tribune,* October 16–17.

Lewis, J. Lowell (1995). 'Genre and Embodiment: from Brazilian Capoeira to the Ethnology of Human Movement', *Cultural Anthropology* 10(2): 221–43.

Lindquist, Galina (1997). *Shamanic Performances on the Urban Scene.* Stockholm Studies in Social Anthropology, 39. Stockholm: Almqvist & Wiksell International.

Livingston, Tamara E. (1999). 'Music Revivals: Towards a General Theory', *Ethnomusicology* 43(1): 66–85.

Lloyd, David (1993). *Anomalous States: Irish Writing and the Post-Colonial Moment.* Durham, NC: Duke University Press.

———. (1999). 'The Recovery of Kitsch', in *Ireland After History.* Notre Dame: University of Notre Dame Press in association with Field Day Essays.

Löfgren, Orvar (1993). 'Materializing the Nation in Sweden and America', *Ethnos* 3–4: 161–96.

———. (2000). 'Motion and Emotion: The Microphysics and Metaphysics of Landscape Experiences in Tourism', in A. Hornborg and G. Pálsson (eds), *Negotiating Nature.* Lund: Lund University Press.

———. (2002). *On Holiday: A History of Vacationing.* Berkeley: University of California Press.

MacAloon, John J. (1981). *This Great Symbol.* Chicago: University of Chicago Press.

———. (ed.) (1984). *Rite, Drama, Festival, Spectacle.* Philadelphia: Institute for the Study of Human Issues Press.

McCarthy, Mark (ed.) (2005). *Irelands Heritages: Critical Perspectives on Memory and Identity.* Aldershot: Ashgate.

McLean, Stuart (2003). 'Céide Fields: Natural Histories of a Buried Landscape', in P.J. Stewart and A. Strathern (eds), *Landscape, Memory and History.* London: Pluto Press.

———. (2004). *The Event and Its Terror: Ireland, Famine, Modernity.* Stanford, CA: Stanford University Press.

MacMahon, Bryan (1954). *The Vanishing Ireland.* Dublin: O'Brien Press.

MacMahon, Deirdre (1998). 'Ireland: Theatrical Dance', in S.J. Cohen (ed.), *International Encyclopedia of Dance* 3: 519–20.

McNeill, William H. (1995). *Keeping Together in Time: Dance and Drill in Human History .* Cambridge, Mass.: Harvard University Press.

MacRéamoinn, Seán (1987). 'Saint Patrick', Dublin: Saints Alive Series.

MacReamoinn, Seona (2002). 'A New Crossroads', *irish theatre magazine* 3(12): 27–33.

———. (2003). 'Phoenix Rises in Belfast: Phoenix Dance Theatre Made an Enchanting Irish Debut in Belfast', *The Sunday Tribune,* 23 March.

MacUistin, Liam (1999). *Exploring Newgrange.* Dublin: The O'Brien Press.

McWilliams, Anthea (2001). 'Remembering and Recovering the Case of Sir Richard Wallace, Benefactor and Art Collector: Why and How Lisburn should Reclaim his Cultural Legacy', MA thesis. Derry: University of Ulster.

Madden, Christine (2002). 'A Festival for Ireland', *irish theatre magazine* 3(12): 10–18.

Magowan, Fiona (2005). 'Drums of Suffering in Belfast's European Capital of Culture Bid: John Blacking on Music, Conflict and Healing', in V. Rogers and D. Symons (eds), *The Legacy of John Blacking*. Perth: University of Western Australia Press.

Maher, Anne (2002). 'Classical Ballet in Step with Audience Taste', *The Irish Times*, May 17.

Man, Paul de (1970). 'Literary History and Literary Modernity', *Daedalus* 99: 384–404.

Manning, Frank E. (1992). '*Spectacle*', in R. Bauman (ed.), *Folklore, Cultural Performances, and Popular Entertainments*. New York: Oxford University Press, pp.291–299.

Marcus, George E. (1998[1995]). 'Ethnography in/of the World System: The Emergence of Multi-Sited Ethnography', in *Ethnography through Thick and Thin*. Princeton, NJ: Princeton University Press.

Margolis, Maxine L. (1994). *Little Brazil*. Princeton, NJ: Princeton University Press.

Media Information Pack (1998). *Riverdance – The Show*. Unpublished brochure.

Mendoza, Zoila S. (2000). *Shaping Society through Dance: Mestizo Ritual Performance in the Peruvian Andes*. Chicago: Chicago University Press.

Messenger, John (1983 [1969]). *Inis Beag: Isle of Ireland*. Prospect Heights, Il: Waveland.

Meyer, Moe (1995). 'Dance and the Politics of Orality: A Study of the Irish *Scoil Rince*', *Dance Research Journal* 27(1): 25–39.

Mitchell, J. Clyde (1956). *The Kalela Dance*. Livingstone: Rhodes-Livingstone Papers No. 27.

Morris, Gay (ed.) (1996). *Moving Words: Re-writing Dance*. London: Routledge.

Moylan, Terry (2002). '"Bouncing Around" on the Green', *The Irish Times*, 16 March.

Mulrooney, Deirdre (2006). *Irish Moves: An Illustrated History of Dance and Physical Theatre in Ireland*. Dublin: The Liffey Press.

Murphy, Pat (1995). *Toss the Feathers: Irish Set Dancing*. Dublin: Mercier Press.

———. (2000). *The Flowing Tide: More Irish Set Dancing*. Dublin: Mercier Press.

Musiat, Anja (2002). 'Not "Irish" at All', *irish theatre magazine* 3(12): 18–21.

Narayan, Kirin (1989). *Storytellers, Saints, and Scoundrels: Folk Narrative in Hindu Religious Teaching*. Philadelphia: University of Pennsylvania Press.

Ness, Sally Ann (1992). *Body, Movement and Culture: Kinesthestic and Visual Symbolism in a Philippine Community*. Philadelphia: University of Pennsylvania Press.

Neveu Kringelbach, Hélène (2005). 'Encircling the Dance: Social Mobility through the Transformation of Performance in Urban Senegal'. PhD thesis. Oxford: University of Oxford.

Nic Craith, Máiréad (2002). *Plural Identities – Singular Narratives: The Case of Northern Ireland*. New York: Berghahn Books.

———. (2004). 'Local Cultures in a Global World', in U. Kockel and M. Nic Craith (eds), *Communicating Cultures*. Münster: LIT Verlag.

Ní Dhuibhne, Éilís (1999a). *The Dancers Dancing*. Belfast: The Blackstaff Press.

———. (1999b). 'The Irish', in Å. Daun and S. Jansson (eds), *Europeans: Essays on Culture and Identity*. Lund: Nordic Academic Press.

Novack, Cynthia J. (1990). *Sharing the Dance: Contact Improvisation and American Culture*. Madison: University of Wisconsin Press.

———. (1995). 'The Body's Endeavour's as Cultural Practices', in Susan L. Foster (ed.), *Choreographing History*. Bloomington: Indiana University Press

O'Brien, Flann (1988). *The Poor Mouth*. London: Paladin Books.

O'Brien, Victoria (2002). 'The Abbey School of Ballet', MA thesis. Limerick: University of Limerick.

Ó Catháin, Séamas (1995). *The Festival of Brigit: Celtic Goddess and Holy Woman*. Dublin: DBA Publications.

Ó Cinnéide, Barra (1999). 'The *Riverdance* Phenomenon: Crosbhealach an Damhsa', in F. Vallely, H. Hamilton, E. Vallely and L. Doherty (eds), *The Crossroads Conference 1996*. Cork: Ossian Publications.

———. (2002). *Riverdance – The Phenomenon*. Dublin: Blackhall Publishing.

O'Connor, Barbara (1993). 'Myths and Mirrors: Tourist Images and National Identity', in B. O'Connor and M. Cronin (eds), *Tourism in Ireland*. Cork: Cork University Press.

———. (1997a). 'Riverdance', in M. Peillon and E. Slater (eds), *Encounters with Modern Ireland*. Dublin: Institute of Public Administration.

———. (1997b). 'Safe Sets: Women, Dance and "Communitas"', in H. Thomas (ed.), *Dance in the City*. New York: St. Martin's Press.

———. (2003a). 'Ruin and Romance: Heterosexual Discourses on Irish Popular Dance, 1920–1960', *Irish Journal of Sociology*, 12(2): 50–67.

———. (2003b). '"Come and daunce with me in Irlande": Tourism, Dance and Globalisation', in M. Cronin and B. O'Connor (eds), *Irish Tourism*. Clevedon: Channel View Publications.

———. (2005). 'Sexing the Nation: Discourses of the Dancing Body in Ireland in the 1930s', *Journal of Gender Studies* 14(2): 89–105.

Ó Giolláin, Diarmuid (2000). *Locating Irish Folklore: Tradition, Modernity, Identity*. Cork: Cork University Press.

O'Keefe, J.G. and Art O'Brien (1902). *A Handbook of Irish Dances*. Dublin: O'Donoghue.

Okely, Judith (2005). 'Written Out and Written In: A Past Text Re-visited'. Paper for the American Anthropological Association, Washington, D.C., 30 November – 4 December, 2005.

Ó Laoire, Lillis (2005). 'Irish Music', in J. Cleary and C. Connolly (eds), *Modern Irish Culture*. Cambridge: Cambridge University Press.

O'Mahony, John (2005). 'Ballet in the Bog', *The Guardian*, February 23.

O'Neill, Charlie (2000). 'Famine, Dance and Desecration', *Ballads* programme. Unpublished brochure.

Ó Súilleabháin, Micheál (1998). '"Around the House and Mind the Cosmos": Music, Dance and Identity in Contemporary Ireland', in R. Pine (ed.), *Music in Ireland 1848–1998*. Dublin: Mercier Press.

O'Toole, Fintan (1997a). 'Unsuitables from a Distance: The Politics of *Riverdance*', in *The Ex-Isle of Erin*. Dublin: New Island Books.

———. (1997b). 'Perpetual Motion', in P. Brennan and C. de Saint Phalle (eds), *Arguing at the Crossroads*. Dublin: New Island Books.

———. (1999). *The Lie of the Land: Irish Identities*. London: Verso.

———. (2003). 'Foreword', in D. Theodores (ed.), *Dancing on the Edge of Europe*. Cork: Institute for Choreography and Dance (icd).

Peace, Adrian(1989). 'From Arcadia to Anomie: Critical Notes on the Constitution of Irish Society as an Anthropological Project', *Critique of Anthropology* 9(1): 89–111.

———. (1997). *A Time of Reckoning: The Politics of Discourse in Rural Ireland*. Social and Economic Studies, 59. St. John's, Newfoundland: Institute of Social and Economic Research.

———. (2001). *A World of Fine Difference: The Social Architecture of a Modern Irish Village*. Dublin: University College Dublin Press.

Persson, Eva A. (2002). 'Croagh Patrick – berättelser på ett berg', in A. Eriksen, J. Garnert and T. Selberg (eds), *Historien in på livet*. Lund: Nordic Academic Press.

Peterson, Richard A. (1997). *Creating Country Music: Fabricating Authenticity*. Chicago: Chicago University Press.

Power, Patrick C. (1988). 'Translator's Preface', in Flann O'Brien, *The Poor Mouth*. London: Paladin.

Power, T. and Kevin Whelan (eds) (1990). *Endurance and Emergence: Catholics in Ireland in the Eighteenth Century*. Dublin: Irish Academic Press.

Programme for 30th Irish World Dance Championships, Ennis (1999). Unpublished brochure.

Quinn, Tom (1997). *Irish Dancing: A Guide to Céili, Set and Country Dancing*. Glasgow: Harper Collins.

Rapport, Nigel and Andrew Dawson (1998). 'Home and Movement: A Polemic', in N. Rapport and A. Dawson (eds), *Migrants of Identity*. Oxford: Berg.

Reed, Susan A. (1998),'The Politics and Poetics of Dance', *Annual Review of Anthropology* 27: 503–32.

Riverdance – The Show. n.d. Official Programme. Unpublished brochure.

Robb, Martha (1998). *Irish Dancing Costume*. Dublin: Country House.

Robinson, Jacqueline (1999). Modern Dance in Dublin in the 1940's (yes, there was ...). Unpublished manuscript.

Rojek, Chris and John Urry (eds) (2000). *Touring Cultures: Transformations of Travel and Theory*. London: Routledge.

Royce, Anya Peterson (2000[1977]). *The Anthropology of Dance*. London: DanceBooks.

Salazar, Carles (1996). *A Sentimental Economy: Commodity and Community in Rural Ireland*. Oxford: Berghahn.

Scheper-Hughes, Nancy (1979). *Saints, Scholars and Schizophrenics: Mental Illness in Rural Ireland*. Berkeley: University of California Press.

Scott, Michael (1997[1986]). *The Children of Lir*. London: Mammoth.

Seaver, Michael (1998). 'Dublin – *Ballads*', *Dance Europe* February/March: 29.

———. (2000). '*Riverdance* – The Army Drill', *The Irish Times*, July 11.

———. (2002). 'Do we need Ballet Ireland?', *The Irish Times*, April 16.

———. (2003). 'Edging Towards Centre Stage: Living Dance History in Contemporary Ireland', in D. Theodores (ed.), *Dancing on the Edge of Europe*. Cork: Institute for Choreography and Dance (icd).

Sherlock, Joyce (1999). 'Globalisation, Western Culture and *Riverdance*', in A. Brah, M.J. Hickman and M. Mac an Ghaill (eds), *Thinking Identities*. London: Macmillan Press.

Shryock, Andrew (ed.) (2004). *Off Stage/ On Display: Intimacy and Ehnography in the Age of Public Culture*. Stanford, CA: Stanford University Press.

Skinner, Jonathan (2004). *Before the Volcano: Reverberations of Identity on Montserrat*. Kingston, Jamaica: Arawak Publications.

———. (Forthcoming). 'Modernist Anthropology, Ethnic Tourism and National Identity: The Contest for the Commoditization and Consumption of St Patrick's Day, Montserrat', in K. Meethan, A. Anderson and S. Miles (eds), *Anthropology and the Production and Consumption of Tourism*. London: CAB International.

Sklar, Deirde (2001). *Dancing with the Virgin: Body and Faith in the Fiesta of Tortugas, New Mexico*. Berkeley: University of California Press.

Sluka, Jeffrey A. (1989). *Hearts and Minds, Water and Fish*. Greenwich, Conn.: JAI Press.

Smyth, Sam (1996). *Riverdance: The Story*. London: Andre Deutsch.

Spencer, Paul (ed.) (1985a). *Society and the Dance: The Social Anthropology of Process and Performance*. Cambridge: Cambridge University Press.

———. (1985b). 'Introduction: Interpretations of the Dance in Anthropology', in P. Spencer (ed.), *Society and the Dance*. Cambridge: Cambridge University Press.

Spooner, Brian (1986). 'Weavers and Dealers: The Authenticity of an Oriental Carpet', in A. Appaduari (ed.), *The Social Life of Things*. Cambridge: Cambridge University Press.

Stewart, Pamela J. and Andrew Strathern (2003). 'Introduction', in P.J. Stewart and A. Strathern (eds), *Landscape, Memory and History*. London: Pluto Press.

Stillman, Amy Ku'uleialoha (1996). 'Hawaiian Hula Competitions: Event, Repertoire, Performance, Tradition', *Journal of American Folklore* 109(4): 357–80.

Stokes, Martin (1994). 'Introduction: Ethnicity, Identity and Music', in M. Stokes (ed.), *Ethnicity, Identity and Music*. Oxford: Berg.

———. (1997). 'Voices and Places: History, Repetition and the Musical Imagination'. *JRAI*, 3(4): 673–91.

Sutton, Julia (1998). 'Galliard', in S.J. Cohen (ed.), *International Encyclopedia of Dance* 3: 106–11. New York: Oxford University Press.

Swan, Sean (2005). 'Where is the Irish Border? Theories of Division in Ireland', *Nordic Irish Studies*, 4: 61–87.

Swift, Carolyn n.d. 'Dance in Ireland, 1900–2000'. Unpublished manuscript.

———. (1995). 'Standing Ovation for Stunning Steps', *The Irish Times*, 10 February.

———. (1997). '*Ballads*', *The Irish Times*, 24 November.

———. (1998). 'Joan Denise Moriarty as Choreographer', in R. Fleischmann (ed.), *Joan Denise Moriarty*. Cork: Mercier Press

———. (1999). 'CoisCéim Dance Theatre', *The Irish Times*, 18 June.

———. (2000). 'The Flowerbed', *The Irish Times*, 8 September.

Taylor, Julie (1998). *Paper Tangos*. Durham, NC: Duke University Press.

Taylor, Lawrence J. (1992). 'Irish', in *Encyclopedia of World Cultures* vol. IV: 151–54, Boston, Mass.: G.K. Hall & Co.

———. (1995). *Occasions of Faith: An Anthropology of Irish Catholics*. Philadelphia: University of Pennsylvania Press.

Theodores, Diana (1996). 'Report-A Dance Critic in Ireland', *Dance Chronicle: Studies in Dance and the Related Arts* 19(2):191–211.

———. (ed.) (2003). *Dancing on the Edge of Europe: Irish Choreographers in Conversation*. Cork: Institute for Choreography and Dance (icd).

Tovey, Hilary and Perry Share (2000). *A Sociology of Ireland*. Dublin: Gill & Macmillan.

Tsing, Anna (2004). *Friction: An Ethnography of Global Connection*. Princeton: Princeton University Press.

Turner, Victor (1982). *From Ritual to Theatre: The Human Seriousness of Play*. New York City: Performing Arts Journal Communication.

Urry, John (2000). *Sociology beyond Societies: Mobilities for the Twenty-first Century*. London: Routledge.

Valera, Eamon de (1943). 'Language Must Be Saved: Call to Nation', *Irish Press*, 18 March.

Valley, Finton (1995). 'A Nation on its Feet', *Sunday Tribune Magazine*, 5 February.

———. (ed.) (1999). *The Companion to Irish Traditional Music*. Cork: Cork University Press.

Valois, Ninette de (1959). *Come Dance With Me: A Memoir 1898–1956*. London: Hamish Hamilton.

Van Niuewkerk, Karin (1995). '*A Trade like Any Other': Female Singers and Dancers in Egypt*. Austin: University of Texas Press.

Vertovec, Steven and Robin Cohen (2002). 'Introduction: Conceiving Cosmopolitanism', in S. Vertovec and R. Cohen (eds), *Conceiving Cosmopolitanism*. Oxford: Oxford University Press.

Wainwright, Steven P. and Turner Bryan S. (2003).'Narratives of Embodiment: Body, Ageing and Career in Royal Ballet Dancers', in H. Thomas and J. Ahmed (eds), *Cultural Bodies*. Malden, Mass: Blackwell.

Walker, Brian (1996). *Dancing to History's Tune: History, Myths and Politics in Ireland*. Belfast: Institute of Irish Studies, Queen's University of Belfast.

Wardle, Huon (2000). *An Ethnography of Cosmopolitanism in Kingston, Jamaica*. Lampeter: Edwin Mellen.

Waters, John (1991). *Jiving at the Crossroads*. Belfast: The Blackstaff Press.

Watson, C.W. 1999. 'Introduction: The Quality of Being There', in C.W. Watson (ed.), *Being There*. London: Pluto Press.

Werbner, Pnina (1999). 'Global Pathways: Working Class Cosmopolitans and the Creation of Transnational Ethnic Worlds', *Social Anthropology*, 7: 17–35.

Whelan, Kevin (2005). 'The Cultural Effects of the Famine', in J. Cleary and C. Connolly (eds), *The Cambridge Companion to Modern Irish Culture*. Cambridge: Cambridge University Press.

Williams, Drid (1976). 'Deep Structures of the Dance', *Journal of Human Movement Studies* 2: 123–44.

———. (2003[1991]). *Anthropology and the Dance. Ten Lectures*. Urbana: University of Illinois Press.

Willis, Roy G. and K.B.S. Chisanga (1999). *Some Spirits Heal, Others Only Dance*. Oxford: Berg.

Wilson, Thomas M. (1984). 'From Clare to the Common Market: Perspectives on Irish Ethnography', *Anthropological Quarterly* 57: 1–15.

Wilson, Thomas M. and Hastings Donnan (2006). *The Anthropology of Ireland*. Oxford: Berg.

Wulff, Helena (1988). *Twenty Girls: Growing Up, Ethnicity and Excitement in a South London Microculture*. Stockholm Studies in Social Anthropology, 21. Stockholm: Almqvist & Wiksell International.

———. (1995a). 'Introducing Youth Culture in Its Own Right: The State of the Art and New Possibilities', in V. Amit-Talai and H. Wulff (eds), *Youth Cultures*. London: Routledge.

———. (1995b). 'Inter-racial Friendship: Consuming Youth Styles, Ethnicity and Teenage Femininity in South London', in V. Amit-Talai and H. Wulff (eds), *Youth Cultures*. London: Routledge.

———. (1998). *Ballet across Borders: Career and Culture in the World of Dancers*. Oxford: Berg.

———. (1999). 'Riverdance – historien om en global succé', *Danstidningen* 2: 4–6.

———. (2000). 'Access to a Closed World: Methods for a Multi-Locale Study of Ballet as a Career', in V. Amit (ed.), *Constructing the Field*. London: Routledge.

———. (2001). 'Dance, Anthropology of', in N.J. Smelser and P.B. Baltes (eds.), *International Encyclopedia of the Social and Behavioral Sciences*, Oxford: Pergamon/Elsevier Science, pp. 3209–12.

———. (2002). 'Aesthetics at the Ballet: Looking at "National" Style, Body and Clothing in the London Dance World', in N. Rapport (ed.), *British Subjects*. Oxford: Berg.

———. (2003). 'The Irish Body in Motion: Moral Politics, National Identity and Dance', in N. Dyck and E.P. Archetti, (eds), *Sports, Dance and Embodied Identities*. Oxford: Berg.

———. (2004). 'The Critic's Eye: Ethics and Politics of Writing Dance Reviews', in E. Anttila, S. Hämäläinen, T. Löytönen and L. Rouhiainen (eds), *Making a Difference in Dance*. Helsinki: Theatre Academy.

———. (2005a). '"High Arts'and the Market: An Uneasy Partnership in the Transnational World of Ballet", in D. Inglis and J. Hughson (eds.), *The Sociology of Art*. Basingstoke: Palgrave.

———. (2005b). Review of *At Play in Belfast: Children's Folklore and Identities in Northern Ireland* by Donna M. Lanclos, *Social Anthropology* 13(3): 356–57.

————. (2006). 'Experiencing the Ballet Body: Pleasure, Pain, Power', in S.A. Reily (ed.), *The Musical Human: Rethinking John Blacking's Ethnomusicology in the 21st Century.* Aldershot: Ashgate Press.

————. (Forthcoming). 'To Know the Dancer: Formations of Fieldwork in the Ballet World', in N. Halstead, E. Hirsch and J. Okely (eds), *Knowing How to Know.* Oxford: Berghahn.

Yeats, William Butler (1990[1928]). 'Among School Children', in *Collected Poems.* London: Picador.

————. (1990[1933]). 'I am of Ireland', in *Collected Poems.* London: Picador.

Zimmermann, Georges Denis (2001). *The Irish Storyteller.* Dublin: Four Courts Press.

Television programme

Dance Lexie Dance. BBC Northern Ireland (1996).
Emerald Shoes: The Story of Irish Dance. UTV (1999).

Web sites

www.coisceim.com
www.knowth.com/newgrange.htm
www.riverdance.com
www.thefabulousbeast.net

Films

Dancing at Lughnasa, Capitol Films, video, 1998.
The Field, Granada Film, dvd , 2001.

Index

Lightning Source UK Ltd.
Milton Keynes UK
25 February 2010

150600UK00001B/38/P